Policy Transfer in Global Perspective

Edited by

MARK EVANS
University of York, UK

ASHGATE

Published by
Ashgate Publishing Limited
Gower House
Croft Road
Aldershot
Hants GU11 3HR
England

Ashgate Publishing Company
Suite 420
101 Cherry Street
Burlington, VT 05401-4405
USA

Ashgate website: http://www.ashgate.com

British Library Cataloguing in Publication Data
Policy transfer in global perspective
   1. Political planning 2. Culture diffusion
   I. Evans, Mark, 1965-
   320.6

Library of Congress Cataloging-in-Publication Data
Policy transfer in global perspective / [edited] by Mark Evans.
     p. cm.
   Includes bibliographical references and index.
   ISBN 0-7546-3206-7
   1. Comparative government. 2. Policy sciences--Cross-cultural studies. 3. Political planning--Developing countries. 4. Diffusion of innovations--Developing countries.
I. Evans, Mark, 1965-

JF51.P645 2004
320.6--dc22

2004007444

ISBN 0 7546 3206 7

Printed and bound by Antony Rowe Ltd, Chippenham, Wiltshire

POLICY TRANSFER IN GLOBAL PERSPECTIVE

To my Mother, Anne,
with love

Contents

1 Introduction: Is Policy Transfer Rational Policy-making?
Mark Evans

2 Understanding Policy Transfer
Mark Evans

PART I: POLICY TRANSFER BETWEEN DEVELOPED COUNTRIES

3 Policy Transfer Networks: An Insider Perspective
Mark Evans with Paul McComb

List of Tables and Figures

Tables

Figures

List of Contributors

Richard Common is a Lecturer in public management and Head of Organizational Behaviour and Human Resource Management in the Business School at Hull University in the United Kingdom.

Mark Evans is a Professor in public policy and Head of the Department of Politics at the University of York in the United Kingdom.

Pedro Flores-Crespo is a Lecturer in the Research Institute for the Development of Education (INEDE) of the Universidad Iberoamericana in Mexico.

Veronica Ivanova is a PhD student in the School of Social Sciences at the University of Southampton in the United Kingdom.

Stella Ladi is a Lecturer in politics in the Department of Politics at the University of Sheffield in the United Kingdom.

Xenia Lana is a postgraduate student in the Department of Politics at the University of York in the United Kingdom.

Paul McComb is a Senior Civil Servant in the Department of Social Security in the United Kingdom.

Anthony Nedley is Country Director of Action Aid Mozambique.

Andrew Street is a Senior Research Fellow in the Department of Health Economics at the University of York in the United Kingdom.

Acknowledgements

In compiling this book, I have benefited enormously from conversations over the years at Economic and Social Research Council sponsored seminars with David Marsh, Charles Raab and David Dolowitz, with colleagues in the Department of Politics at the University of York, particularly Keith Alderman, and, with five of my PhD students, Richard Common, Pedro Flores-Crespo, Oscar Huerta Melchor, Stella Ladi and Khariah Mokhtar. The Department's MA in Public Administration has also proved to be an important forum for the development of ideas on the study of policy transfer, thanks to the high quality of student participation. I also owe intellectual debts to Jonathan Davies and Philip Cerny. Several of the chapters in this volume refer to collaborative work that I completed with Jonathan in 1998 and 1999 on policy transfer. In particularly, I gratefully acknowledge the influence of his ideas on the importance of validation in policy transfer analysis and in the formulation of my methodological arguments. Chapter Four also draws on collaborative work that Phil and I have conducted on the rise and development of the competition state in the United Kingdom (1999; 2003; and, 2004) and, thus I acknowledge a huge debt to his exhaustive work in this area.

My debts to all of these people are considerable. However, I would particularly like to thank Jim Buller and Rob Hulme for their input at the beginning of this project. Jim provided me with some insightful commentary on early versions of two of the case study chapters and conversations with Rob have helped to shape some of my thoughts on the structure of the volume. As always, however, the responsibility for shortcomings in this work rests entirely with my co-authors and me.

Finally, the love and support of my wife Lorna, my son Jack and my daughter Caitlin was, as always, invaluable during long periods spent locked away in my study.

List of Abbreviations

ABC	Agência Brasileira de Cooperação (*Brazilian Agency of Technical Cooperation*)
AMI	American Enterprise Institute
AMREF	African Medical Research Foundation (Kenya)
ANDIP	Development Company of the Municipalities of Piraeus (Athens, Greece)
AUC	Association of Ukrainian Cities
BFI	Benefit Fraud Inspectorate (UK)
BFR	Budgeting for Results (Singapore)
CA	Contributions Agency (UK)
CAPAM	Commonwealth Association for Public Administration and Management
CBHC	Community Based Health Care Policy (Tanzania)
CIS	Commonwealth of Independent States
CMPS	Centre for Management and Policy Studies (UK)
COSLA	Confederation of Scottish Local Authorities
CSA	Child Support Agency (UK)
DETR	Department of the Environment, Trade and the Regions (UK)
DfEE	Department for Education and Employment (UK)
DfID	Department for International Development (UK)
DSS	Department of Social Security (UK)
ESRC	Economic and Social Research Council (UK)
EU	European Union
FAPs	Feldsher and Accoucher Stations (Kyrgyzstan)
FMI	Financial Management Initiative (UK)
FOIA	Freedom of Information Act (Canada/US/UK)
GATS	General Agreement on Trade in Services
GATT	General Agreement on Tariffs and Trade
GOSL	Government of Sri Lanka
HAZs	Health Action Zones (UK)
IBGE	Instituto Brasileiro de Geografia e Estatística (*Brazilian Institute of Geography and Statistics*)
IDB	Inter-American Development Bank
IDS	Institute for Development Studies (University of Sussex, UK)
IIED	International Institute for Environment and Development (UK)
ILO	International Labour Organization
IMF	International Monetary Fund
IPEA	Instituto de Pesquisas Econômicas Aplicadas (*Institute of Applied Research in Economics/Brazil*)
ISCED	International Standard Classification of Education

ITs	Office of the Technological Institutes (Mexico)
IULA	International Union of Local Authorities
IWS	Industrial Welfare State
KI	Knowledge Institution
LAs	Local Authorities (UK)
LDC	Lesser Developed Country
LGA	Local Government Association (England)
MAMPU	Administrative Modernisation and Information Technology Unit (Malaysia)
MBS	Ministerio de Bienestar Social (*Ministry of Social Welfare/Ecuador*)
MBS	Modified Budgeting System (Malaysia)
MDG	Millennium Development Goals
MoS	Minister of State (UK)
NAO	National Audit Office (UK)
NES	New Economic School of Moscow
NGO	Non-governmental Organization
NHS	National Health Service (UK)
NPM	New Public Management
NTAN	National Institute of Public Administration (Malaysia)
OAED	Organization for the Employment of the Working Force (Greece)
OCE	Observatorio Ciudadano de la Educación (Mexico)
OECD	Organization for Economic Cooperation and Development
PLA	Participatory Learning and Action
PPBS	Performance Program Budgeting System (Malaysia)
PPs	Performance Pledges (Hong Kong)
PPS	Programa de Protección Social (*Social Protection Programme/Ecuador*)
PSR	Public Sector Reform (Hong Kong)
PTNs	Policy Transfer Networks
PUMA	Public Management Programme (OECD)
RPHCs	Rural Primary Health Care Centres (Kyrgyzstan)
SAP	Structural Adjustment Programme (IMF)
SAR	Strategic Administrative Region (Hong Kong)
SBA	Social Security Benefits Agency (UK)
SELBEN	Sistema de Selección de Beneficiarios (*Beneficiary Selection System*)
SEP	Secretariat of Public Education (Mexico)
SIU	Service Improvement Unit (Singapore)
SMEs	Small and Medium Sized Enterprises
SoS	Secretary of State (UK)
TIC	Technological Information Centre (Denmark)
TMP	Target-Based Management Process (Hong Kong)
UK	United Kingdom
UnB	Universidade de Brasília (*University of Brazil*)
UNCTAD	United Nations Conference for Trade and Development

UNDP	United Nations Development Programme
UNESCO	United Nations Educational, Scientific and Cultural Organization
UNICEF	United Nations International Children Emergency Fund
UPHGs	Primary Health Care Groups in Urban Areas (Kyrgyzstan)
US	United States of America
USAID	United States Agency for International Development
V/CHW	Village or Community Health Care Worker (Tanzania)
WB	World Bank
WBS	Weekly Benefits Saving (UK)
WHO	World Health Organization
WITS	Work Improvement Teams (Singapore)
WLGA	Welsh Local Government Association
WTO	World Trade Organization

Chapter 1

Introduction:
Is Policy Transfer Rational
Policy-making?

Mark Evans

First, if any individual points have been well made by previous writers, let us try to follow them up; then from the collection of constitutions we must examine what sort of thing preserves and what sort of thing destroys cities and particular constitutions, and for what reasons some are well administered and others are not.
Aristotle (384 to 322 BCE), *Nicomachean Ethics* (X, 1181b).

Evolving Opportunity Structures for Policy Transfer

There is nothing new about the concept of policy transfer or its practice. As early as 315BCE Aristotle in his *Nicomachean Ethics* advised us of the rationality of engaging in lesson-drawing from positive and negative administrative experiences elsewhere. Policy transfer, a generic concept that refers to a process in which knowledge about institutions, policies or delivery systems at one sector or level of governance is used in the development of institutions, policies or delivery systems at another sector or level of governance, has thus been habitual practice since the dawn of civilization. Nonetheless, it has become increasingly common to observe that the scope and intensity of policy transfer activity has increased significantly as a consequence of changes to the field of action in public policy-making (see Common, 2001; Dolowitz and Marsh, 2000; and, Evans and Cerny, 2003). It is claimed that this is largely the function of the world of public policy becoming increasingly small due to dramatic changes in global political and economic institutional structures and to nation states themselves.

These changes at the structural level have impacted upon the work of public organizations either directly or indirectly and have created new opportunity structures for policy transfer. The following empirical statements illustrate the scope of change and the emergence of new opportunity structures for policy transfer.

i. *A process of external 'hollowing-out' has occurred to different degrees in different states as a consequence of the differential impact of processes of globalization on domestic policy formation such as changes in the nature of geopolitics, political integration, the internationalization of financial markets and global communications.*

ii. *A process of internal 'hollowing-out' of the state has occurred to different degrees in different countries as a consequence of the differential impact of processes of privatization, the marketization of public services, and, decentralization on both the institutional architecture of the state and domestic policy formation.*

iii. *New technology has impacted on the work, services and commercial activities of public organizations and has created attractive new ways of delivering public goods.*

iv. *The shift from traditional government to collaborative governance has increased the range of non-state actors involved in delivering public goods and has created an opportunity structure for cross-sector policy learning.*

v. *The increasingly multi-cultural and multi-ethnic character of liberal democracies have created new challenges for public administrators that are best dealt with through drawing rational lessons from positive and negative international experiences.*

vi. *The policy agenda in many, but not all, nation states has become increasingly internationalized with regard to: stable economic management and economic prudence; public management based upon economy, efficiency and effectiveness; a change in the emphasis of government intervention so that it deals with education, training and infrastructure and not industrial intervention; reform of the welfare state through managed welfarism; and, reinventing government through decentralization and the opening-up of government.*

At the same time, these changes at the structural level have precipitated a range of problems at the organizational level such as: issues of cost containment; increased pressure on public organizations to engage in income generating activities; the need for more effective coordination of policy systems across sectors and levels of governance; new patterns of need caused by the widening gap between rich and poor, changing social and demographic patterns (e.g. longer life expectancy, smaller sized families) and greater ethnic diversity and conflict within urban areas; the formation of stronger regional identities through processes of administrative decentralization; and, rising expectations of public services due to the pervasiveness of quality management (e.g. performance indicators).

Policy Transfer as Rational Policy-making

Public organizations in both developed and developing countries do not always possess the expertise to tackle the problems they confront and increasingly look outside the organization to other governments or non-governmental organizations for the answers to problems. The public expects more from government than ever before and this expectation has been mediated through politicians to civil servants:

> This government expects more of policy-makers. More new ideas, more willingness to question inherited ways of doing things, better use of evidence and research in policy-making and better focus on policies that will deliver long-term goals (UK Cabinet Office, 1999).

Given this emphasis on the importance of evidence-based policy-making, policy transfer has become a rational choice for most developed countries (see Davies *et al.*, 2000 and Pawson, 2002).

The story, however, is less clear for developing countries, transition societies or countries emerging from conflict. Policy transfer remains largely a rational process in the sense that such states still need to engage in lesson drawing from successful exemplars in order to engineer effective national development or reconstruction planning and programming. However, governments in developing countries are often compelled by influential donor countries (e.g. countries that give large amounts of aid to developing countries such as the United States, Britain or Japan), supra-national institutions (e.g. the European Union), global financial institutions (e.g. the World Bank and the International Monetary Fund), international organizations (e.g. the Organization for Economic Co-operation and Development) or transnational corporations (e.g. Time Warner), to introduce policy change in order to secure grants, loans or forms of inward investment. For example, in the past the securing of loans by developing countries from the International Monetary Fund (IMF) has become conditional on the introduction of structural adjustment programmes (SAPs) including initiatives such as administrative reform, privatization, competition policy and other forms of market liberalization. Such programmes are predicated on a western interpretation of 'Good Governance' and give rise to negotiated processes of policy transfer that often undermine the sovereignty of nation states to make public policy in the national interest. The history of failed SAPs is testimony to the omnipresence of poorly conceived processes of policy transfer in developing countries. At the same time, however, it is evident that such countries can improve their bargaining position with international organizations and donors if they have the capacity to engage in evidence-based policy discourses (see Stiglitz, 2002: 26-33). Sadly this is not often the case which is why building the human resources necessary to attain this position should be a key goal of any national development plan.

This book evaluates the implications of these changes and challenges for both the study and the practice of policy transfer. It provides: an understanding of policy transfer as a process of organizational learning; an insight into how and why such processes are studied by policy scientists; and, an evaluation of its use by policy practitioners. This will allow for the development of a better understanding of the phenomenon of policy transfer and its relationship with global and domestic processes of economic, social and political change.

Argument

The book develops two central arguments. The first is a normative argument, policy transfer can be a rational and progressive learning activity but only if the policy that is transferred is compatible with the value system of the recipient organization, culturally assimilated through comprehensive evaluation, and, builds on existing organizational strengths. In most instances, locally sensitive solutions must be found to local problems. There are, of course, exceptions to this rule. For example, while the British Empire contributed much to its former colony, Sri Lanka, in terms of transferring an effective administrative system, the present ethnic conflict in Sri Lanka is a manifestation of a crisis of the state that has its roots in British imperialism. The British left behind a majoritarian constitution that privileged one ethnic group over all others and ensured its dominance in politics, economy and society. As a GOSL Minister (Evans, 2004) puts it, '[u]ntil we have a constitution that reflects the multi-ethnic character of Sri Lankan society and protects the rights of minorities, the conflict will continue'. As a rule of thumb, however, policy transfer must be able to work with the grain of the indigenous policy system.

The second argument centres on the domain of enquiry in policy transfer analysis. The study of policy transfer can only be distinctive from the analysis of normal forms of policy-making if it focuses on the remarkable movement of ideas between systems of governance through policy transfer networks and the intermediation of agents of policy transfer. It is claimed that these two arguments hold in both developed and developing countries.

Bridging the Gaps

Policy Transfer in Global Perspective has three main aims that seek to bridge significant gaps in the existing literature on policy transfer.

The first aim is to provide an interdisciplinary framework for studying processes of policy transfer. The recent literature analysing policy convergence, policy diffusion, policy learning and lesson drawing assesses the nature of different forms of policy transfer from the perspective of a host of disciplines ranging from domestic and international political science to comparative politics. The study of policy transfer has a truly interdisciplinary character. Yet what is commonly viewed as a strength can also be identified as a weakness. As a consequence of the diffuse nature of this field of study, policy transfer analysts do not have the benefit of a common idiom or a unified discourse of theoretical or methodological discussion and reason from which lessons can be drawn and hypotheses developed.

Indeed, despite often having complementary research agendas these disciplines have continued to speak past each other. Our starting point then is that policy transfer analysis can provide a context for integrating common research concerns of scholars of domestic, comparative and international politics.

The second aim is to provide an explanatory model of policy transfer. The study of policy transfer is an area of research that remains under theorised and weak in explanatory power or what we will term *additionality* (Stone, 1999; Page, 2000). Specifically, it may be asked of policy transfer, what does it tell us which we did not know before? Max Weber (Gerth and Wright-Mills, 1948: 145) once cautioned:

> Consider the historical and cultural sciences...they give us no answer to the question, whether the existence of these cultural phenomena have been and are worthwhile. And they do not answer the further question, whether it is worth the effort required to know them.

Policy transfer analysis must become more distinctive from the analysis of normal forms of policy-making if it is not simply to rearticulate other ideas. It must justify itself in the theoretical and the empirical domain. Indeed, it will be argued in the next chapter that the survival of policy transfer as a framework of understanding relies on its ability to be adapted into a multi-level, interdisciplinary perspective which both recognizes the importance of global, international, transnational and domestic structures and their ability to constrain and/or facilitate policy development and allows for the possibility that policy transfer may purely be the product of interpersonal relations in a policy transfer network.

The third aim is to present a broad range of detailed empirical case studies of policy transfer:

- between developed countries;
- from developed to developing countries; and,
- from developing countries to developing and developed countries.

There is presently a dearth of literature on the study of policy transfer in the last two categories (see Stone, 1999). The empirical investigation that follows will therefore involve chapters on new public management, welfare policy, health policy, local government reform, youth employment policy, health policy, and education policy in countries as diverse as Britain, Brazil, Ecuador, France, Germany, Greece, the special administrative region of Hong Kong in China, Kyrgyzstan, Malaysia, Mexico, Singapore, Tanzania, the Ukraine, and, the United States.

Policy Transfer in Global Perspective thus provides the first account of policy transfer in the global sphere. Drawing on the first published collection of case studies of policy transfer between first, second and third world countries, it presents a multi-level explanatory model that accounts for the emergence and development of processes of policy transfer between nation states. In addition, its findings provide a guide to best practice for practitioners engaged in policy transfer activity that highlights the importance of finding local solutions to global policy problems.

The Structure of the Argument

The discussion that follows is organized around a critical review of the policy transfer literature, ten empirical chapters and a concluding chapter. The final chapter reviews the book's empirical findings and establishes a set of empirically testable hypotheses to guide the identification of potential independent and dependent variables in future policy transfer research.

Chapter Two provides an insight into the main components of the theory of policy transfer in order to prepare the ground for the empirical investigation to follow. The existing literature is organized into four main approaches to the study of policy transfer: process-centred approaches, ideational approaches, comparative approaches, and, multi-level approaches. It is argued that the first three of these approaches are virtuous in their descriptive powers but weak in their explanatory power and it emphasizes the merits of following a multi-level perspective. The chapter then moves on to present a defence of policy transfer analysis from recent criticisms and to identify some theoretical propositions and methodological techniques that should inform the analysis of processes of policy transfer.

The empirical investigation is then divided into three parts: policy transfer between developed countries; policy transfer from developed to developing countries; and, policy transfer from developing countries. From Chapters Three to Eleven a broad range of empirical cases of policy transfer are presented. These case studies have been selected for four main reasons. First, with the exception of Chapter Ten, they provide illustrations of the application of multi-level approaches to the study of policy transfer. Secondly, they provide a truly global perspective on the policy transfer phenomenon. Thirdly, they include case illustration of failed as well as successful processes of policy transfer and 'in-process' as well as completed processes of policy transfer. And, finally they involve an evaluation of the three basic forms of policy development – 'policy', 'programmes' and 'delivery' issues. In this context we refer to 'policy' as a course of action or plan that has been conceived to deal with a particular political problem, while a programme involves an action oriented activity which in combination with other action oriented activities will, at least in theory, lead to the implementation of the policy and ultimately provide a solution to the problem(s). Hence, a policy is an attempt to define a rational basis for action or inaction. 'Delivery' issues focus upon the mechanics of policy or programme design that deal directly with delivery issues and are rarely subject to public scrutiny but remain wholly political.

In Part One, *Policy Transfer Between Developed Countries*, three case studies of voluntary processes of policy transfer mediated through policy transfer networks are presented. In Chapter Three, Mark Evans and Paul McComb provide an account of the emergence and development of a performance measurement and resource allocation programme within the UK Department of Social Security

(DSS) to counter social security fraud. The chapter draws on the unique, insider perspective of the Project Leader and his team at the Benefit Fraud Inspectorate (BFI). It argues that the structure of the policy transfer network was the key determinant of policy transfer outcomes. In Chapter Four, Mark Evans presents data from a case study of policy transfer in the Welfare policy arena – the New Deal. It is argued that the study of the New Deal provides fertile ground for investigating the significance of the theory of the competition state as a lens for observing both the changing nature of the nation state and the role of state actors and institutions in promoting new forms of complex globalization through processes of policy transfer. In the final chapter in this section, Chapter Five, Stella Ladi conducts an empirical investigation of an attempt to transfer an environmental employment project, *Ecotrans*, from Denmark to Greece and to Germany. The policy transfer process proves to be unsuccessful in Greece and successful in Germany.

Part Two, *Policy Transfer from Developed to Developing Countries*, consists of four chapters. In Chapter Six, Veronica Ivanova and Mark Evans examine the applicability of the policy transfer approach to a state in transition using local government reform in the Ukraine as an example. It contends that policy transfer is not only a useful but also a necessary tool for analysing transition societies. In Chapter Seven, Andrew Street examines why UK General Practitioner Fund-holding was placed on the Kyrgyz policy agenda and evaluates the prospects for implementation of the scheme. The case study is analysed using three competing analytical frameworks – rational decision-making, public choice theory, and indirect coercive transfer. He argues that analytical bias pervades policy transfer analysis as the case study demonstrates that the selection of a particular analytical position pre-determines the conclusions drawn about the process and outcome of policy transfer. In Chapter Eight, Pedro Flores-Crespo investigates the transfer of the French model of the Institute Universitaire de Technologie in the creation of the Mexican Technological Universities using the policy transfer framework. He argues that while it would be irrational to ignore foreign experiences in the development of indigenous public policy processes, policy learning must work with the grain of indigenous policy systems and be compatible with social norms, values and behaviour. In the final chapter in this section, Richard Common presents an account of the diffusion of public management in South-east Asia. The chapter challenges the notion that New Public Management (NPM) is being globalized and exposes the weaknesses of globalization studies that assume homogeneity in policy development across all countries.

The final section, *Policy Transfer from Developed Countries*, consists of two chapters. In Chapter Ten, Anthony Nedley argues that to date policy transfer analysis has evolved in a vacuum of its own making that exhibits myopic tendencies by failing to see the full extent of knowledge available to it. Indeed, the exclusion by Northern policy-makers of developing country experience suggests an unhealthy lack of willingness to access what 'the-other-half' knows. This approach inhibits the opportunity for genuine global dialogue and, in turn, confines both policy learning and transfer to easily accessible jurisdictions determined by language, historical legacies and/or institutional and political similarities. This chapter has been included in this volume because it demonstrates the importance of broadening search activity in the North to encompass successful southern policy exemplars.

In the final empirical chapter, Xenia Lana and Mark Evans build on Nedley's argument – the tendency to ignore the study of the transfer of policies, programmes and ideas outside the North American-European axis. The main theoretical contribution of this chapter is to evaluate the applicability of the policy transfer approach to the analysis of transfers between developing countries. They argue that policy transfer analysis is a useful framework for studying transfers between developing countries and present a multi-level framework for examining such processes. It is further argued that knowledge institutions play an important role in facilitating and implementing 'South-to-South' transfers. The main empirical contribution of the chapter is the development of an original case study of the voluntary transfer of the *Bolsa-escola* (School Scholarship) programme from Brazil to Ecuador, where it is called the *Beca escolar* programme.

The book's conclusion provides an overall assessment of the utility and prospects of policy transfer analysis as a heuristic theory of policy development. It establishes the domain of enquiry for policy transfer analysis, highlights certain theoretical and methodological weaknesses and presents a set of empirically testable hypotheses in order to guide the identification of potential independent and dependent variables for future policy transfer research. These include some normative, as well as analytical propositions.

The Authors

The idea for this book arose out of discussions during the Masters in Public Administration and Public Policy, hosted by the Department of Politics at the University of York, over the relationship between systemic globalizing forces and the increasing scope and intensity of policy transfer activity. Five of the students participating in these discussions went on to complete PhD theses on different aspects of the study of policy transfer (Richard Common, 1999; Khariah Mokhtar, 2001; Pedro Flores-Crespo, 2002; Veronica Ivanova, 2003; and, Stella Ladi 2002) or to pursue academic careers. Andrew Street, for example, is a senior research fellow in the internationally renowned Centre for Health Economics at the University of York. Others, such as Xenia Lana, Paul McComb and Anthony Nedley are practitioners in the field actively engaged both in researching and implementing processes of policy transfer. This book hopes to crystallize the best of those ideas that emerged in discussion and on paper from 1999 to 2003.

In summary then, through a combination of theoretical and empirical enquiry this book attempts to advance beyond the existing literature in the following ways. It provides: a critical literature review on the study of policy convergence and diffusion, learning or transfer (Bennett 1991a and b, Bennett and Howlett 1992, Dolowitz and Marsh 1996, Rose 1991 and 1993); the first attempt to develop multi-level explanatory models of policy transfer; a rigorous model of validation and evaluation in order to better identify cases of policy transfer; and, the first published collection of case studies on policy transfer between developed countries, from developed to developing countries, and, from developing countries.

Chapter 2

Understanding Policy Transfer

Mark Evans

Introduction

Policy transfer analysis is a theory of policy development that seeks to make sense of a process or set of processes in which knowledge about institutions, policies or delivery systems at one sector or level of governance is used in the development of institutions, policies or delivery systems at another sector or level of governance. Different forms of policy transfer such as band-wagoning (Ikenberry, 1990), convergence (Coleman, 1994), diffusion (Majone, 1991), emulation and harmonization (Bennett, 1991), learning (P. Haas, ed., 1992; Greener, 2001; Common, 2004) and lesson-drawing (Rose, 1993) have been identified in a wide ranging literature which has attracted significant academic attention from domestic (Dolowitz *et al.*, 2000; Evans and Davies, 1999), comparative (Wolman, 1992; ESRC 2000); and, international political scientists (Stone, 2000; Ladi, 2003).

In this chapter I will sketch some of the main components of the theory of policy transfer in order to prepare the way for the empirical investigation to follow. Its purpose is to evaluate the character of this interdisciplinary approach to cross-national policy development and to assess its strengths, weaknesses and potential theoretical and methodological development. It therefore considers: the domestic and international circumstances that are likely to bring about policy transfer; the key approaches to the study of policy transfer that have emerged over the past decade; and, the scope and dimensions of the policy transfer process. The chapter is organized around a consideration of five central research questions:

- how is policy transfer studied?
- why do public organizations engage in it?;
- what form of policy oriented learning emerges in processes of transfer?;
- does the policy transfer framework provide useful insights into contemporary policy development?; and,
- in what ways can the policy transfer approach be improved?

This will advance our investigation in two main ways. First, it will provide the reader with a contextual understanding of the phenomenon of policy transfer, its relationship with global and domestic processes of economic, social and political change and an insight into how it is studied. Secondly, it will allow for an assessment of which aspects of the framework should and should not be pursued in empirical work, which will inform the empirical investigation to follow.

Studying Policy Transfer

I begin by describing the scope of enquiry in policy transfer analysis before moving on to a presentation of the main approaches that are currently utilized in this mode of enquiry.

The Scope of Enquiry

Policy analysts deploy the policy transfer approach as a generic concept that encompasses quite different claims about why public organizations engage in policy learning. Typically policy transfer analysts refer to three different processes of transfer: voluntary transfer or lesson-drawing; negotiated transfer; and, direct coercive transfer. The first is a rational, action oriented approach to dealing with public policy problems that emerge from one or more of the following: the identification of public or professional dissatisfaction with existing policy as a consequence of poor performance; a new policy agenda that is introduced due to a change in government, minister or the management of a public organization; a political strategy aimed at legitimating conclusions that have already been reached; or, an attempt by a political manager to upgrade items of the policy agenda to promote political allies and neutralize political enemies.

The second and third processes of transfer involve varying degrees of coercion. Negotiated policy transfer refers to a process in which governments are compelled by influential donor countries, global financial institutions, supra-national institutions, international organizations or transnational corporations, to introduce policy change in order to secure grants, loans or other forms of inward investment. Although an exchange process does occur it remains a coercive activity because the recipient country is denied freedom of choice. The political economy of most developing countries throughout the 1980s and 1990s has been characterized by the implementation of SAPs in return for investment from the IMF, or the World Bank (WB). This is a reflection of the pervasiveness of negotiated forms of policy transfer to developing countries. Another form of indirect policy transfer can be identified when government's introduce institutional or policy changes due to a fear of falling behind neighbouring countries. For example, Japan's economic miracle in East Asia proved inspirational to neighbouring countries such as Singapore, South Korea and Malaysia. John Ikenberry (1990: 102) terms this process 'bandwagoning'.

Direct coercive policy transfer occurs when a government is forced by another government to introduce constitutional, social and political changes against its will and the will of its people. This form of policy transfer was widespread in periods of formal imperialism and its implications can still be seen today in contemporary Mexico, Kenya, India, Pakistan, Sri Lanka, Zimbabwe and South Africa, to name but a few.

The contemporary study of policy transfer originates from policy diffusion studies, a sub-set of the comparative politics literature. Research in this area focused on identifying trends in timing, geography, and resource similarities in the diffusion of innovations between countries, and, in the United States, between states (see Walker, 1969 and Gray, 1973). However, this research revealed next to nothing about the process of transfer apart from its identification of mechanisms of diffusion or, indeed, the content of the new policies. In contrast, much of the contemporary literature on policy transfer has primarily focused on studying voluntary policy transfer between developed countries as a process of policy development, identifying a process in which policies implemented elsewhere are examined by rational political actors for their potential utilization within another political system (Dolowitz and Marsh, 2000). As Richard Rose (1991: 3) puts it:

> Every country has problems, and each thinks that its problems are unique...However, problems that are unique to one country...are abnormal...confronted with a common problem, policy makers in cities, regional governments and nations can learn from their counterparts elsewhere responded.

Up until recently the study of policy transfer from developed to developing countries and, from developing countries to developing and developed countries, has largely been ignored.

The literature on policy transfer analysis may be organized into two discernible schools: one which does not use the label 'policy transfer' directly but deals with different aspects of the process using different nomenclature; and, one which uses the concept directly. The former includes the literatures on: band-wagoning (Ikenberry, 1990); convergence (Bennett, 1991; Coleman, 1994); diffusion (Eyestone, 1977; Majone, 1991); evidence-based practice (Davies *et al.*, 2000 and Pawson, 2002); learning (P. Haas, ed., 1992; Greener, 2001; Common, 2004); and, lesson-drawing (Rose, 1993). The latter includes the work of domestic policy scientists (Dolowitz *et al.*, 2000; Evans and Davies, 1999; and, Page, 2000), comparativists (Common, 2001; Peters 1997; and, Wolman, 1992); and, international policy scientists (Cerny and Evans, 2002; Stone, 2000; and, Ladi, 2003). Indeed the breadth of policy transfer research is reflected in the Economic and Social Research Council's (ESRC) *Future Governance Programme* in the UK, which was launched in January 2000 (see http://www.hull.ac.uk/futgov/). It consists of 30 research projects that examine the scope for drawing policy lessons from cross-national experience. In addition to the projects, the Programme organizes cross-national comparative meetings aimed at promoting lesson-drawing on the basis of systematic social science research (see: J. Bachtler *et al.*, 2001; P. Carlen, 2001; P. Furlong, 2001; A. Gilbert, 2001; T. Jones and T. Newburn, 2001; M. Levi, 2001; K. Mossberger and H. Wolman, 2001; R. Rose, 2001; A. Rutherford and M. Telford, 2001; and, A. Tickell and G. Clark, 2001).

Policy transfer analysis encompasses the traditional domain of policy analysis: the study of the broad macro-environs of the policy process such as the economic context, Europeanization (in the case of EU member states and associates) or processes of globalization (e.g. geopolitics, political integration, global communications, and, the internationalization of capital); meso-level or intergovernmental forms of policy analysis (e.g. policy transfer network analysis); and, micro-level stages of the policy process (e.g. formulation, implementation, evaluation) and methods of analysis (e.g. prospective policy evaluation, implementation theory). Policy transfer analysts are therefore interested in: decision-making processes and the key actors which shape policy-making; policy implementation and causes of policy 'failure'; issues involved in researching and studying policy change, and, enhancing the capacity of public administrators to formulate and implement policy decisions. Policy transfer analysis therefore focuses on three areas of study that are commonplace in normal policy analysis:

- description – how policy transfer is made;
- explanation – why policy transfer occurs;
- prescription – how policy transfer should be made.

It needs to be noted here, however, that most political scientists, particularly in Europe, deliberately avoid the third area of study in the aspiration of maintaining social scientific impartiality. In sum, as Harold Lasswell (1970) would put it, policy transfer analysis is about providing 'knowledge of and knowledge in policy making'.

Approaches

There are four main approaches employed in policy transfer analysis: process-centred approaches; ideational approaches; comparative approaches; and, multi-level approaches (see Table 2.1).

Process-centred approaches Policy scientists who focus on the process of policy transfer directly in order to explain the voluntary, or coercively negotiated importation of ideas, policies or institutions use process-centred approaches. This approach argues that policy learning is largely based on the interpersonal interaction between agents of transfer, bureaucrats and politicians within interorganizational settings. In these settings there exists a pattern of common kinship expressed through culture, rules and values. Hence, an emphasis is placed on analysing the structure of decision-making through which policy transfer takes place and relationships between agents of transfer and their dependencies. It therefore centres on state and non-state actors who are actively engaged in policy learning such as bureaucrats and think tanks. It has also tended to be a predominantly inter-state approach that emphasizes the role of state actors as active agents seeking solutions to policy problems rather than the passive agents depicted in pluralist or corporatist decision literatures. The role of the agent of transfer (e.g. policy entrepreneurs such as think tanks, knowledge institutions (KIs), or pressure groups) is considered critical within this approach.

Table 2.1   The main approaches to the study of policy transfer

Approach and Emphasis	Strengths and Weaknesses
Process-centred approaches argue that policy transfer is almost solely based on personal interaction in decision settings where there exists a 'common kinship' and 'agreed culture'. Bennett (1991) uses policy transfer as an independent variable focusing on the transfer of policy goals and content, instruments or administrative techniques, while Rose (1991; 1993) uses policy transfer as a dependent variable attempting to explain why transfer occurs, and, how lessons are incorporated into a political system.	This is an approach that is strong on descriptive and prescriptive analysis and assumes rationality. The research demonstrates who has relationships with whom and it can describe how these relations impinge on the making of policy. Focuses too much on the role of individuals and how they see the process of transfer rather than upon transfer networks and exogenous structures (with the exception of technology) and institutions that can influence policy outcomes.
Ideational approaches are united in arguing that it is systems of ideas which influence how politicians and policy-makers learn how to learn and they all address, in different ways, the problem of when and how policy-makers and societies learn how to learn (Hall, 1993; Common, 2004; Stone, 1996; and, Ladi, 2002).	This approach is particularly useful in helping policy analysts to identify potential obstacles to policy transfer and insights into how to develop a learning organization. However, policy analysts tend to assume that systems of ideas influence policy transfer rather than demonstrate it empirically.
Comparative approaches involve both single comparative case study analysis (Wolman, 1992) and cross-national aggregate comparison (Peters, 1997).	Such approaches provide the benefit of comparison e.g. generalizability but overemphasize broader structural factors over agency factors that account for processes of transfer.
Multi-level approaches are characterized by a concern with understanding outcomes of policy transfer through combining macro and micro (Dolowitz and Marsh, 1996; 2000), or, macro, meso and micro (Common, 2001; Evans and Davies, 1999) levels of enquiry.	These approaches provide comprehensiveness but can be criticized for being too complex due to the identification of too many variables and explaining everything and nothing. Such approaches require careful theorization and appropriate integration of levels of analysis.

Two key applications can be identified within this approach that have proved particularly influential – the work of Richard Rose (1991; 1993), and Colin Bennett (1991). A brief account of both of these approaches will be presented here. In 1991, following a panel at the American Political Science Association, a special edition on lesson-drawing was published by the *Journal of Public Policy*, which dealt with voluntary processes of policy transfer in the Europe-North-America axis.

Rose and Bennett's work deserves special attention, because they presented two of the first attempts to explain the reasons why countries voluntarily engage in policy transfer and the process by which they utilize foreign experience to develop new programmes. Moreover, they have both had a significant influence on subsequent policy transfer research.

Richard Rose (1993: 6) uses the concept of lesson-drawing (voluntary policy transfer) as a dependent variable. He attempts to explain why it occurs and how lessons are incorporated into a political system through various processes of copying, emulation, hybridization, or inspiration. He deploys the concept of lesson-drawing as a method for learning from past and/or extra organizational experiences and emphasizes the role of the bureaucrat and the programme itself in the process of policy learning:

> A Programme is a creation of public law; a statute identifies its purposes and the conditions under which it operates. Money to finance the programme is appropriated in the budget. A specific public agency and employees are responsible for administering a programme. The outputs of a programme can take many forms: money (a social security benefit); services of public employees (health care or education); or normative rules (laws about environmental pollution). A programme is an instrument of public policy, because it is a necessary means of achieving policy intentions.

Rose's work on lesson-drawing has contributed greatly to our understanding of the programme as an instrument of public policy, and the conditions in which programmes can be effective in non indigenous settings. For Rose, the important features of this process are the circumstances surrounding the learning of lessons from other sources, the extent to which they are adopted, and, crucially, the impact they have on the new policy environment. He also provides a set of useful tools for helping policy actors to draw lessons from other jurisdictions (Rose, 2001). Anthony Nedley will look at Rose's work in more detail in Chapter Ten, for he rightly argues that the lesson-drawing approach is the most useful for practitioners engaged in policy transfer activity as it provides the basis for a rigorous model of prospective policy evaluation (see Mossberger and Wolman, 2001).

Colin Bennett (1991) employs the process of policy learning as his key independent variable for explaining why a particular policy is adopted. He conducts empirical research on, amongst other areas, how and why evidence about the United States Freedom of Information Act (FOIA) was utilized in Canada and Britain. He observes that the FOIA was used as an exemplar in Canada and the reverse in Britain. His research focuses on the transfer of policy goals, content and instruments (e.g. privatization programmes). The importance of Bennett's research lies in his questioning of the political neutrality of the advocacy of foreign lessons. In his study of the transfer of the FOIA to Canada and the United Kingdom, he emphasizes the subjective views of elites in the recipient country in influencing the adoption of the American policy (what he terms 'the interests of the pullers'). He also makes an important methodological contribution in his refutation that there is only evidence of policy learning when there is evidence of the diffusion of a programme (1991: 32). He therefore argues for greater empirical rigour in the gathering of evidence for the establishment of causal pathways from knowledge (or awareness) to utilization and then to the adoption of a foreign policy.

Both of these applications has its merits. They are virtuous in their descriptive understanding of policy development and can be used to explain certain aspects of the process of transfer. The research ably demonstrates who has relationships with whom and it can describe how these relations impinge on the making of policy (e.g. why some actors are influential and others are not). However, while both of these approaches are important to our understanding of the nature of the process of transfer, they have shortcomings in explaining why policy transfer takes place in the first place due to the absence of any reflection on the putative role of exogenous forces in processes of policy transfer. Moreover, both authors provide limited empirical evidence to support their main empirical assertions and focus completely on voluntary processes of transfer between developed countries.

Ideational approaches There are four main accounts of policy development using ideational based studies that are worthy of brief discussion here: the social learning approach; the organizational learning approach; the epistemic community approach; and, discursive approaches. These approaches are united in arguing that it is systems of ideas which influence how politicians and policy-makers learn how to learn and they all address the problem of when and how politicians, other policy makers and societies learn how to learn.

It is important to note at the outset that social learning approaches, with the exception of Freeman (1996 and 1999), do not make explicit reference to the concept of policy transfer but rather seek to provide a general theory of policy change. The relationship between the two literatures, however, is self-evident as policy transfer is an intentional activity involving the movement of ideas between systems of governance in the aspiration of forging policy change. Peter Hall's (1993) social learning approach disaggregates the policy-making process into three dimensions: the overarching goals that guide policy in a particular field (third order change); the techniques or policy instruments used to attain these goals (second order change); and, the precise settings of these instruments (first order change). So to provide an illustration that is presently topical in the UK context. One of the goals of the Blair government is to establish world-class universities in the UK. The main obstacle to achieving this aim, however, is the ability to generate sufficient finance. One of the policy instruments that the British government has decided to use to secure appropriate levels of funding is the tuition fee. The British government has changed the settings of the policy by giving universities the freedom to charge the level of fees that they want to for home students.

Hall argues that in order to make sense of how policy learning takes place we need a theory of the policy process that takes into account the role of ideas. For

Hall, public policy deliberation takes place within a broader system of ideas that is understood and accepted by the policy-making community. This system of ideas specifies not only the goals of policy and the instruments used to attain them, but also the very nature of the issues that are important and need to be addressed. Keynesianism or monetarism may be viewed as two illustrations of systems of ideas or what Hall also terms 'policy paradigms' emerging in periods of third order change. The rise of a competition state ethos under New Labour in the UK may be viewed as another. Here a macro-level commitment to competition state principles creates opportunity structures for policy transfer to occur (Evans and Cerny, 2003). Economically, the competition state constitutes a move away Keynesianism and the belief in the concept of the industrial-welfare state through the introduction of a distinctive economic project that embraces the pressures of international markets through the adjustment of domestic as well as foreign economic policies. The competition state pursues increased marketization in order to make national economic activities more competitive in both international and national terms. This strategy has manifested itself in the reduction of public spending, the control of inflation and general neo-liberal monetarism, combined with the deregulation of economic activities (especially financial markets). Moreover, in order to complete such an ambitious economic project, the instruments of public policy-making have been changed, new forms of statecraft have emerged and institutional structures and political practices reshaped with the aim of enhancing the steering capacity of the state.

Hall's work has proved particularly influential in the study of policy change but is yet to be applied to the study of policy transfer. Its potential utilization in this field, however, is rich with possibilities.

The organizational learning approach is largely a product of management studies and its concern with public sector learning from the private sector. Indeed, it has superseded Total Quality Management as the key strategy for improving public sector performance (Tushman and Nadler, 1996). It is based on the proposition that the quality of an organization rests on its ability to demonstrate that it can learn collectively through the application of new knowledge to the policy process or innovation in policy implementation. As Olsen and Peters (1996: 4) note, organizational learning involves the 'development of structures and procedures that improve the problem-solving capacity of an organization and make it better prepared for the future'. The literature distinguishes between the notions of organizational learning and the learning organization. The former is based on observing learning processes within organizations, while the latter provides an action-oriented perspective for improving the performance of public organizations.

It is noteworthy, that recent research in this area by Reschenthaler and Thompson (2001: 53) concludes that 'governments and organizations within government have been, and are, seriously disadvantaged as learning organizations'. This approach has only very recently been introduced in the study of policy transfer through Richard Common's (2004) study of the British government's attempt to become a learning organization. It is particularly useful in helping policy analysts to identify potential obstacles to policy transfer and in providing insights to practitioners on how to develop the type of learning organization conducive to the facilitation of successful policy transfer (see Pedler *et al.*, 1991).

The study of epistemic communities as a method of understanding the movement of ideas in the international domain is a central preoccupation in the study of international relations (E. Hass, 1980; P. Hass 1989; E. Adler and P. Haas, 1992). Diane Stone's influential research on think tanks has been central in integrating the concerns of this literature with the study of policy transfer (see Evans and Davies, 1999, for an alternative account). Stone (1996a; 1999; 2000a&b) identifies think tanks as key agents of policy transfer within what are termed 'epistemic communities'. Epistemic communities are comprised of natural and social scientists or individuals from any discipline or profession with authoritative claims to policy relevant knowledge that reside in national, transnational and international organizations. The function of these communities is to facilitate the emergence of policy learning that may lead to policy convergence. Her research provides an understanding of the mechanisms by which think tanks have been successful in influencing the formulation of public policies, specifically the spread of privatization ideas. The epistemic communities literature has also been used to explain how international policy has converged in areas such as GATT, food aid, financial regulation and environmental protection.

Stella Ladi's (1998; 2000; and 2002) recent work on the role of think tanks in mediating policy transfer in the EU emphasizes the influential role of the discourses of globalization and Europeanization in processes of policy transfer. Ladi argues that an understanding of the belief systems that agents of transfer hold with regard to globalization and Europeanization is crucial in order to evaluate the influence of the discourse within which a process of policy transfer takes place. In her research on the role of a knowledge institution (*Understandingbus*) in processes of policy transfer in Germany and Greece, she notes that it had an extremely positive approach towards advancing the European and globalization projects. However, although the discourses of globalization and Europeanization were influential in both Germany and Greece, the outcome of the policy transfer process varied due to mitigating political factors. She concludes that although the ideational sphere is important, it is interwoven with the material sphere and processes of policy transfer can only be successful if the material sphere is also satisfied. The sustainability and vitality of transfer networks rests on the forging of a consensus between policy actors and agents of transfer that a programme has been found that will deal with the problems that they are facing. In order to achieve such a consensus, policy-makers must be convinced that the programme is technically feasible and in keeping with the dominant value systems of the domestic policy domain.

Comparative approaches   All studies of policy transfer should adopt a comparative methodology but unfortunately few do. In most cases thick description is provided to account for the indigenous policy environment and detail of the non-indigenous policy environment is largely ignored. Comprehensive policy transfer analysis requires thick description but this does make for tiresome narrative and few journal editors are likely to countenance it. Two explicitly comparative approaches can be identified in the literature.

Harold Wolman (1992) uses policy transfer as an explicit tool of comparative political enquiry. He argues that the adoption of similar policies can result from common processes occurring within nations (such as levels of social and economic modernization), which lead states either to independently adopt similar policies or to engage in conscious imitation. This conscious imitation is what Wolman (1992: 28) takes to be policy transfer. His empirical research focuses on a single comparative case study, which analyses the transfer of the American Urban Development Action Grant programme (UDAG) to Britain as the Urban Development Grant (UDG) in the early 1980s. Wolman's work has been particularly influential in urban studies but it can be criticised for providing a limited methodology for studying the process of policy transfer and, in particular, poor validation to support the occurrence of policy transfer. Indeed, Davies and Evans (1998) demonstrate that this particular process of policy transfer, the transfer of the UDAG to Britain as the UDG, was already underway prior to the period of policy change identified by Wolman in his account. Nonetheless, as we shall see later, it must be noted that proving that policy transfer has taken place is a particularly thorny problem in policy transfer analysis.

A distinct categorization of analysis for cross-national aggregate comparison may also be identified in policy transfer analysis. However, such studies, while using the concept of policy transfer directly, do not study the process of transfer itself. Guy Peters (1997), for example, examines the diffusion of administrative reform policy transfers through the member countries of the Organization for Economic Co-operation and Development (OECD). He argues that policy learning is a common activity in governments around the world, but that there are differences in the rates at which countries are able to learn and adapt. He attributes these differences to structural factors such as economic, ideological, cultural and institutional similarities. Those states that share common features are more likely to engage in policy transfer with one another. He concludes that cultural variables play an extremely important role in the transfer of policy innovations among countries, particularly in relation to geographical proximity and political similarity. However, another set of policy ideas, those associated with political parties and ideologies, appear to have much less of a relationship with the spread of management reforms.

As always Peters's work is highly scholarly and provocative but it does fall foul of the criticism that it is impossible using this methodology to prove that policy transfer has taken place. Hence, his explanation of why the diffusion of administrative reform has occurred through the member countries of the OECD is at best impressionistic. This appears a classic case of where quantitative analysis proves useful in highlighting potential critical variables for qualitative analysis. In other words cross-national aggregate comparisons of this sort are best contained within a mixed methods approach.

Multi-level approaches Multi-level approaches to the study of policy transfer are characterized by a concern with understanding outcomes of policy transfer through combining macro and micro (Dolowitz and Marsh, 1996 and, 2000; and, Flores-Crespo, 2002), or, macro, meso and micro (Common, 2001; Evans and Davies, 1999; Evans with McComb, 1999; Ladi, 2000; and, Mokhtar, 2001) levels of enquiry. The most influential accounts using this approach have been developed by David Dolowitz and David Marsh (1996; 2000), Richard Common (2001), and Mark Evans and Jonathan Davies (1999).

Dolowitz and Marsh (1996) have led efforts within British political science to develop a comprehensive theory of policy transfer. In essence, they have drawn together a general framework of heterogeneous concepts, including policy diffusion, policy convergence, policy learning and lesson-drawing, under the umbrella heading of policy transfer, which is mainly derived from the work of Rose (1991; 1993), Bennett (1991a & b), Robertson (1991) and Wolman (1992). They therefore use policy transfer as a generic concept, which encompasses quite different claims about the nature of policy development. Rose (1991: 9), for example, characterizes lesson-drawing as 'voluntaristic', whereas policy diffusion and policy convergence tend to be associated with 'structural' dynamics which Rose associates with 'technocratic determinism' (Ibid.). Alternatively, Wolman argues that similar policies can arise in different countries either from common process or through conscious imitation – both structure and agency. As Eyestone (1977: 441) observes, [d]iffusion patterns may reflect either the 'spread of necessity' or the 'emulation of virtue'.

Dolowitz and Marsh suggest that all these phenomena occur and can be organized into one framework as 'dimensions of policy transfer'. Thus lesson-drawing is categorized under the sub-heading 'voluntary transfer' and structured change is categorized within 'voluntary', 'perceptual' and 'direct' or 'indirect' coercive policy transfer. Dolowitz and Marsh provide an extremely useful framework which invites others to criticize and develop it – a map of the process of policy transfer which can only ever be a representation of a reality which needs to be proved or disproved through empirical investigation: '[w]e have suggested a series of questions which can be used both to organize our current knowledge of the process and to guide future work'. The framework developed by Dolowitz and Marsh is clearly designed to incorporate a vast domain of policy-making activity by classifying all possible occurrences of transfer, voluntary and coercive, temporal and spatial. Policy transfer is common in this scheme and processes such as the 'rapid growth in communications of all types since the Second World War' have accelerated the process (1996: 343). This is not, however, a claim that policy transfer is pervasive nor do Dolowitz and Marsh comment on the difference between policy transfer and normal forms of policy innovation, or whether policy transfer falls entirely within the parameters of policy succession. We will discuss the question of boundaries to the study of policy transfer further below.

Dolowitz and Marsh's approach is generally regarded to be more inclusive than previous studies for two main reasons. First, their definition of transfer is broad enough to encompass both voluntary and coercive processes and transferences within and between nations. Secondly, the concept of policy transfer is used as both a dependent and an independent variable. In other words, they seek to explain what causes and impacts on the process of transfer as well as how processes of policy transfer lead to particular policy outcomes. As Dolowitz's (1997) analysis of how the British government learned from American employment policy demonstrates, the framework is extremely useful for organizing research questions and classifying the process of transfer under scrutiny. Similarly, Dolowitz *et al.* (2000), provide a compelling account of policy transfer and British social policy development.

Dolowitz and Marsh have made a significant contribution to the study of policy transfer, particularly in organizing a fragmented literature into a coherent whole and suggesting their own preferred interpretation. Indeed, their work has heavily influenced subsequent multi-level approaches to the study of policy transfer (see Common, 2001; and, Evans and Davies, 1999). Dolowitz and Marsh's definition of transfer, however, is far too broad to give the concept distinctive analytical validity. It is extremely difficult to distinguish between their theory of policy transfer and normal forms of policy development. Furthermore, the explanatory power of the model is limited both in terms of its articulation of the relationship between structure and agency and in its account of the role of actors in processes of agenda setting and transference. The weakest aspect of the approach lies in the presentation of a continuum of policy transfer development in which rational/voluntary and non-rational/coercive policy transfer activity may be found at each end of a spectrum, with negotiated or obligated forms of policy transfer lying in the middle of the axis. While one of the central arguments advanced in this book is the normative proposition that policy transfer activity is likely to be more successful if it builds upon and reinforces indigenous practices, it is important to note that some of the most enduring and rational legacies of formal imperialism have emerged from coercive processes of transfer such as administrative systems, irrigation and sanitation systems and road networks. In short, coercive forms of policy transfer do not *always* have to be non-rational.

Richard Common (2001) applies a multi-level policy transfer framework in a comparative study of the spread of NPM strategies in Malaysia, Hong Kong and Singapore. The analytical framework used in this research consists of three overlapping elements: a model of administrative change, policy transfer analysis as a method for analysing an observable and measurable process and NPM as public policy output to be observed. Qualitative and quantitative methods are employed effectively to challenge the popular misapprehension that NPM has been globalized (Dunleavy, 1994). Common concludes that although the rhetoric of NPM strategies can easily be identified in the three countries he analysed, NPM can only be regarded as a global phenomenon if the impact of its implementation is tangible to bureaucrats and to the public across all nations (see Chapter Nine for a broader exposition).

The shortcomings in Common's work are those that are common to all comparative approaches to the study of policy transfer. While his work is impressive in terms of the scope of its empirical investigation and the integration of management and policy science literature, it is unsurprisingly stronger in its account of structural and organizational dynamics of policy change than those emanating from processes of policy oriented learning. In sum, his approach lacks the detailed empiricism of the processes of policy transfer to sustain his knowledge claims about the occurrence or otherwise of the spread of new public management in Malaysia, Hong Kong and Singapore.

The multi-level approach to policy transfer analysis developed by Mark Evans and Jonathan Davies in 1999 represented an attempt to transcend some of the problems identified with the aforementioned approaches. Evans and Davies argued that the survival of policy transfer as a theory of policy-making rested on its ability to be adapted into a multi-level, interdisciplinary perspective on policy change. They observed that the literature on policy transfer analysis only provided a definitional criteria of what policy transfer involves, together with a set of dependent variables to inform empirical investigation. They further argued that the approach needed to advance beyond this and develop a conception of policy transfer analysis that allowed for the investigation of the role of global, international and/or transnational forces; state-centred forces; the role of policy transfer networks in mediating policy change; and, micro-level processes of policy oriented learning. In short, an approach that allows for a multi-level empirical investigation of the relationship between structure and agency.

Evans and Davies therefore developed a multi-level model of policy transfer that built upon and integrated accounts of international structure and agency and the epistemic community approach, domestic structure and agency, policy network analysis and process-centred policy transfer analysis. The utilization of the notion of a policy transfer network is integral to their account of the cognitive dimension of decision-making – i.e. how decision makers acquire knowledge. They developed the concept of a policy transfer network to depict an ad hoc, action oriented policy-making structure set up with the specific intention of engineering rapid policy change. They exist only for the time that a transfer is occurring. By implication policy transfer networks matter because without them other policies might be adopted.

The policy transfer network approach involves the application of an 'ideal-type' policy cycle to case study investigation. By this they refer to the stages through which a political issue can pass. As this emphasis infers, this stages approach is associated with what has been traditionally termed the rational model of decision-making in bureaucratic organizations. The authors adopt this approach for organizational rather than pedagogic reasons, as the intellectual shortcomings of the rational model are legend. For instance, the proposition that decision makers can control the environment in which policy formulation and implementation takes place is clearly difficult to square empirically. Indeed, the major challenge of modern policy analysis is to analyse decision-making under conditions of uncertainty. They use the notion of a policy cycle purely as a heuristic method for mapping processes of transfer through a combination of decision and delivery analysis.

Decision analysis focuses on analysing: the nature of agenda setting; problem definition (or 'deciding how to decide'); decision-making structures (policy transfer networks); and, options analysis (the review of evidence based practice). Delivery analysis centres on the interaction between policy-making and policy implementation. A particular focus here is placed on sub-systems (policy transfer networks) and policy delivery systems (managerialism) and on how policy is evaluated i.e. whether a policy transfer has been successful in achieving the outcomes desired in contrast to securing the desired outputs. This approach also lends itself usefully to comparative policy analysis as each stage can be analysed through the lens of comparison.

As Table 2.2 illustrates, a series of empirically testable hypotheses can be deduced from the above characterization of the process of voluntary policy transfer. Following Marsh and Rhodes (1992b), these may be organized into a set of independent and dependent variables in which structures should be viewed as independent variables and functions as dependent variables. Any variation in the dependent variable (function) may be the result of variation in either the structure (independent variable) or in the intervening variable (process or mechanism).

Table 2.2   Multi-level policy transfer analysis

1 *Global, International and Transnational Structures* Economic, technological, ideological and institutional structures constrain but do not determine the behaviour of state actors at levels 2 and 3.   2 *The State Project (e.g. the UK Competition State)* The state has some autonomy from structural forces (economic, technological, ideological and institutional) at the level of strategic selectivity   3 *Meso-Level: the Policy Transfer Network* A network of indigenous and exogenous agents in resource dependent relationships with some level of autonomy from structural forces at the level of options analysis and implementation in processes of policy transfer. Events at level 3 can often be explained by reference to the interaction of 1 & 2.

Source: developed from Evans and Davies (1999).

For example, exogenous or network environment changes may lead to the creation of a policy transfer network leading to policy change. These may be economic/market, ideological, knowledge/technical, or institutional effects. If economic factors constitute the catalyst for change, the form of the response may be influenced by, for example, the ideology of the competition state or the developmental state, depending, of course, on the type of state under study. It may also be deduced that policy changes, which emerge from a policy transfer network, can be the product of endogenous factors such as the influence of the agent of transfer. However, as the multi-level nature of this approach dictates, policy transfer networks are but one component of an explanation of policy change. Evans and Davies also developed the first model for analysing processes of coercive policy transfer using the policy transfer network approach. How does this schema differ from a process of voluntary policy transfer? In overview, the authors argue that a coercive policy transfer network is even more action oriented than a normal transfer network as it '...involves one government or supranational institution pushing, or even forcing, another government to adopt a particular programme' (Dolowitz and Marsh 1996: 344). As such a coercive agent is likely to be involved in the process of transfer from the beginning. This will confine the search activities of policy actors to their immediate regime and it is likely that an agent of transfer, such as a representative of an epistemic community (the OECD, for example) will strongly guide their thinking throughout the process of transfer, as such, inputs will be closely monitored and controlled at all stages of the process. Having said that, it is equally clear that cultural effects can influence the evaluation and implementation stages of the transfer process.

Thus through its emphasis on structural (organizational rules and imperatives) and interpersonal relationships (information and communication exchange) within networks, together with an acceptance of accounting for structural factors exogenous to the network (e.g. ideology, economy, technology and resource exchange) a method is provided for understanding forms of policy development within a multi-organizational setting. In this sense policy transfer networks provide a context for evaluating the complex interaction of domestic and international policy agendas forged through the interaction of state and non-state (transnational and/or international) actors.

Policy Transfer Analysis and Its Critics

Policy transfer analysis is not without its critics. There are four main areas in which the policy transfer approach is subject to critique. First, that policy transfer analysis cannot be distinguished from normal forms of policy-making in general (Evans and Davies, 1999; James and Lodge, 2003) and rational approaches to policy-making in particular (James and Lodge, 2003), and, therefore it has no distinctive domain of enquiry. Secondly, that policy transfer analysts fail to advance an explanatory theory of policy development, or, as Ed Page (2000: 12) puts it, the researcher should not expect from the literature 'firm guidance about how to frame the research questions or how to pursue them empirically' (see also: Dolowitz and Marsh, 2000; Evans and Davies, 1999; and, James and Lodge, 2003).

This criticism is in keeping with Keith Dowding's (2001: 89) depiction of non-formal models, such as policy transfer analysis, as 'time consuming', 'expensive' and prone to 'trivial findings'. Thirdly, that policy transfer analysts fail to provide rigorous tools for evaluating whether policy transfer has occurred or not (Evans and Davies, 1999). And, fourthly, that policy transfer analysts focus too much attention on policy transfers between developed countries and are largely ignorant of policy transfer activity in the developing world. This final substantive section of the chapter will evaluate the credibility of each of these criticisms in more detail.

The Domain of Enquiry

Given its easy fit with traditional forms of policy analysis what kind of a theory is policy transfer analysis and how distinctive is it from normal models of policy-making? Minimally, a theory is 'a systematically related set of statements, including some law-like generalizations, that is empirically testable' (Rudner, 1966: 10). Given this definition, policy transfer analysis does not constitute an explanatory theory in the sense that it has established a set of law-like generalizations on cross national policy development. In most instances, it is used as an analogical or heuristic model in the sense that it refers to the suggestion of substantive similarities between a particular form of policy-making and mechanisms of transfer, diffusion, convergence, emulation, or learning. It is also a meso-level concept that links the micro-level of analysis, which deals with the role of interests and levels of government in relation to particular policy decisions, and the macro-level of analysis, which is concerned with broader questions concerning the distribution of power within contemporary society.

The 1990s have witnessed an upsurge of interest in meso-level analysis, particularly in British Political Science (see Dowding, 1995). The reasons for this are both political and intellectual. Politically it has been a response to what Rhodes (1996: 652) has termed 'the New Governance: Governing without Government', which refers to policy-making through multi-layered, self-organizing, interorganizational networks. Intellectually it reflects the challenge of studying the New Governance. The meso-level is exhorted as the most fertile level for analysing policy-making in Britain for two main reasons. Macro-level theories are often abstract and frequently applied to concrete situations with little attention to mediating processes, while micro-level theories tend to ignore the impact of broader structural factors on micro-decision-making settings. Hence, operating at the meso-level acts as a corrective device for ensuring that policy scientists do not lose sight of the macro- or micro-level questions, while simultaneously observing that much policy-making takes place within multi-layered, self-organizing, interorganizational networks. Meso-level analysis has thus become a crucial analytical tool for analysing policy-making.

But how weak is policy transfer analysis in terms of what I will term *additionality*? It is clearly necessary to classify the policy transfer phenomenon by its domain of enquiry in order to assess its analytical utility. Analysing the domain of the policy transfer framework necessarily depends upon assumptions about its purpose that may not be shared by its adherents. However, I will present a number of assumptions here concerning the limits of policy transfer as a tool of research and analysis. It is not an inclusive model of policy development and it is not a model concerned with the general diffusion of knowledge among humankind. It is best concerned with discernible and remarkable features of contemporary policy change. I am sceptical about the utility of intraorganizational policy transfer, in particular its temporal dimension. This view is predicated on four basic assumptions.

First, policy transfer is a theory of action oriented policy change. It is therefore better focused on identifying processes of change than on the measurements of continuity and change that intraorganizational transfers point toward. Much policy development literature suggests either directly or indirectly that forms of transfer are common and on the increase (see Hay and Marsh, 1997). As early as 1983, Hogwood and Peters asserted that policy succession was increasingly pervasive. There were, they argued, few, if any policy areas in which governments are not active. These arguments certainly imply that 'policy transfer', at least from an organization's past, will be extremely common. Rose's (1993: 120-136) voluntaristic approach to lesson-drawing also suggests that unique policies and programmes are rare although he does not discount major change – particularly where lessons are drawn transnationally. Rose does not state whether this leads him to conclude that lesson-drawing is pervasive as Hogwood and Peters argue of policy succession. However, he argues that the first logical response of a policy maker in attempting to deal with a problem will be to look for similar examples elsewhere.

These observations beckon the question: if policy transfer has become such an every day part of policy-making is it a normal form of policy development? Rose is clear that lesson-drawing is an intentional exercise involving research – suggesting that personal past experience does not count. Thus, a policy-maker who moves from organization A to organization B and then draws instinctively or deliberately upon some fragment his/her past experience in organization A cannot be said to have drawn a lesson. Rose's caveat is important for otherwise there is no boundary to what counts as lesson-drawing or policy transfer. Even policy innovations will be bound to rely on prior knowledge to some degree. It would, in any case, be impossible to identify lessons at this level of detail. No group or individual can reasonably be asked to identify all the influences that led to a particular complex decision. Thus, policy transfer should be defined in Rose's terms as an action oriented intentional activity.

Secondly, it is assumed that policy transfer must seek to identify and classify remarkable phenomena not otherwise explained. The day-to-day diffusion of knowledge, intentional or otherwise, at the micro-level within organizations is not remarkable in the context of policy transfer either in terms of process or of fact. These transfers are better the subject of normal policy analysis or management studies.

Thirdly, when remarkable intraorganizational transfers occur it is likely to be extraorganizational factors which are remarkable, rather than the intraorganizational process of transfer.

Fourthly, investigating the dynamics of international policy transfer falls outside the frameworks of normal forms of policy-making. This argument is supported by much of the prior and contemporary literature which focuses on inter/transnational transfers (see Stone, 1996 and 2000a). Hence, the temporal dimension of policy transfer is likely to be remarkable only in the context of a spatial variable, which excludes most intraorganizational transfers from consideration. A qualification to this proposal is the potential for intraorganizational transfer analysis across spatial dimensions, although this does not seem appropriate to current institutions of governance either at the supranational or international levels. By a process of elimination, it may be concluded that the great majority of remarkable policy transfers will occur between distinct organizations at the international or transnational levels. Five levels of political spatiality are commonly referred to in political science: transnational, international, national, regional and local. International policy transfer might conceivably take place at and between any of these levels. As Table 2.3 illustrates, theoretically it is possible to conceive of at least twenty-five cross-national transfer pathways along which transfers might occur. The frequency with which transfers along each pathway happen is evidently a subject for empirical analysis. However, the study of systemic context might reveal whether transfer along a particular pathway is likely.

Table 2.3 Policy transfer pathways

International - International	Regional - International
International- Transnational	Regional - Transnational
International - National	Regional - National
International - Regional	Regional - Regional
International - Local	Regional - Local
Transnational - Transnational	Local - International
Transnational - International	Local - Transnational
Transnational - National	Local - National
Transnational - Regional	Local - Regional
Transnational - Local	Local - Local

National - International
National - Transnational
National - National
National - Regional
National - Local

These four assumptions provide policy transfer analysis with a distinct domain of enquiry. However, policy transfer analysis also contributes a great deal more to the broader study of policy-making. As an interdisciplinary approach, policy transfer analysis has certainly proved that it has the capacity for integrating the common research concerns of scholars of domestic, comparative and international politics in the sense that it provides a lens for observing the role of state actors and non-state actors in promoting new forms of complex globalization.

It thus provides the scope for observing new opportunity structures for policy transfer and evaluating the claim that globalization leads to convergence or divergence in public policy-making (Stone, 1999 and 2000). Moreover, as a descriptive theory of policy development it proves useful in helping us to understand how decision-makers acquire knowledge, and, it encourages comprehensive policy analysis in that it provides a holistic approach; inviting policy scientists to analyse the whole process of policy-making from awareness to impact rather than discrete aspects of the process. However, as a predictive theory the usefulness of policy transfer analysis to practitioners largely rests on the development of policy transfer analysis into a tool for prospective policy evaluation. There have been attempts to develop policy transfer analysis in this way (see Rose, 2001 and Mossberger and Wolman, 2001), however, more work needs to be done on integrating implementation and evaluation analysis with policy transfer analysis in order to provide more penetrative tools of enquiry for evidence based learning. Much can be learnt from the organizational learning literature in this regard (Common, 2004). But, what of the ability of policy transfer analysis to explain policy development?

Explaining Policy Transfer

It is quite simply incorrect to argue that policy transfer analysts do not advance explanations for policy change. However, it is accurate to criticize policy transfer analysts for failing to clearly stipulate their critical variables. Most approaches to policy transfer are unclear in their specification of independent and dependent variables and messy in their theorization of the relationship between variables and between levels of enquiry. This is largely because most explanations of policy transfer emerge from inductive reasoning rather than deductive formal modelling. This is an inevitable corollary of applying heuristic models of policy development.

What are the knowledge claims of policy transfer analysis? The claim that policy transfer activity is on the increase is normally attributed to one or more of the following sources of policy change: global, international and/or transnational forces; state-centred forces; the role of policy transfer networks in mediating policy change; and, micro-level processes of policy oriented learning.

Global, international and transnational sources of policy change   Global, international and transnational sources of policy change   provide opportunity structures for policy transfer to occur. Of course, the terms transnational and international should not be used interchangeably. I recognise as international those structures and processes which inform state-to-state relations such as the United Nations (UN) and as transnational the increasing importance of non-state actors, such as multi-national corporations and knowledge institutions, in policy-making at all levels of governance (Risse-Kappen ed., 1995 and Stone, 1996). The phenomenon globalization is clearly more problematic. The lack of an agreed understanding of the term is one of the most commonly asserted problems in contemporary political science (Amin and Thrift, 1994: 1), yet even the growing band of critics of globalization explicitly place the study of the term at the centre of their analyses (Callinicos, 2003 and Hirst and Thompson, 1996 and 2000).

Irrespective of one's position within the globalization debate no serious scholar would deny that patterns of increased internationalization have occurred and that these have posed significant constraints on the ability of most nation states to forward independent national economic strategies. In particular, there have been significant changes in the organization of production and patterns of economic power in which a closer integration of national economies has been brought about by the reduction of the costs of transportation and communication and the breaking down of barriers to the flow of goods, services, capital, and, fundamentally to this book, knowledge, across borders.

Knowledge of policy initiatives in a wide variety of policy arenas at different levels of governance in nation states throughout the world is more accessible than ever before. Policy tourism via the Internet is now in the easy reach of most policy-makers, as the majority of public organizations provide detailed information of their activities on their web sites. If we wish to explore the latest economic development initiatives in Atlanta, Leeds, Delhi or Shanghai, they are available to use through our desktop search engines. Just ten years ago, with the possible exceptions of the United States and the Netherlands, it would have been impossible to access such information via the Internet.

The advent of the Internet has also provided a unique opportunity for policy entrepreneurs, knowledge institutions and think tanks to sell their expertise to governmental organizations throughout the world. The Internet has exposed a hitherto private realm of policy oriented learning – global networks of epistemic communities. At the same time, the Internet has also established a rich source for non-governmental policy oriented learning for individuals and groups wishing to question the views of government. Government is no longer the expert. Of course, such a development poses threats as well as opportunities. The Internet does not provide a free market of ideas. Ideas are in imperfect competition with one another. Indeed, the think tanks with the highest profile on the Internet tend to be deeply ideological, cloaking dangerous policies in creative evidence-based practice. Hence, policy analysis needs to be more rigorous than ever in discerning appropriate policy transfers.

The economic dynamic of globalization has been underpinned by a political process of global institution building in which the activities of the three main institutions that govern economic globalization – the IMF, the WB and the WTO – have increased in scope and intensity. It is, of course, no coincidence that processes of economic globalization and the power of global economic institutions have gained in strength as alternatives to the liberal paradigm have declined in popular influence since the break-up of the former Soviet Union and the end of the

Cold War. The influence of these global economic institutions has been particularly pronounced in developing countries, transition states and states emerging from conflict, which all depend heavily on external aid, loans and investment.

The IMF's mandate is to provide the basis for collective action at the global level to ensure economic stability. It was created in the aftermath of the Second World War to avoid further global economic depressions. In other words it was founded on the Keynesian belief that markets were inherently unstable and required intervention to offset structural inequalities. Its main policy instrument is the provision of loans to countries confronting economic decline funded through the tax base of its member countries. However, by the 1980s the influence of free market oriented Reaganomics in the United States led to the IMF's wholesale rejection of Keynesianism and it became a champion of market liberalism. Despite the absence of any formal changes to its original mandate, the IMF has acted as a predatory agent of free market policy transfer in the developing world compelling poor countries to introduce structural adjustment programmes (SAPs) or other conditions in return for loans and forcing the pace of globalization with scant regard for the need for cultural adaptation. Indeed, up until the recent introduction of participatory assessments, the IMF paid little heed to the views of indigenous publics in the design of SAPs. Fiscal discipline (maintaining strict controls on the money supply), the privatization of state owned enterprizes and market liberalization (the elimination of protectionist measures such as tariffs) became the watchwords of IMF thinking throughout the 1980s and 1990s.

The IMF's attitude towards developed countries, however, has been rather different. It has coerced poor countries into removing trade barriers, while allowing rich countries such as Australia, Japan, France, the United States, and others to retain protectionist practices. Further, the IMF has pressurized developing countries in Asia and Latin America to loosen capital market controls thus benefiting Western dominated financial markets and destroying indigenous banking sectors.

Has the IMF's policies been successful in maintaining global economic stability? Clearly the answer to this question depends on where you are sitting. While most Western countries have experienced unprecedented economic growth in the 1990s, SAPs did not bring sustained growth to developing countries in Africa or Latin America and after the 1997 Asian crisis, IMF policies deepened the crises in Thailand and Indonesia resulting in social and political chaos. Moreover, the IMF inspired practice of shock therapy (rapid market reform involving tight monetary policies, capital market liberalization and privatization) in post Soviet Russia and other former soviets has led to increased poverty and inequalities that have undermined processes of democratization and caused profound social instability. Indeed, as Joseph Stiglitz (2002: 151) observes, only Poland, Hungary, Slovenia and Slovakia have a GDP equal to that of a decade ago.

Chinese experience, however, has demonstrated that there is an alternative to shock therapy. In a gradualist institutional reform process that has spanned a 20-year period, a virtually new administrative system has been established to underpin

China's socialist oriented market economy and society. Its main achievements have included: the strengthening of social macro-management and planning; the transformation of state-owned enterprises into private enterprises; the redefining of the relationship between central and local governments through a process of functional decentralization; the dramatic reduction of the number of public organizations and personnel; and, the development of a meritocratic system of appointment and promotion in the Chinese civil service.

These successes have been the product of a considered, incremental development strategy that has rested on three main assumptions about transition planning and programming. First, that national economic transition plans should focus on the reconstruction of public infrastructure and economic management and developing the human resources, appropriate institutions of governance and forms of public management to deliver on development goals. Secondly, that the civil service must be the prime mover in economic transitions. Paradoxically, given the dominant neo-liberal belief in limited government, successful market transition requires the establishment of a strong, efficient and effective central administrative system. This normally involves restructuring through administrative reform aimed at improving efficiency, effectiveness and responsiveness. As Turner and Hulme (1997: 1) observe, '[i]t seems that all are agreed on the proposition that the nature and performance of public sector organizations are critical elements in determining developmental success'. Indeed countries that have experienced the most rapid and sustained development such as South Korea, Taiwan, Singapore, Thailand and Malaysia, all have highly effective public sector organizations, strong centres, entrepreneurial elites, relatively autonomous states, effective economic planning ministries, certain aspects of 'Good Governance', and have engaged in civil service reform (see Leftwich, 2001). Thirdly, that successful economic transition requires engaging in progressive lesson-learning from international experience but that ultimately indigenous solutions must be found to indigenous problems. Public administrators must engage in rational policy transfer and draw on the best overseas expertise that fit their own circumstances.

The close adherence to these three assumptions, allied to an incremental approach to market transition, has enabled China to avoid the catastrophe that has beset economy and society in most former Eastern bloc countries as a consequence of shock therapy. While China has consistently made the development of its economy its highest priority, it has recognized the importance of restructuring the institutional superstructure in order to deliver on its broader economic development goals (Xia, 1998: 412). This has led to a dramatic period of institutional reinvention to underpin the incremental process of market reform (Chen, 1998: 229). The administrative system of a country is closely tied to its economic and political system, hence administrative reform is normally guided by a country's historical and cultural development. In the process of transition, however, China has not always had an institutional memory to draw upon. China has therefore had to combine lesson-drawing from positive and negative international experiences with the best of its own administrative traditions in the formulation and delivery of the reform process. This has been the key, thus far, to its success.

As the defects of economic globalization have taken hold in developing countries, these processes of inequitable economic and political globalization have been accompanied by a renewed interest in both the legitimacy of public institutions such as the IMF and the activities of intergovernmental institutions such as the UN, the World Health Authority (WHA) and the ILO. Although globalization has had an uneven impact on the international political system it has had significant social implications. International civil society has become radicalized both in order to respond to the opportunities afforded by globalization and to oppose them. The work of new organizations such as the Jubilee Movement advocating debt reduction in the developing world is evidence of the former and violent protests organized by new social movements at virtually every major meeting of the IMF, the WB and the WTO illustrates the latter. Moreover, established international organizations such as the OECD have become proactive in pushing neo-liberal policy agendas in the international domain particularly in the areas of economic and administrative reform. The OECD is an international organization consisting of 30 member countries that share a commitment to democratic government and the market economy. With active relationships with some 70 other countries, NGOs and civil society, it has a global network of members and associates. The OECD is a committed agent of policy transfer with the stated aim of assisting '...governments in building and strengthening effective, efficient and transparent government structures through its Public Management Programme (PUMA)' (see www.oecd.org).

Of course, this pattern of increased internationalization and transnationalization has not been confined to the economic arena, strong and weak claims of globalization can also be found in relation to studies of changing trends in culture (Smith, 1990), political integration (Camilleri and Falk, 1992), geopolitics (Rosenau and Czempiel, 1992), technology (Dosi, Pavitt and Soete, 1990), knowledge (Strange, 1988), and domestic governance and statecraft (Cerny and Evans, 2003; Common, 2001; Rhodes, 1997).

In sum then, if we take Philip Cerny's (1998: 2) definition of globalization as our starting point, '...the sum total of the wide range of political, economic and social processes of transnationalization and internationalization taking place in the world today', our primary concern becomes the analysis of those institutional and ideational structures and processes which can shape the behaviour of international, state and non-state actors and constrain or facilitate processes of policy transfer. The existence of the following institutional and ideational structures and the processes that emanate from them provide increased opportunity structures for policy transfer to occur:

- ideational discourses such as globalization, Europeanization, and neo-liberalism – the Washington Consensus (Ladi, 2002);
- the activities of global economic institutions such as the IMF, the WTO and the WB and accompanying regulatory systems (Stiglitz, 2002);
- the activities of international financial markets and their accompanying regulatory systems (Cerny, 1994);

- the activities of international intergovernmental organizations such as the UN and the ILO (Haagh and Helgo, eds., 2002);
- the institutions and processes of Europeanization (Buller *et al.*, 2002);
- international treaties such as the General Agreement on Tariffs and Trade (GATT) and the North American Free Trade Area (NAFTA) allowing for the freer movement of goods, investment and services between Canada, Mexico and the United States; and,
- transnational and non-state organizations promulgating particular international policy agendas in the international domain (see Stone, 1996).

As well as acting as potential opportunity structures for policy transfer these institutional and ideational structures and the processes that emanate from them can also act as sites of struggle between competing conceptions of globalization. For example, unaccountable bureaucrats have designed the global economic architecture, such as the development of banking standards that govern economic globalization, and this has engendered significant resentment in the developing world. The securing of loans by developing countries from the IMF and elsewhere has become conditional on the introduction of SAPS that are predicated on a western interpretation of 'Good Governance' that also give rise to significant resentment.

State-centred explanations of policy change State-centred explanations of policy change can be disaggregated into a set of changes that emanate from systems change (electoral, institutional, and ideological), historical legacies and the sharing of similar problems.

Changes in government provide a significant opportunity structure for policy transfer activity in what Hall (1993) refers to as periods of third order change that give rise to new policy paradigms. For example, the assent of the Blair government to power in the UK in July 1997 led to a proliferation of policy transfer activity between Britain and the United States and signalled the rise of some new policy paradigms although there was also a significant degree of continuity with Conservative government policy particularly in economic matters. The close relationship which developed between the Blair and Clinton administrations was reflected in a long list of common policy initiatives that included: education (reduction of class sizes), crime (zero-tolerance, anti-truancy drives), and welfare (welfare to work and creation of work incentives) reform. In addition, the UK's Chancellor of the Exchequer, Gordon Brown, became convinced of the need for Bank of England independence after discussions with Alan Greenspan, Chair of the independent US Federal Reserve Board (Central Bank), and Robert Rubin, Clinton's Treasury Secretary. Indeed, Brown's working family tax credit system is a direct copy of the American earned income tax credit scheme. Many of these items may be viewed as part of an international policy agenda for the centre-left which was forged by Blair, Clinton, and their advisors. On 6 February 1998 Blair addressed the US State Department outlining what he termed the 'five clear principles of the centre-left' common to both New Labour and the New Democrats:

1. stable management and economic prudence in order to cope with the global economy;
2. a change in the emphasis of government intervention so that it dealt with education, training, and infrastructure and not things like industrial intervention or 'tax and spend';
3. reform of the welfare state;
4. reinventing government, decentralization, opening-up government; and,
5. internationalism in opposition to the right's isolationism.

It is within this international agenda for the centre-left that we are most likely to find examples of policy transfer between Britain and America. For example, in NPM (Common, 2001; James, 2001), urban (Wolman, 1992) or welfare (Dolowitz *et al.*, ed., 2000) policies.

Hence, the upsurge of policy transfer activity between the two countries may be attributed partly to the sharing of similar policy problems, and, partly because of ideological similarities between the New Democrats and New Labour. It was made possible, however, because elites in the two countries share a common ontology and language, together with the existence of longstanding historical legacies that are embedded economically, socially and culturally.

As we observed in the previous section, a significant degree of policy transfer activity involving third order change is also common in countries that are engaged in state transformation through processes of modernization (e.g. Mexico), democratization (e.g. Russia) or market reform (e.g. China). Ikenberry (1990) also draws our attention to the argument that a fear of being left behind one's neighbours often stimulates policy transfer between clusters of countries in particular geographic regions. He uses the diffusion of privatization policy in South-east Asia and Central and Latin America to illustrate his argument. The existence of indigenous as well as international agencies of technical cooperation in developing countries also provides opportunity structures for policy transfer between developing countries that share similar social, political and/or economic problems. It should also be noted that developing countries often engage in policy transfer for tactical reasons to increase their relative autonomy from international forces (Flores-Crespo, 2002 and Ikenberry, 1990), although, this often leads to the transfer of rhetoric rather than substantive policy content (Common, 2001).

In many developed countries, particularly in Europe, processes of 'hollowing-out' have created new opportunity structures for policy transfer. The term 'hollowing-out' infers that the political powers of the central state are being eroded in particular ways. Rhodes (1994: 138-39) has argued that there are four key interrelated trends which illustrate the reach of this process in the UK: privatization and limiting the scope and forms of public intervention; the loss of functions by central government departments to alternative service delivery systems (such as Next Steps Agencies) and through market testing; the loss of functions from the British government to EU institutions; and, the emergence of limits to the discretion of public servants through a public management that emphasizes managerial accountability, and clearer political control created by a sharp distinction between politics and administration. A further dimension can be added to these four – the global trend towards regionalization and devolution. The rise of this new form of governance has facilitated cross-sectoral opportunities for policy transfer. Hence, the private sector is increasingly used as a source of policy learning due to its expertise in particular areas (e.g. Banks and credit card fraud detection, management, risk assessment or logistics). Indeed policy transfer is more likely to occur in an era of what Rhodes (1996: 652) has termed 'the New Governance: Governing without Government'. In this context, New Governance refers to the increasing pervasiveness of 'self-organizing, interorganizational networks' which Rhodes argues compliment markets and hierarchies as governing structures for authoritatively allocating resources and exercising control and co-ordination in public policy-making. In times of uncertainty policy-makers at the heart of networks will look to the 'quick fix' solution to public policy problems that policy transfer can provide.

Organizational-centred explanations for policy change　The most common explanation for the occurrence of policy transfer is that micro-level dissatisfaction with existing policy systems identified through monitoring systems or broader policy evaluation frameworks provide opportunity structures for policy transfer to occur. However, public organizations in both developed and developing countries often do not have the expertise to tackle all the problems they confront and increasingly look outside their organizations for the answers to their problems (Stone, 1999). This depicts policy-makers as wholly reactive beings. There is evidence, however, that some governments have started to emphasize the importance of governmental organizations being rational learning organizations engaged in an ongoing process of evidence based learning (Common, 2004). In 2001, the UK government's Cabinet Office established an International Comparisons in Policy-making project, as part of its agenda to modernise the civil service. The project is located in the Centre for Management and Policy Studies (CMPS) in the Cabinet Office which was created to help improve executive policy-making in British government. The aim of the project is to:

> …help improve the quality of public policy development and delivery by promoting the use of international examples where relevant, easing access to reliable information about international policy-making experience, and increasing the capability of practitioners to learn useful lessons from that experience (Wyatt and Grimmeisen, 2002).

The CMPS has created a policy transfer toolkit to act as practical guidance for UK policy-makers engaged in policy transfer activity and have established a 'Policy Hub' web site to act as a resource base. In short, the British government has created a permanent opportunity structure for policy oriented learning and possible transfer. Given this emphasis on the importance of evidence-based policy-making, policy transfer has become a rational choice for most developed countries (see

Davies *et al.*, 2000 and Pawson, 2002).

There are, of course, other organizational-centred explanations for policy change that are highlighted in the literature. Changes in organizational leadership often provide an opportunity structure for policy change to occur (Rose, 1993). Moreover, policy transfer may be introduced for political reasons to legitimate conclusions already reached by the organization (Robertson, 1991). It may also be observed that processes of policy transfer can precipitate further processes of policy transfer. For example, it can be observed in the UK context in the case of New Labour's New Deal for unemployed 18 to 24-year-olds, that new service delivery approaches have been adopted including one-stop-shops on the United States Iowa model and the introduction of a single gateway to the benefit system (see Dolowitz *et al*, 2000).

Policy oriented learning as a mechanism of policy change   Recent studies of processes of policy transfer have emphasized the role of policy transfer networks as key instruments of policy oriented learning (Evans and Davies, 1999; Evans with McComb, 1999; Ladi, 2002; Mokhtar, 2001). These are collaborative decision structures comprised of state and non-state actors that are set up with the deliberate intention of engineering policy change. It is argued that policy transfer networks matter because they shape the nature of policy outcomes emerging from the process of transfer. Moreover, the creation of a policy transfer network provides an opportunity structure for the creation of further policy transfer networks. In this sense policy transfer activity can have a momentum of its own through a process of functional spill-over.

Policy transfer networks can act as agents of globalization or counteragents to globalization, for agents of policy transfer are often carriers of particular policy belief systems (e.g. new public management, privatization etc.) and use their membership of formal and informal international policy networks to disseminate international policy agendas. Indeed, the content of policy transfers is often informed by notions of 'best practice' disseminated by international organizations, KIs and think tanks in the international domain, suggesting that ideological considerations play a key role in informing the content of policy transfers.

International organizations, KIs and think tanks play a key role in facilitating policy-oriented learning through imparting technical advice, for the content of policy transfers normally reflect areas where indigenous state actors lack expertise. This observation has particular resonance in developing countries as the content of policy transfers often takes the form of conditions imposed by the IMF in return for grants or loans. Hence, developing countries can become dependent on the technical expertise and other resources of non-state actors. Agents of policy transfer that can bridge the indigenous knowledge gap can become important players in policy transfer networks. However, the degree of autonomy that state actors can demonstrate from the expertise of non-state actors tends to be broadly representative of their state of development. For example, in most instances, voluntary forms of policy transfer demonstrate the relative autonomy of state actors in decision processes, while coercive forms of policy transfer demonstrate the incapacity of a state to maintain its national sovereignty over decision-making.

A necessary criterion for identifying policy transfer is therefore to identify the agent(s) of transfer, to specify the role played by agent(s) in the transfer and the nature of the transfer that the agent(s) is/are seeking to make. At least eight main categories of agents of transfer can be identified in the literature on policy transfer: politicians; political parties; bureaucrats; policy entrepreneurs including think tanks, KI's, academicians and other experts; pressure groups; global financial institutions; international organizations; and, supra-national institutions (Stone, 2000)

Table 2.4 provides a range of examples of potential agents of policy transfer that seek to influence policy agendas. The list includes think tanks and KI's, which aim to influence the policy agenda through the publication or research and policy advocacy.

Table 2.4   Potential agents of policy transfer

Type of Agent of Transfer	Illustration
Politicians	Senator John Kerry, Democrat Presidential candidate (http://www.johnkerry.com/)
Political Parties	The British Conservative Party (http://www.conservative-party.org.uk/)
Bureaucrats	Department of Health and Human Services, United States (http://aspe.hhs.gov/)
Pressure Groups	Amnesty International (http://www.amnesty.org/)
Policy entrepreneurs	The Institute for Public Policy Research (http://www.ippr.org.uk/)
Global Financial Institutions	The International Monetary Fund and the World Bank (http://www.imf.org/external/np/exr/facts/sia.htm)
International Organizations	The Public Management Service of the OECD (http://www.oecd.org/).
Supra-national Institutions	The European Union (http://www.europe.org.uk/info/enlargement/default.asp)

The literature identifies four different forms of policy oriented learning emerging from the process of transfer. First, *copying* – where a governmental organization adopts a policy, programme, or institution without modification. Secondly, *emulation* – where a governmental organization accepts that a policy, programme, or institution overseas provides the best standard for designing a policy, programme, or institution at home. Thirdly, *hybridization* – where a governmental organization combines elements of programmes found in several settings to develop a policy that is culturally sensitive to the needs of the recipient. And, fourthly, *inspiration* – where an idea inspires fresh thinking about a policy problem and helps to facilitate policy change. However, it should be noted that copying is very rare and the bulk of the case study evidence suggests that hybrid and emulated forms of transfer tend to be the norm.

The content of policy transfers can include: first order change in the precise settings of the policy instruments used to attain policy goals (marginal adjustments to the status quo); second order change to the policy instruments themselves such as the development of new institutions and delivery systems; and third order change to the actual goals that guide policy in a particular field (negative ideology, ideas, attitudes and concepts). Of course, negative lessons can be drawn in each form of policy change.

But what factors can constrain policy transfer and policy oriented learning? As Figure 2.1 illustrates, three broad sets of variables can be identified in the case study literature: 'cognitive' obstacles in the pre-decision phase, 'environmental' obstacles in the implementation phase and international and public opinion. These variables do not exist in a vacuum; they interact in complex and often unexpected ways and inform the process of policy transfer. Cognitive obstacles refer to the process by which public policy problems are recognized and defined in the pre-decision phase and refer to the receptivity of existing policy actors and systems to policy options and the complexity of such options. The most significant cognitive barrier for agents of transfer to overcome at this stage of policy development is the prevailing organizational culture.

Environmental obstacles refer to the absence of effective cognitive and elite mobilization strategies deployed by agents of transfer and the mergence of a cohesive policy transfer network, the range of broader structural constraints (institutional, political, economic and social) that impact and shape the process of policy transfer and the normal technical implementation constraints that constrain or facilitate the process of policy transfer. The latter would include: coherent and consistent objectives; the incorporation of an adequate causal theory of policy development; the sensible allocation of financial resources; hierarchical integration within and among implementing organizations; clear decision rules underpinning the operation of implementing agencies; the recruitment of programme officers with adequate skills/training; sufficient technical support; and, the use of effective monitoring and evaluation systems including formal access by outsiders.

Most developing countries engaged in processes of policy transfer are heavily dependent on the support of the international community, particularly the US, the IMF, the WB, the UN, and key donors. The capacity of such governments to maintain international attention is thus crucial in order to raise sufficient funding for policy transfer. It is equally important, however, in both developed and developing countries to build a societal consensus across elites and masses on transfer imperatives in order to ensure the effective implementation of the new policy.

The interaction between these 'cognitive' and 'environmental' obstacles and the forces of international and domestic public opinion (depending on the nature of the state) inform the completion or otherwise of the process of policy transfer.

Cognitive Obstacles in Pre-decision Phase

- *Limited search activity*
- *Cultural assimilation through commensurable problem recognition and definition*
- *The degree of complexity involved in the process of transfer*

Environmental Obstacles During the Process of Transfer	**Public and International Opinion**
• *Ineffective cognitive and elite mobilization strategies by agents of transfer*	• *International opinion –* Washington Consensus, UN, key donors *
• *The absence of a cohesive policy transfer network*	• *Elite opinion –* political, bureaucratic, economic, religious
• *Structural constraints –* socio-economic, political, institutional	• *The attitudes and resources of constituency groups*
• *Normal technical implementation constraints arising from limited policy design, resources and technical support*	

Process of Policy Transfer

---

* This is an interactive model in the sense that these sets of variables do not exist in a vacuum; they interact in complex and often unexpected ways.

Figure 2.1 Mapping potential obstacles to processes of policy transfer*

Demonstrating Policy Transfer

Dolowitz and Marsh (1996) rightly argue for a clear scheme for measuring the occurrence of policy transfer. To achieve this, they identify five sources through which the existence of policy transfer might be observed: the media, reports, conferences, visits and government statements. However, these categories should be treated more as sources of learning than as sources of evidence that policy transfer has occurred. Unfortunately, the existing literature does not provide adequate techniques for demonstrating policy transfer. Indeed, given adequate standards of validation, proof of policy transfer may be more difficult than is commonly assumed by those arguing that it is on the increase. This is because rigorous validation would demand excellent access to key informants, which is often beyond the reach of policy scientists. Consequently, much of the existing literature rests too much on abstracting perfect fit cases of policy transfer. This is why greater attention must be paid to investigating cases of non-transfer and in-process transfer in order to improve our understanding of the process of policy development. The following sequence of steps can be used as a safeguard against exaggerated claims about the nature and extent of policy transfer.

The subject of analysis   At the outset, it is important to be clear about the phenomenon under study. In primary empirical work, a range of possibility exists. One might consider attempts to facilitate/enforce policy transfer, the process of transfer, as it is occurring, or a claim that policy transfer has occurred in the past.

Who or what is identified as the agent(s) of transfer – who wants it, what do they want from it, how are they going about effecting it, to whose benefit, and why? An agent is essential to the voluntary and coercive dimensions of policy transfer given that policy transfer involves action oriented intentional learning. Hence, transfer must be a conscious process, whether this is undertaken voluntarily or whether the subject of coercion.

Is there evidence of non-transfer?   There are two potential dimensions of non-transfer to be taken into account in any validation exercise. Elements of an idea or a programme which are borrowed from domestic antecedents or which are innovative can be described as non-transfers.   Parts of an original idea or programme discarded or filtered out by the subject/agent are also non-transfers. Detailed comparison of the subject policy against both domestic and original settings is therefore essential if the real extent of transfer in a particular case is to be discovered.

What is the evidence offered to support the claim? How good is it?   Researchers should look for a preponderance of evidence, which demonstrates or refutes a process of policy transfer. Clearly, evidence will differ depending on the nature of the subject. For example, in seeking to demonstrate whether an idea or an attitude has been transferred, a researcher will seek to examine the views and interpretations of the recipient subject(s).   If on the other hand it were being argued that a programme has been copied, one would expect to find more concrete 'physical' evidence. One can only say that a programme has been copied by another programme if they have been compared.   The question of whether the programme has been carried out might then be subjected to implementation analysis to determine how far the transfer has permeated. A distinction should be made between *soft* transfers (ideas, concepts, attitudes) and *hard* transfers (programmes and implementation).

The question then follows as to how good the evidence on offer is. Of course, this is a problem of empirical analysis in general, but it is of particular importance here, given the different kinds of transfer and different evidence, which might support them.

What conclusion can be drawn from the above about the nature and extent of transfer, which has taken place? Here, answers are given to questions about the subject of analysis – is it ideas, programmes or implemented programmes which have/not been or are/not being transferred? If policy transfer is found to have occurred, one might then determine the degree of transfer – copying, emulation, hybridization, or inspiration.

Area Bias in Empirical Research

It is self-evident from this review of the literature that most policy transfer analysts tend to focus on policy transfer activity between developed countries and largely ignore policy transfer activity from developed to developing countries, and, from developing countries to developing and developed countries. Moreover, there is also a tendency to investigate 'perfect fit', 'completed' processes of policy transfer. The empirical investigation that follows will attempt to help bridge the gap in providing cases of 'completed', 'in-process' and 'non transfer' in policy arenas as varied as new public management, welfare policy, health policy, local government reform, youth employment policy, health policy, and education policy, in countries as diverse as Britain, Brazil, Ecuador, France, Germany, Greece, the special administrative region of Hong Kong in China, Kyrgyzstan, Malaysia, Mexico, Singapore, Tanzania, the Ukraine, and, the United States.

In Conclusion – How Useful is Policy Transfer Analysis as an Understanding of Contemporary Policy Development?

Policy transfer analysis is a useful analogical model employed for cognitive purposes to suggest something about the properties and relations understood to exist within the process of transfer. It has *additionality,* because policy transfer analysis does tell us something that we did not know before. We now have a good idea about the domestic and international circumstances which are likely to bring about policy transfer, the scope and dimensions of policy transfer and which aspects of the framework should and should not be pursued in empirical work.

However, much policy transfer analysis does exhibit an inability to determine with *precision* the phenomenon it is trying to explain. This argument does not negate the importance of the policy transfer approach. As James Gregor (1977: 193-4) puts it, analogical models are 'sustained metaphors', 'promissory notes' on theories to emerge from within the analytical process. A sound model is not necessarily one that purely explains or predicts with precision. It is one rich with implications. Brian Barry (1975: 86) argues, '[o]ur understanding of a subject may be advanced if concepts and processes can be translated into other terms more readily grasped and fruitful analogy will suggest new lines of enquiry by provoking the speculation that relationships found in the one field may hold, mutatis mutandis, in the other as well'. It therefore follows that we should be able to extract novel hypotheses from studies of policy transfer, which must then be articulated in a systematic fashion in order to provide the basis for future empirical research. The remaining chapters in this book endeavour to meet this aim.

Part I

Policy Transfer Between
Developed Countries

Chapter 3

Policy Transfer Networks:
An Insider Perspective

Mark Evans with Paul McComb

Introduction

This chapter makes three central claims about the importance of the study of policy transfer. First, it provides a rich source for investigating structures and processes of collaborative governance, involving governmental and non-governmental actors. For policy transfer is the outcome of collaborative policy oriented activities between governmental and non-governmental actors that has gained in salience in an era of New Governance. Secondly, the Blair administration in the UK has pushed initiatives involving collaborative governance as part of its public participation agenda, arguing that they are exemplars of participatory democracy. However, we contend that structures of collaborative governance, such as policy transfer networks, can extend and limit participation; empower and disempower affected societal groups. Thirdly, we draw on previous work (Evans and Davies, 1999), to argue that the policy transfer network approach provides a useful lens for studying this particular structure and process of collaborative governance. The chapter explores these three claims through a case study of the emergence and development of a performance measurement and resource allocation programme within the Department of Social Security (DSS) to counter social security fraud. The chapter draws on the unique, insider perspective of the Project Leader and his team at the Benefit Fraud Inspectorate (BFI). It therefore benefits from access to key informants in an in-process case study of policy transfer.

The Policy Transfer Network Approach

In an article published in 1999 in the journal *Public Administration* Jonathan Davies and I mapped out a multi-level, interdisciplinary approach for understanding policy transfer (Evans and Davies, 1999). Our main submission was that policy transfer analysis provides a context for integrating some key concerns of domestic, comparative and international political science. It was observed that the increasing complexity and uncertainty that underpins modern governance has increased the tendency for policy-makers at all levels of governance to engage in policy transfer activity. The article focused on the tactics of research in policy transfer analysis and concluded that the process of policy transfer should be examined through a structure and agency approach with three dimensions: global, international and transnational levels, the macro-level and the inter-organizational level. This three-dimensional model employs the notion of a policy transfer network as a middle-range level of analysis which links a particular form of collaborative governance (policy transfer), micro-decision-making in organizations, macro-systems and global, transnational and international systems. The development of the policy transfer network approach was primarily a response to the absence of an adequate methodology within the existing literature for analysing processes of policy transfer, the role of agent(s) of policy transfer within processes of policy transfer; and, policy oriented learning.

Analysing Processes of Policy Transfer

As policy transfer takes places within a multi-organizational setting the analysis of policy transfer requires a methodology that provides empirical tools for understanding inter-organizational politics. It was argued that the policy network and the epistemic community approaches provide policy transfer analysts with such a method. The reasoning behind this assertion was based on the observation that most empirical examples of policy transfer tend to emphasize the crucial role of elite decision-makers within close-knit policy communities (a form of policy network) including consultants, other forms of policy entrepreneur, key bureaucrats, politicians and privileged groups (see Dolowitz and Marsh, 1996). Moreover, the epistemic community approach deals directly with many of the same agents of transfer that play a pivotal role in policy evolution within transfer networks, for example, natural and social scientists or individuals from any discipline or profession with authoritative claims to policy relevant knowledge that reside in national, transnational and international organizations. Table 3.1 maps out the relationship between the Marsh and Rhodes (1992) conception of a policy community and the Adler and Haas (1992) conception of an epistemic community. Table 3.2 presents our conception of a policy transfer network. There are key similarities between the first two characterizations of policy development in terms of membership, the nature of elite integration and the resources its members possess. However, the membership and values of both a policy community and an epistemic community tend to persist over time, while our understanding of policy transfer networks is that they are an ad hoc phenomenon set up with the specific intention of engineering policy change. They exist only for the time that a transfer is occurring. By implication policy transfer networks matter because without them other policies might be adopted.

Table 3.1 The characteristics of policy communities and epistemic communities

Dimension	A policy community (Marsh and Rhodes)	An epistemic community (Adler and Haas)
Membership *number of participants*	Limited, a shared set of causal and principled beliefs (analytic and normative) act as a filter mechanism to preclude certain inputs.	Limited, a shared set of causal and principled beliefs (analytic and normative) act as a filter mechanism to preclude certain inputs.
type of interest	Normally includes representatives of governmental interests, economic groups, and/or professional interests in tight-knit decision structure.	Includes natural and social scientists from any discipline or profession with authoritative claims to policy relevant knowledge which reside in international regimes.
Integration *frequency of interaction*	Frequent, high-quality, interactions on all matters related to the policy arena.	An ongoing process of bargaining within and between epistemic communities.
continuity	Membership, values and outcomes persist over time.	Membership and values persist over time as long as reputation survives.
consensus	All participants share basic values and accept the legitimacy of the outcome.	All participants share a consensual knowledge base and a common policy enterprise.
Resources *distribution of resources (within network)*	All participants have resources in an exchange relationship.	All participants have knowledge resources in an exchange relationship.
distribution of resources (within participating organizations)	Hierarchical; leaders can deliver members.	Policy-makers are dependent on the intelligence gathering skills and knowledge resources of the epistemic community.
Power	A balance of power exists among members – although one group may dominate, it must be a positive-sum game if the community is to persist.	The view of policy-makers ultimately determines the influence of an epistemic community and its status of acceptance.

Source: Adapted from Marsh and Rhodes (1992b) and Adler and Haas (1992).

Studying Agents of Policy Transfer

We further argued that policy transfer analysis should be restricted to action oriented intentional learning – that which takes place consciously and results in policy action. In this sense policy transfer is a potential causal phenomenon – a factor leading to policy convergence. This element of intentionality in our definition of policy transfer makes an agent essential to both voluntary and coercive processes. Intentionality may be ascribed to the originating state/institution/actor, to the transferee state/institution/actor, to both, or to a third party state/institution/actor. Agents from different levels of government participate in transfer networks for a variety of reasons: (1) the need to solve objective policy problems; (2) to gain access to other organizational networks; (3) further motivating values (such as economic, political or ideological factors); and (4) to find certain essential skills and knowledge resources. A necessary criterion for identifying policy transfer is therefore to identify the agent(s) of transfer, to specify the role played by agent(s) in the transfer and the nature of the transfer that the agent(s) is/are seeking to make.

The application of a version of policy network analysis, which incorporates the strengths of the epistemic community approach, was thus considered an essential research tactic because it allows policy transfer analysts to analyse the role of agents in the process of policy transfer. The notion of a policy transfer network can also help us to evaluate the cognitive dimension of decision-making – i.e. how decision-makers acquire knowledge. Thus through its emphasis on studying structural (organizational rules and imperatives) and interpersonal relationships (information and communication exchange) a method is provided for understanding forms of policy development within a multi-organizational setting.

The Policy Transfer Cycle

Figure 3.1 illustrates how, for analytical purposes, the voluntary policy transfer process can be broken down into twelve stages. Stages one to three involve the identification of a public policy problem and the search for ideas. Stages four to nine and twelve represent potential periods of policy-oriented learning. Stages ten and eleven signify periods in which the policy enters formal policy processes. Each of these putative stages within the process of voluntary policy transfer will be analysed in detail within the ensuing case study. It must be noted that we are making no claims here about the rationality or otherwise of the policy transfer process. The capacity for a policy to pass through these stages is contingent on environmental factors (e.g. prevailing economic conditions, changes in government) and the type of agent of transfer involved. Moreover, processes of policy transfer can break-off at any point past 'search' and still result in a form of transfer (e.g. the drawing of a lesson or the transfer of rhetoric). The scheme that we present is thus wholly illustrative and provides a frame for organising empirical research.

Table 3.2 The characteristics of policy transfer networks

Dimension	A policy transfer network
Membership *number of participants* *and type of interest*	Limited, a shared set of causal and principled beliefs (analytic and normative) act as a filter mechanism which precludes certain inputs, emphasis on bureaucratic and technocratic elites or agents of policy transfer, affected politicians and bureaucrats.
Integration *frequency of interaction*	Within set time scale, frequent, high quality interaction of insider participants on all matters related to the policy transfer.
continuity	Ad hoc action-oriented networks set up with the specific intention of engineering policy change.
consensus	All participants share basic values.
Resources *distribution of resources* *(within network)*	All participants have resources in an exchange relationship.
distribution of resources *(within participating* *organizations)*	Policy makers are dependent on the intelligence gathering skills and knowledge resources of the agent of transfer and the donor organization.
Power	The success of a policy transfer network rests on the ability of the agent of transfer to satisfy the objective policy problem of the client, there must be a positive-sum game if the network is to be successful.

The policy transfer network approach is now applied to our case study of the development of new policies for performance measurement of social security fraud.

Case Study: Social Security Fraud – Performance Measurement and Resource Allocation

The potential for voluntary policy transfer exists at any spatiality of government as long as enough dissatisfaction or necessity exists and providing that an entrepreneurial elite is ready to manipulate these grievances and establish a policy transfer network.

1	2	3
Problem recognition	**The search for ideas**	**Contact with potential**
economic crisis	*regime*	*agents*
globalization	*international*	*of transfer*
modernization	*transnational*	
policy failure	*national*	
electoral change	*regional*	
conflict	*local*	
legitimation	*cross- sectoral*	
⇒	⇒	⇒
4	5	6
The emergence of an	**Cognition**	**The emergence of a**
information feeder	**and reception**	**policy transfer network**
network	*(identification of agents of transfer)*	
⇒	⇒	⇒
7	8	9
Elite and cognitive	**Interaction**	**Evaluation of options**
mobilization		
(agenda-setting)		
⇒	⇒	⇒
10	11	12
Decision enters	**Formal policy processes**	**Implementation to**
formal policy		**outcome**
stream		
⇒	⇒	⇒

**Figure 3.1 The emergence and development of a voluntary policy transfer
network**

The emergence of a policy transfer network begins with the recognition by a
decision-making elite, politician or bureaucrat, of the existence of a public policy
problem that requires, due to contextual factors, pressing attention.

Problem Recognition

The Department of Social Security (DSS) pay over £90 billion a year to over 30
million people (SoS for Social Security, 1999: iii). In 1996, the Major government
expected to invest up to £300 million over the ensuing three years in activities to
combat fraud, anticipating in return savings to the benefits bill of around £2 billion

(DSS, 1996). In practice, much more was invested for a greater return. In 1997/98 alone around £450 million was invested in return for benefit savings of almost £2.5 billion (SoS for Social Security, 1998). The Government White Paper, *New Ambitions For Our Country: A New Contract For Welfare* (SoS and MoS for Social Security, 1998), set out New Labour's plans for a radical reform of the welfare state. It argued that one of the three key problems with the existing system was that fraud is taking money out of the system and away from genuine claimants. It goes on to state that '...the most effective approach [to stopping fraud] is to prevent it from occurring in the first place...' (Ibid: 67).

However, the primary approach to tackling benefit fraud has focused on detection activities, for example, following-up on tip-offs from Social Security Benefits Agency (SBA) staff and members of the public. When the circumstances of an investigation fit set criteria (this is not reproduced here for public interests reasons), a fraud will be deemed to have been committed. And in almost all of these cases an amount of benefit will be claimed as having been saved as a result. This amount would have been estimated from the value of the weekly benefit in payment multiplied by 32 weeks (Social Security Benefits Agency, 1996). For example, if £50 per week of benefit is in payment and a fraud is deemed to have been committed the administrator will claim that £1600 benefit has been saved. This measure is termed the Weekly Benefits Saving (WBS) and is both the primary metric for determining the total level of benefit savings and the level of performance achieved by administrators.

The measure also has a secondary role in establishing the amount of resources that the administrator can 'earn' to undertake counter-fraud activities. SBA will bid for funds within the general public expenditure survey on the basis of how much WBS they aim to achieve. The situation for local authorities is similar and differs only in the sense that they earn a percentage of the WBS they score as a cash subsidy. There are evident problems with the WBS system. The National Audit Office (NAO), for instance, in their report on housing benefit fraud was highly critical of the WBS system as it '...rewards fraud detected, creates undesirable incentives and has adverse consequences'. Significantly, '...it holds limited incentives...to prevent and deter fraud, or to detect complex fraud' (1997: 7). The NAO (Ibid: 41) reported four key weaknesses in the WBS system:

1. a shortfall of fraud was detected against estimates of fraud;
2. there was error in, and possible abuse of the WBS system – the validity of 30 per cent of the claims they examined were doubtful, suggesting over claiming by the administrator;
3. deficiencies were identified in the 32 week multiplier – it was based on one benefit only (income support), yet was applied to all benefits; and,
4. heavy-handed conduct of fraud investigations was reported as a consequence of the relationship between the resources allocated and the amount of WBS identified.

There was therefore significant evidence that innocent people who have been overpaid benefits may be suffering as a result of over-zealous anti-fraud strategies.

From the Blair Government's perspective the most serious weakness with the WBS measure was that it concentrated on 'quick wins – short-term savings which result from fraud detection' (SoS and MoS for Social Security, 1998: 67) and did little to encourage fraud being prevented. Indeed this was considered the only way permanent reductions in the level of fraud could be achieved. This view was endorsed in the 27th Report of the Committee of Public Accounts (1998) which found it 'totally unacceptable that...the DSS do not have information on whether fraud is increasing: measures introduced...have not helped to prevent fraud: and suspected fraudsters have a 99 per cent chance of getting off scot-free' (Committee of Public Accounts, 26 March 1998).

In brief then, the British Government has a stated objective of a permanent reduction of fraud across the social security system. It has three main aims. In the first instance it wants to deter the would-be fraudster from having a go. In the second instance, it wants to prevent the fraudster from breaking-in to the benefit system. And in the third instance, should the fraudster manage to commit a fraud, they want him/her detected and punished. In the Government's own words (SoS for Social Security, 1998: 45-46), the WBS system as a means of measuring performance and allocating resources to meet these objectives, was at its best an '...imperative...to kick start action within a system that ignored fraud' and at its worst 'rewarded administrative systems which let in fraud – which can then be found – rather than... prevented'.

In December 1997, the DSS undertook a review of its anti-fraud strategy. It had five strands including risk management, delivery systems and human resource management; performance measurement, improving public confidence, and, developing organizational structures that facilitate effective service delivery. The third strand on performance measurement was led by the BFI, a unit within the DSS established to inspect and report on the anti-fraud and security performance of local authorities and DSS agencies. It is notably independent from the organizations it inspects (BFI, 1998a). The co-author of this chapter, Paul McComb, was the leader of the project that developed the new policy proposals which would ultimately form an important component of the Blair Government's anti-fraud strategy. The main objective was to develop a measurement framework that allowed the DSS to:

- measure the level of programme loss and its causes on an ongoing basis;
- determine the overall capability of DSS and Local Authorities (LAs) to minimize social security programme loss;
- identify, resource, target and measure the activity necessary to reduce this loss.

It also aimed to:

- establish the value of the current measurement system used by the DSS and LAs;
- ensure that any new proposals could help to meet stakeholder needs both within

and outside the DSS; and,
* identify early opportunities for making improvements (BFI, 1998b: 7).

The relatively short time-scale for the completion of this work (three months), and the need for its findings to integrate with other strands of the anti-fraud review meant that some of the recommendations would need further refinement during the implementation stage.

The Search for Solutions

The absence of acceptable alternative policy responses or solutions may lead an agent to engage in a search for policy ideas. This is quite often an ad hoc process characterized by trial and error. We would define searching an organization's past as normal policy development. Search activity is a key feature of the process of policy transfer. For as we shall see it is within this process that the nature of information gathering enters new arenas and forms of collaborative governance emerge. The BFI deliberately involved as many interests and stakeholders as necessary to ensure the best possible chance of coming up with some new lasting and innovative proposals (BFI, 1998a). Indeed it is here that we can identify a real commitment on its part to developing a broad based policy transfer network. Table 3.3 maps out the initial structure of the network devised for the organization of this project. It is evident that the BFI was attempting to search across as many different sectors for similar circumstances as possible within the confines of the three-month search period. Moreover, the organizational design of the project was geared towards engaging in intensive search activity in a short period of time.

The Project Sponsor (Director General of the BFI) was also a member of the general review committee and as such provided high-level strategic management for the overall review. The Project Board provided strategic management for the measurement project. McComb was assisted by a consultant from Ernst and Young, and had personal responsibility for taking the project forward. His responsibilities included ensuring that there was adequate planning and involvement of internal and external stakeholders. McComb was also responsible for delivering the aims of the project to a strict timetable and was personally accountable to the Project Sponsor. The primary responsibility of the Project Analysts was to bring independent expertise and a degree of objectivity to what was a very sensitive and complex piece of work. The team included two consultants from the private sector (one from Ernst and Young and one from Andersen Consulting) and a senior academic expert from University of Wales College, Cardiff.

In the past a wide range of approaches had been taken to address the problem of measuring benefit fraud activity, which reflected different concerns of different stakeholders. McComb decided to organize these approaches into three types of stakeholder: policy, operational and commercial. The 'policy' participant mainly focused on definitional and moral issues.

Table 3.3   The composition of the policy transfer network in the search phase of the project

Project Board: Director General of DSS/BFI (Chair and Sponsor); Director of Projects, SBA; Officer, HM Treasury; Officer, DSS Counter Fraud Unit; Officer, DSS Branch Security; Academic Advisor, University of Cardiff; Paul McComb, DSS/BFI, Measurement Project Leader; Officer, DSS; and, Officer, DSS Finance Division.

Project Analysts: Academic Advisor, University of Cardiff; Researcher, DSS; Consultant, Ernst and Young; Consultant, Andersen Consulting.

Policy Approach:
Leaders: Academic Advisor, York University; Director, NAO
Network: Officer, DSS Counter Fraud Unit; Officer, DSS Counter Fraud Unit; Officer, DSS Housing Benefit Security; Officer, DSS Planning & Finance Division; Officer, LGA; Officer, COSLA; Officer, WLGA; Officer, SBA Security Officer, CA Policy Director; and, Officer, DSS Analytical Services Division.

Operational Approach:
Leaders: District Manager, SBA; Officer, SBA District Office and assisted by consultant from Ernst & Young
Network: Officer, SBA Security Branch; Officer, SBA Directorate; three SBA Managers; Customer Services Manager, SBA; Officer, SBA Organized Fraud Investigation; Officer, CA Northern Region; Officer, CSA; and, four local government officers.

Commercial Approach:
Leaders: Consultant, Anderson Consulting
Network: four consultants; four private sector contractors; Representative, Association of Payment Clearing Services; Representative, Institute of Chartered Accountants; and, Director, Software Company.

Examples of the former would involve questions such as: how can we determine the nature of the loss resulting from a fraud?; where should we spend public money to prevent the loss? The latter would involve consideration of a government's moral and political obligation to the electorate – i.e. it is the moral and political obligation of the DSS to attempt to bring fraudsters to justice. The 'operational' participant emphasized the importance of experience. This strand of expertise was largely made up of implementing officials who are able to draw lessons from past successes and failures and assess their implications for the current deliberation. Finally, the 'commercial' participant addressed the issue of policy definition from an orthodox economic perspective – 'fraud costs money; what conceptual tools of performance measurement can we introduce to prevent this from happening?' Here the project sought to draw lessons from successful practice in the private sector (e.g. the credit card industry).

Each group had its own leader(s) who were personally responsible for the work on their approach and were supported by an ad-hoc development network made up of groups or individuals who either had an interest or value to add to the work. As it was recognized that with this type of approach some duplication was likely, the Project Leader was instructed to keep that to a minimum but not at the expense of stifling progress or free thinking. It is important to note that many of the external organizations consulted were drawn from a group convened in September 1997 at a DSS Fraud Seminar (Andersen Consulting, Coopers and Lybrand and Ernst and Young, for example). At the same time practitioners from SBA, the Contributions Agency (CA), the Child Support Agency (CSA) and two local authorities were invited to participate.

As Table 3.3 illustrates, in the initial policy transfer network, the BFI was the primary agent of transfer who undertook search activity on behalf of its client, the DSS. However, due to the complex nature of the policy problem the BFI broadened the scope of its search activities. Hence the BFI's search strategy reflected the absence of expertise it possessed in the measurement area. As Paul McComb puts it, '[w]e didn't have the expertise so we contracted people in who did. This created the scope for much more creative thinking'. Indeed it was quite a novel approach to search activity, for typically a project like this would be tackled by a dedicated in-house team with the Project Manager largely determining the outcome.

This had three very important implications for the policy outcomes that would follow. First, it meant that it was likely that multiple agents of transfer would emerge which reflected the imperatives of each strand of participant ('policy', 'operational', 'commercial'). Secondly, due to the existence of multiple agents of transfer the outcome of the process was likely to be a hybrid policy transfer; one which combines elements from other programmes already in process. Thirdly, the co-ordinating role of the Project Leader was absolutely essential for each strand had a different problem definition and hence a different solution to the problem. The most important aspect of the Project Leader's work was thus to harness the creative energy of each strand in a positive way.

There was also an important political motivation for adopting a multi-level approach to search activity. It was deemed crucial to the success of the project to involve all the key bureaucratic players with a stake in the policy from the outset. In this case these were identified as the NAO and the Treasury and those who operated the current policy (i.e. DSS agencies and local authorities). This made it possible, where it was deemed to be politically expedient, both to identify and circumvent objections and accommodate their interests prior to the development of concrete proposals.

Contact with Potential Agents of Transfer

During the search process an organization may come across a potential agent of transfer with specialist 'cognitive' and 'elite' mobilization skills (e.g. an epistemic community residing within an international organization). In this context, 'cognitive' mobilization refers to the ability of the agent of transfer to develop the necessary political and knowledge resources to satisfy successful policy development. 'Elite' mobilization refers to the ability of the agent of transfer to gain access to knowledge elites and bring their expertise into the transfer network. At this juncture the potential agent of transfer will only be interested in disseminating basic information to the potential client with the aim of seducing them into a dependency relationship. It must be noted that for some agents (e.g. Ernst and Young), policy transfer is a lucrative business. Hence from their part a significant deal of strategic calculation will go into closing a lead. The nature of contact which takes place is ultimately dependent on whether the agent is independent of both client and donor organization. It is conceivable, for instance, that the agent might be part of the search organization itself. This was the case with regard to the principal agent of policy transfer within our case, the BFI.

Through its multi-level approach to search activity the BFI was initially able to facilitate the involvement of a broad range of stakeholders from both the public and the private sector. This generated a significant degree of information and debate on the key issues of concern. Indeed the most interesting ideas were followed-up by the Project Leader through face-to-face meetings. Academics and experts from the private sector were then invited to analyse the strengths and the weaknesses of those ideas. It was now time for the DSS to evaluate the quality of the information, which had been gathered on its behalf by the BFI.

The Emergence of an Information Feeder Network

If the curiosity of the client (in this case the DSS) is aroused through preliminary contact the principal agent of transfer will develop an information feeder network in order to increase both the volume and the detail of information. At this stage the agent will be intent on demonstrating the quality of their access to communication and knowledge networks and further opportunity structures for transfer. The main role of the Project Leader at this juncture was primarily a reactive one. As the DSS expressed an interest in particular ideas it made requests to the Project Leader for further contextual information. This included case studies of other organizations at home and abroad. The Project Leader also began to identify an elite group of agents (all of whom may be considered potential agents of transfer with the exception of DSS officials) who had the necessary political and knowledge resources to satisfy the objectives of the review.

Cognition, Reception and the Emergence of a Policy Transfer Network

The client will evaluate the information that has been provided through the information feeder network. Cognition and reception will then usually depend on both client and agent of transfer sharing a commitment to a common value system. In this sense policy transfer networks tend to be the preserve of elite activity and involvement in the game is wholly dependent on the resources, which an agent of transfer possesses. Table 3.4 provides an overview of the key characteristics of the policy transfer network, which emerged in our case study. The network combined bureaucrats with technocrats and was established due to the skills shortage of the recipient organization (the DSS). The 11 members of the network included: the accountable DSS official for the review; the Project Sponsor (Director-General BFI); the Project Leader; a consultant from Ernst and Young; an academic from the University of Wales College, Cardiff; two consultants from Andersen Consulting; a representative from the DSS Analytical Services Division; an academic from the Social Policy Research Unit at the University of York; the Director of the NAO and a District Manager of the SBA.

The DSS spent six weeks evaluating the information provided by the Project Leader and made further requests for information and clarification. It was at this stage that the DSS and the principle agent of transfer (the BFI) started to work more closely on the development of the policy proposals. As a consequence an inner circle developed within the network comprised of the Director General of the BFI, the DSS Director of Fraud Strategy, the Project Leader and three experts (one from academia and two consultants).

Elite and Cognitive Mobilization

The process of elite and cognitive mobilization is critical to the success of the transfer network. It is here that the quality of the agent's knowledge resources is put to the test. The agent will be expected to provide detailed information about programmes elsewhere which have addressed a similar problem. In the seminal work on systems theory, David Easton (1965) argues that in order to maintain the status quo within a decision-making structure mechanisms exist to filter out, or exclude input which would be dysfunctional, or which would overload the system. He referred to these regulators as gatekeepers who exclude from the system excessive or unacceptable demands. The same argument can be applied to this stage of the policy transfer process where agents of policy transfer can act as gatekeepers who exhibit a bias against certain inputs.

In this case there were two key determinants of the policy agenda. First, time evidently played a crucial role in focusing search activities on specific exemplars. Although a broad range of stakeholders were involved, the three-month search cycle meant that fewer illustrations were considered from abroad than might have been the case with a longer period of review. Secondly, the elite representatives from the three groups of stakeholders emerged as the gatekeepers of the agenda. The interests of the citizen or the consumer are noticeably absent. Moreover, a cost containment discourse underpinned the nature of the review and provided the 'ideological glue' that bound the key network participants together in a common overarching value system. By this we refer to the Chancellor of the Exchequer Gordon Brown's emphasis on the control of inflation and his deployment of general neo-liberal monetarism. This has become the touchstone of state economic management and interventionism. For example, two traditional categories of economic policy – monetary and fiscal policy – have undergone significant change.

Table 3.4   The key characteristics of the counter social security fraud policy transfer network

Dimension	Case Study Characteristics
Membership *number of participants*	An exemplar of collaborative governance. In the early stages a large number of participants were involved (90), but as the new policy began to emerge the number decreased to 11 key players representing three strands of participant – policy, operational and commercial.
type of interest	The agents of transfer included bureaucrats, private sector consultants and academics.
Integration *frequency of interaction*	The process of transfer occurred within a three-month action plan.
continuity	The network was disbanded after the formulation of policy.
consensus	All participants did not share basic policy values as some participants (e.g. private sector contractors and consultants) stood to gain financially – a motivation not present within the network at large. The project leader had significant influence in terms of shaping the belief system, which underpinned the proposals.
Resources *Distribution of resources (within network)*	This was critical to the determination of the composition of the policy transfer network and its inner circle.
Distribution of resources (within organizations	The process of collaborative governance was established due to the skills shortage of the recipient organization (the DSS).
Power	The agent of transfer had little direct power other than that gained as a result of satisfying the objective of formulating a new policy; and having access to the knowledge resources to help implement it.

The relative priorities between the two have been reversed with tighter monetary policy being pursued alongside looser fiscal policy through tax cuts. We have also witnessed a shift from macro-economic to micro-economic interventionism, reflected not only in deregulation and industrial policy but in new social policy initiatives such as 'Welfare to Work' schemes (see Evans and Cerny, 2003). It would be wrong, however, to depict this loose-knit value system purely as a neo-liberal one. It very much represents the historic compromise between the Thatcher project and New Labour's attempt to achieve 'globalization with a human face'.

The new policy proposals, presented three months later, consisted of four main elements that reflected the influence of the three groups of participant. The first was called programme review. In essence this was the development of a model which analysed DSS data on known 'frauds' and other data from the county courts, family expenditure survey and credit industry. The concept was a direct transfer from a statistical and forecasting model that had been developed for use in the financial sector (in the main, credit card and insurance sectors). The recommendation was to develop programme review by further developing this model as a collaborative public/private sector initiative. This would help the DSS to estimate the level of social security fraud by geographical location, client type or benefit. In sum, this would be the overall outcome measure of the level of fraud. Although programme review would allow others to judge the success of the DSS in outcome terms (i.e. whether the level of social security fraud was going up or down), as a measure it would be impacted by external factors such as the level of unemployment or the level of benefits relative to earning. It was for this reason that additional measures were required.

The second element of the new policy package was the development of a strategic scorecard. The strategic scorecard was a measure of the capability of the DSS as an organization to control and minimize the amount of social security fraud. Scorecards are common particularly in private sector partnerships, where there is a need to judge each partner's contribution to 'success'. The concept was used on the advice of inner circle consultants who knew of a number of examples where scorecards had been developed and were found to be particularly effective. A further search across other governments found them to be employed in social security contexts in Australia and the United States. Hence, the strategic scorecard proposal was not drawn from one particular donor but was constructed from the experience of a number of donor organizations that adopted similar systems.

The third element of the new policy proposals was less significant in terms of innovation. For DSS operational purposes, activity-based measures would be needed to establish, resource and target the range of activities and initiatives designed to reduce losses due to fraud. Consultants were employed to search across the public and private sector to determine the characteristics of activity measures; and from this a 'Good Measurement Checklist' was developed. In effect this was a hybrid of what was judged 'good' in practice.

The fourth and final element of the proposals was a mechanism for informing how resources should be allocated to the various activities designed to counter fraud. It was argued that any new methodology for resource allocation should ensure that: activity is linked to problems identified through the programme review; a risk analysis had been undertaken; there was a clear understanding of how the activity would contribute to the capability score in the strategic scorecard;

and that the cost of the activity was outweighed by the benefits, unless there was some compelling public interest issue at stake (such as dealing with organized crime). Two options were presented. The first was fairly simplistic and based on the United States Quality Control Programme. This is a method of resource allocation whereby US State administrators have to bear from their administration budget (or by raising state taxes) excessive losses incurred on their social security programme budget. The second option was based on the overall capability of the organization to control and minimize fraud losses (the score determined by the strategic scorecard). This extension of the scorecard concept was once again drawn from private sector partnership experience and advocated by inner circle consultants (BFI, 1998b).

A mapping exercise was conducted to determine what was new and different between the current and new policy that addressed the question; what was going to change? Despite the protestations of those who operated the current policy (i.e. DSS agencies and local authorities), it demonstrated that the new policy was a significant departure from its predecessor.

Interaction

The agent of transfer will be expected to organize forums for the exchange of ideas between the client and knowledge elites with policy relevant knowledge. These may take the form of representatives of an epistemic community who have similar professional beliefs and standards of judgement and share common policy concerns. A context of interaction may therefore take place through the organization of seminars, fact-finding missions, conferences and the exchange of specialist policy advice documents (e.g. the drafting of legislation). It is through these forms of diffusion activity that agents of transfer can channel particular policy ideas. Of course this characterization is also dependent on the type of agent of transfer under consideration. In this case study, the interaction stage ran in tandem with the elite and cognitive mobilization stage and the Project Leader arranged several meetings with potential donor organizations. The interaction stage did lead to certain refinements to the operational dimension of the policy proposals, which were documented in the previous section.

Evaluation of Options

Once the client is satisfied with the degree of intelligence gathering that they have engaged in, a process of evaluation will commence. The evaluation process is critical in determining: the objects of transfer (e.g. policy goals, structure and content; policy instruments or administrative techniques; institutions; ideology; ideas, attitudes and concepts; policy style or negative lessons); the degree of transfer (e.g. copying, hybridization, emulation, or inspiration); and the prerequisites of transfer (e.g. policy feasibility and political, cultural and institutional conditions) which will condition the nature of a policy programme. In this study because the new policy programme referred to operational issues, no legislative process and thus exposure to parliamentary and public scrutiny was deemed necessary. The DSS thus followed the recommendations of the BFI for a hybrid policy transfer with its four components outlined above.

The Formal Decision Stream

The policy transfer process is not an isolated enterprise, but an integral part of the policy process. Hence it is best understood, in John Kingdon's (1984) terms, as one of a variety of policy alternatives competing in the 'policy' stream of the process. In this sense ideas for policy transfer compete with other alternatives. The inner circle emerged within the policy transfer network in May 1998 and the Blair government's new strategy was published in July 1998. Hence a process of lobbying by DSS agencies and local authorities ran in parallel to the process of policy transfer from the elite and cognitive mobilization phase. They sought to demonstrate to the Director of Fraud Strategy, that despite the criticism, much of what was current policy was in line with the new policies being proposed. The only demonstrable evidence to prove the effect of this process of lobbying is contained within the Green Paper on fraud, 'Beating Fraud is Everyone's Business: Securing the Future' (SoS for Social Security, 1998) which devotes eight out of its ten paragraphs on performance measurement and resource allocation to current activities, with only two covering the new policy. Moreover, in a section, which provides details of the government's 'timetable for action' (Ibid: 49-51), the new policy is mentioned as the last item for action in 1999.

Implementation

The study of policy transfer is incomplete without an implementation perspective. Even if a policy is a faithful programmatic copy of the original, it can ultimately only be said to have been transferred if it is carried out. It is by no means certain that those implementing a programme will do what was intended or specified by those who formulated it. Indeed it may, for reasons of structural incompatibility, be impossible for them to do so. Hence the analysis of policy transfer is incomplete without reference to implementation. Unfortunately this remains the case for our study. The policy has now been implemented but it will remain some time until we are able to develop an implementation perspective, which allows us to assess the impact of post-decisional inputs on the process of policy transfer.

In Conclusion: Policy Transfer as Rational Collaborative Governance

Bill Mackenzie (1975: 142-143) in a seminal work argues that:

> ...the case study method is to establish the facts and let them speak for themselves; put the reader in the position of informed spectator and let him use the material as he pleases. He may wish to judge or generalize; he may merely learn by experience the feeling of a variety of situations...yet a case study is pointless if what it says is

determined by chance. The author in so far as he is skilled, knows how to control his material in accordance with certain criteria of relevance.

The policy transfer network approach has proved a useful heuristic device for organising our case study analysis and studying the process of policy transfer. In Mackenzie's terms it provides a 'criteria of relevance'. It has helped us to simplify a complex process of policy transfer in order to comprehend the multiplicity of factors, which have shaped this unusual policy-making process. Indeed, it is possible to conclude from the evidence presented that the process of policy transfer itself may be treated as an independent variable that explains why this particular raft of policy proposals was adopted.

What does this case study tell us about the nature of this particular process of policy transfer? It is unsurprisingly elite driven and is not about extending democracy but is about finding technical solutions to highly technical problems. This requires technocratic expertise that is not always readily available within public organizations. Moreover, if a highly technocratic process of policy transfer is developed it can prove a useful instrument for absorbing the strength of argument from counter forces elsewhere in the bureaucracy. Initially the policy transfer network included participation from a broad range of stakeholders with 'policy', 'operational' and 'commercial' interests and expertise. An inner circle then emerged within the network comprised of key technocrats and bureaucrats who ultimately determined the nature of the policy proposals. In sum, it was the structure of the policy transfer network, which was the key determinant of policy outcomes. The decision was determined at the third, fourth and fifth stages of the policy transfer process. This was primarily due to the pressing need for a new policy to be announced in the face of mounting criticism from government watchdogs. Having made the decision to adopt the new policies the remainder of the transfer process, although still very relevant, became stages of policy refinement, which operated at a lower level in the decision-making hierarchy.

The policy transfer network approach also proved helpful in assisting our understanding of how decision-makers at the DSS acquired knowledge. Two important conclusions can be drawn. First, the time-scale that is established to search for policy ideas informed the scope of the inquiry. Secondly, multi-level search activity produced multiple agents of policy transfer and ultimately hybrid forms of cross-national and cross-sectoral policy transfer. How can we evaluate the role of the agents of policy transfer within this process of policy transfer? A process of gate keeping took place in which elite players were selected by the primary agent of policy transfer (the BFI) according to their political or knowledge resources. It is here that agents of policy transfer have their most significant influence.

At the inter-organizational level then, the policy transfer network approach appears to have a high degree of relevance. However, two crucial shortcomings can also be identified with the approach. First, consultants are generally paid fees, which presents a financial motive for their involvement in a policy transfer network. This is at odds with the model's expectation that all participants would share basic values. Secondly, it is evident from the case study that it is crucial to conceptualize policy transfer networks as a potential site for a healthy competition of ideas between different bureaucratic interests. Hence, in this study the role of those operating existing policy programmes, DSS agencies and local authorities deserved far greater attention.

Chapter 4

Policy Transfer in a Competition State: Britain's 'New Deal'

Mark Evans

Introduction

My main submission in this chapter is twofold. First, the British Labour government has adopted a policy agenda, which in its most crucial aspects reflects the continuing transformation of the British State into a competition state. Secondly, within a competition state policy actors and institutions increasingly promote new forms of complex globalization through processes of policy transfer in an attempt to adapt state action to cope more effectively with what they see as global 'realities'. The purpose of this chapter is to consider the significance of these two developments. However, given the sheer size of this task I must begin by limiting the scope of my field somewhat. It will be argued in this chapter that the adoption of contracting post-welfarism in Britain is a key feature of the competition state and a rich source of hybrid policy transfer from the United States and elsewhere. Hence, it is claimed that the study of policy transfer in the welfare policy arena provides fertile ground for investigating the significance of the competition state as a lens for observing both the changing nature of the nation state and the role of state actors and institutions in promoting new forms of complex globalization.

The argument is developed cumulatively and organized into three parts. The first presents a brief account of the rise and fall of the Industrial Welfare State (IWS), and, its replacement with forms of the competition state under neo-liberal and centre-left governments in Britain and the United States. It then moves on to outline the key features of the competition state and generates a series of propositions that are subject to a brief empirical investigation. In the second section of the chapter an overview of Welfare reform under the current Labour government is presented together with an assessment of the philosophical foundations to Labour's new thinking, and an evaluation of the sources of its ideas. The final substantive section presents data from a case study of policy transfer in the Welfare policy arena – the New Deal. The chapter concludes with some general observations about what this case study of the emergence and development of a policy transfer network tells us about the impact of the competition state project on welfare policy development in Britain.

The Theory of the Competition State

The main challenge facing governments all over the world is their capacity to adapt to the exogenous constraints and opportunities brought about by different processes of globalization while maintaining a relatively effective domestic policy programme. Within this context, the challenges faced by centre-left parties and governments are particularly problematic. For most of the 20th century these parties have believed in expanding the boundaries of the state to provide public goods for working peoples, minorities, and other socially valued groups and causes. These interventionary strategies have depended historically upon the capacity of states to make domestic policy in ways that preserve key spheres of autonomy for policy-makers *vis-à-vis* international capital. However, such autonomy is increasingly being constrained by processes of globalization. Some theorists of globalization suggest that all states are losing power and coherence (for example, compare McKenzie and Lee, 1991, with Reich, 1991), while others maintain that governments are able to adapt and to transform state structures in ways that alter, but do not fundamentally reduce or undermine, state capacity, not only for neo-liberal governments of the right but also for social democratic governments of the centre-left (for example, compare Hirst and Thompson, 1996, with Garrett, 1998).

The theory of the competition state provides an alternative conception of this problematic which, while accepting that the state is losing power and coherence due to processes of Globalization and transnationalization, argues that the competition state will increasingly become the engine room and the steering mechanism of a political globalization process which will further drive and shape economic, social and cultural globalization (see Cerny and Evans, 2000 and Evans and Cerny, 2003). It should be noted from the outset that the theory of the competition state stands in contrast to the 'Post-Fordist State' of Regulation Theory which asserts that the restructuring of the state as a consequence of globalization effectively permits the state to maintain its 'generic function' of stabilizing the national polity and promoting the domestic economy in the public interest. It presents six main propositions about how states and state actors adapt and respond to the imperatives of globalization that can be used to explain the trajectory of the British State under the Blair government in Britain.

Proposition 1: The Changing Form and Functions of the State

The competition state involves both a restructuring and a qualitative disempowering of the state in the face of processes of globalization and transnationalization. It may also lead to the empowering of the state in certain areas.

By prioritising the promotion of international competitiveness, the state over time loses its capacity to act, in Oakeshott's (1976) term, as a 'civil association' and comes more and more to act merely as a promoter of various 'enterprise associations'. In addition, an endogenous process often referred to as the 'hollowing-out' of the state leads to the loss not just of its previous interventionist role, but also of much of its traditional raison d'être. Rhodes (1994 and 1997) has argued that there are four key interrelated trends which illustrate the scope of this process: privatization and limits on the scope and forms of public intervention; the loss of functions by central government departments to alternative service delivery systems, such as 'next step' agencies and through market testing; the loss of functions to European Community Institutions and national assemblies through devolution; and the emergence of limits to the discretion of public servants through the New Public Management.

Policy networks are central to understanding internal 'hollowing-out' while globalization is central to understanding a concomitant process of external 'hollowing-out' in a world of complex interdependencies. Hence the policy focus of the state shifts from the macro-level of the Industrial Welfare State (IWS) to a micro-level analogous to the space traditionally occupied by local, provincial, regional or US 'state' governments. Indeed the competition state itself becomes a pivotal agent in the erosion of many of those social and economic functions that capitalist states had taken on in the first two-thirds of the 20th century. This outcome stems from the interaction of two main variables. In the first place, we can identify an exogenous independent variable – the horizontal restructuring of the global economy and polity, and, perhaps must crucially, the formation of transnational networks and discourses of power and governance.

This exogenous, cross-cutting process of restructuring sets up a series of fundamental challenges to the vertically organized national state and political economy. More specifically it places less emphasis on the physical forces of production per se and more on other factors of capital, especially globally mobile finance capital, and the emergence of relatively autonomous transnational elites who adopt the discourses and practices of globalization in order to pursue their own goals and values on a wider field of action. In other words, the impact of globalization on the policies and policy-making processes of states increasingly involves attempts by governments to capture the perceived benefits of internationally mobile capital. The competition state is thus itself an authoritative agent of globalization, embedding that process in its domestic practices as well as its international and transnational linkages.

The competition state will also seek to enhance its capacity to steer the nation state. Indeed, the constitutional reform project is a good example of this in Britain. For it constitutes a strategy of integration; a process through which new and old political communities are either defined or redefined, created or discarded in both institutional and attitudinal terms. Indeed, historically devolution has been used as a policy instrument by British governments to assimilate the demands of nationalist movements within the 'nations' seeking greater autonomy (see Evans, 2000). Its main aim is to secure elite attachment to the UK system of governance through the forging of a consensus on national policy goals.

Proposition 2: The Nature of Political Agency

Rather than attempting to insulate states from key international market pressures, as state actors in the National Industrial Welfare State sought to do, political actors in competition states embrace openness and marketization.

State actors and institutions promote new forms of complex globalization in the attempt to adapt state action to cope more effectively with what they see as global 'realities'. Hence they seek to make the domestic economy more prosperous and competitive in international terms while accepting the loss of key traditional social and economic state functions, which were central to the development of the IWS. However, in attempting to meet the challenges of globalization, domestic political and bureaucratic actors increasingly transform the domestic political system into a terrain of conflict underpinned with profound policy debates around alternative responses to globalization (e.g. in Britain the issue of the single European currency). Out of this process of domestic rearticulation, a particular range of policy options comes to represent a restructured, loosely knit consensus. First on the right (many of whose 'neo-liberal' members have always believed deeply in the disarming of the economic state) and then on the left, as traditional alternatives are incrementally eroded. This increasingly familiar consensus involves both an extensive process of deregulation, liberalization, and flexibilization not only of public policy but of the state apparatus itself and a refocusing of the state on supporting, maintaining and even promoting transnational and international market processes and governance structures at home. The latter manifests itself in a moral emphasis on personal responsibility, an economic and political acceptance of the correctness of market outcomes, and, paradoxically, an increase in pro-market regulation and intervention (see Cerny, 1990 and Vogel, 1996). Thus the rationale for state intervention is aimed not only at sustaining the domestic economy but also at promoting its further integration into an increasingly open global economy in the acceptance that the imperatives of international competitiveness and consumer choice have a higher ideological status than issues of domestic social solidarity.

Proposition 3: The Diminishing Role of Ideology

As a result of these changes, some consensual, some coercive, the ideological divide between left and right comes to lose many of its traditional landmarks.

Social democratic and other centre-left parties begin to search for policies, which, while adapting to the new constraints, are intended to promote a diluted form of neo-liberalism, or what has been termed the 'Third Way'. In Britain this represents the outcome of the war of ideas between the forces of social democracy and neo-liberalism.

Proposition 4: The Internationalization of the Policy Agenda

The creation of a competition state involves a policy agenda, which seeks to provide the conditions that will help the state to adapt state action to cope more effectively with what they perceive as global 'realities'.

In terms of the key elements of economic policy transformation, transnational factors have interacted with domestic politics to bring five specific types of policy change to the top of the political agenda. First, there has been an emphasis on the control of inflation and general neo-liberal monetarism – hopefully translating into non-inflationary growth. This has become the touchstone of state economic management and interventionism, reflected in a wider embedded financial orthodoxy. Secondly, a shift from macro-economic to micro-economic interventionism has occurred, as reflected in both deregulation and industrial policy and in new social initiatives such as 'welfare-to-work' schemes. Thirdly, a shift in the focus of interventionism has also occurred at the international level away from maintaining a range of 'strategic' economic activities in order to retain minimal economic self-sufficiency in key sectors to a policy of flexible response to competitive conditions in a range of diversified and rapidly evolving international market places. Fourthly, new regulatory structures have been established to enforce global market-rational economic and political behaviour on rigid and inflexible private sector actors as well as on state actors and agencies. Finally, a shift in the focal point of party and governmental politics away from the general maximization of welfare within a nation (full employment, redistributive transfer payments and social service provision) to the promotion of enterprise, innovation and profitability in both private and public sectors has been initiated.

Proposition 5: The Proliferation of Policy Transfer

Policy transfer has become a key mechanism for delivering the policy agenda of the competition state through elite structures of governance.

This policy agenda is spreading primarily as a consequence of four key developments. Firstly, as a consequence of processes of globalization both external to the nation state and the 'hollowing-out' of the nation state itself have created new opportunity structures for policy transfer. Secondly, a process of Americanization has helped to reinforce key features of the competition state in the UK through bi-lateral forms of policy transfer (see Deacon, 2000). Thirdly, policy transfer is more likely to occur in an era that Rhodes (1996: 652) has termed 'the New Governance: Governing without Government', in which in times of uncertainty policy-makers look to 'quick fix' solutions to public policy problems that policy transfer can sometimes provide. Fourthly, key agents and agencies within the state have also moved up the institutional pecking order in highly significant ways to enforce such changes in emphasis directly. Probably the most important of these are central banks, whose power has increased not only because of their location at the crossroads of the national financial economy and the global financial marketplace, but also because governments of both centre-left and right have come more and more to accept that such agencies should be independent and free of supposedly 'short-termist' political pressures in making key decisions on the setting of interest rates, control of the money supply and regulation of increasingly transnationalized financial institutions and markets.

Proposition 6: The Decline of Social Solidarity

These developments challenge the capacity of state institutions to embody the kind of communal solidarity, which gave the modern nation-state its deeper legitimacy, institutionalized power, and social embeddedness.

The cumulative effect of these various pressures and processes is a redefinition of the boundaries of the political. The restructuring of the political arena forces parties and governments of the left to redefine their conception of the 'social' and the 'public' away from the traditional confines of the 'modern' state. In Britain this has been reflected in two main developments. Firstly, the residual rights approach to citizenship that underpinned Britain's unwritten constitution has been replaced with the introduction of legally enforceable individual rights through the incorporation of the European Convention on Human and Political Rights into British law. Secondly, there has been a paradigm shift in British Welfarism that has been manifested in an attack on welfare dependency and the bonding of welfare rights and obligations. This latter process of reform is the subject of the next section of this chapter.

The Post-Welfare Contracting State

> We understand that economic stability is the prerequisite for radicalism in social policy rather than an alternative to it. We must be the parties of fiscal and economic prudence. Combined with it must be reform of the welfare state... Welfare has become passive; a way of leaving people doing nothing, rather than helping them become active (Tony Blair, speech to the Party of European Socialists' Congress, June 1997).

There are two key features of this crucial dimension of the competition state. First, the ideology of welfare from which subsequent welfare reform has flowed has changed and lessons have directly been incorporated from the United States. The ideological sea change underpinning the philosophy of British welfarism began in earnest with Sir Keith Joseph's (1972 and 1974) attack on the post-war settlement in the mid-1970s which proved particularly influential in shaping Margaret Thatcher's thinking on the welfare state. However, it was the American conservatives, especially Charles Murray, Lawrence Mead and the *New consensus on family and welfare* (AEI, 1987) that gave the critique of welfare dependency greater policy and programmatic expression. Indeed it is also possible to trace a change to the discursive construction of British welfarism from this conjuncture.

The work of the American conservatives also had a profound impact on New Labour's thinking especially in relation to their argument that rights and responsibilities were mutually reinforcing elements of sustainable welfarism. This, of course, challenged the key premises of Labour's post-war conception of welfare entitlements as the key policy instruments for achieving social equality and solidarity. Brian Lund (1999: 447-462) argues that the governing principles of 'Old' Labour's approach to social policy were strongly informed by the legacy of Richard Titmuss who was criticized for placing too much stress on obligation. As Lund (1999: 448) observes, Titmuss adopted the language of 'ultra-obligation' and, according to some communitarian critics, his call for universal altruism failed to establish specific obligations'. Deacon (2000: 11) notes that shortly after becoming Minister for Welfare Reform Frank Field wrote of Titmuss's 'pervasive influence in the political world of social policy [which] resulted in an approach to welfare which helped to make Labour unelectable for so much of my political career…[t]he Titmuss legacy lingered over the political debate with such force that I, for one, felt that it covered me with a form of intellectual treacle which made movement difficult'. Nonetheless, the importance of bonding welfare rights and obligations won the war of ideas in the mind of Blair and 'no rights without obligations' became 'a prime motto for the new politics' under New Labour (Giddens 1998: 65).

The second feature of the Post-Welfare Contracting State can be identified in the shift in welfare policy itself in favour of integrating people into the private sector workforce through active labour market inclusion largely based on the American model. However, it is important to note that once again the development of the post-welfare, contracting state, pre-dates the Blair government. As Anne Gray (1998: 6) argues, 'New Labour has explicitly chosen to continue the Tories' 'workfarist' approach to labour market policy and to encourage adoption of its new labour discipline in other EU states by pressing for a minimalist social chapter and promoting the 'New Deal' as a model policy'. This focus on the need to produce incentives in the welfare state constitutes an appropriation of a key New Right concept – the need to destroy the welfare dependency culture through getting people back to work rather than keeping them on benefits. This emphasis on the virtues of work was central to Blair and Clinton's assault on what Thatcher termed the 'evils of welfare dependency' and despite the considerable differences which exist between the two welfare systems, not to mention political traditions, Blair and Clinton argued that the two countries share a common problem of welfare dependency, which can be tackled through welfare-to-work.

The Case of the New Deal

This chapter now moves on to explore a case study of policy transfer in the welfare reform arena – the New Deal. The case study is evaluated using the policy transfer network approach as presented in the previous chapter. As Figure 3.1 illustrated, for analytical purposes, the policy transfer process can be broken down into twelve stages. Each of these potential stages within the process of voluntary policy transfer will be analysed in detail within the following sections.

Problem Recognition

The emergence of a policy transfer network begins with the recognition by a decision-making elite, politicians or bureaucrats, of the existence of a decision problem, which requires, due to environmental factors, pressing attention. This illustrates the rationale behind Blair's aim of increasing the aggregate skill levels of British peoples in order to compete in the international economy. As Chris Holden (1999: 437) illustrates, 'New Labour's conceptions of social exclusion and globalization thus fit together to produce a labour market policy geared toward increasing labour market participation...in order to increase labour market efficiency within what is perceived to be an ever more competitive world market'. This quotation further illustrates the marriage between the imperatives of a competition state and the government's attitude towards work and by implication welfare to work. In sum, since coming to power New Labour has expanded the scope of the Post-welfare Contracting State through the ending of free higher education and the introduction of 'Workfare' (an American concept from the 1960s and 1970s) and 'Learningfare' as part of what is called the New Deal for unemployed 18 to 24-year-olds. The Blair Government has placed welfare reform at the heart of the competition state project. £5 billion has been spent on the welfare-to-work programme representing by a considerable margin the new Government's largest single public spending commitment. In addition, in successive budgets, Gordon Brown has introduced a raft of financial incentives in an attempt to lift people out of the poverty trap. These measures have included the introduction of the Working Families Tax Credit, and, the lowering of national insurance contributions and tax levels for lower paid workers.

The Treasury has played the key co-ordinating role in the development of the New Deal proposals as the centre-piece of the Government's Welfare to Work strategy. The official reason for why the Treasury led the project rather than the Department for Education and Employment (DfEE), although it was represented in deliberations, was that it symbolized the broader movement of employment policy away from training. However, it may also be argued that it reflected Brown's desire to maintain control over welfare reform in order to steer the competition state. As a Senior Treasury Official put it, '[e]verybody knows that this is about the marketization of the state, that's why Brown's so involved. What we don't know is whether he really thinks that it can have some redistributive effects'. It was also argued that it was evident from similar programmes in the US that the delivery of New Deal would require a co-ordinating body to ensure joined-up delivery across departments at the national, regional and local levels. It was Brown's view that the Treasury was best equipped to perform this role as it had the necessary expertise to take advantage of evidence based learning from the United States and elsewhere.

The Search for Solutions

The absence of acceptable policy responses or solutions may lead an agent to engage in a search for policy ideas. This is quite often an ad-hoc process characterized by trial and error. Search activity is a key feature of the process of policy transfer. For as we shall see it is within this process of search activity that the nature of information gathering enters new arenas and forms of collaborative governance emerge.

The rationale for why ideas and developments in the US have been so influential on the British welfare reform debate has already been discussed in the previous sections of this chapter and have also been well documented elsewhere (see Deacon, 2000). Suffice to say that history, language, ideology, and a shared belief in the competition state project (in particular, macro-economic analysis) have all played a role. Although to term this 'Americanization' of the British Welfare debate (see Walker, 1998) would be a slight exaggeration. As a Senior DSS official observes, '[a]part from the ability to communicate more easily (and this isn't always the case I can assure you) there is really no compelling reason why America is always our first port of call for welfare ideas. After all they have such a different welfare tradition to ours'. This tension between traditions would manifest itself in the evaluation stage of the policy transfer process. Indeed there is plenty of evidence to suggest that the Treasury has also been influenced by initiatives in Australia ('Lone Parents and Partners', 'Working Nation' and 'single gateway/one stop shops' programmes), Sweden ('Working Nation'), the Netherlands ('single gateway/one stop shop' programmes) and Canada (the 'Making Work Pay' scheme). In addition, institutional memory (for example, 'Job Seekers Allowance' and 'Restart' schemes from 1988 and 1996) has also been influential. Nonetheless, the US remains the pioneer in ideas about welfare to work programmes, and, in particular, issues of policy presentation.

It was therefore unsurprising that the Wefare to Work Unit should narrow their search to the United States, the Commonwealth and certain European exemplars such as the Netherlands and Sweden. In an important sense this focused enquiry on easily accessible exemplars where programme success was easily demonstrated through sophisticated forms of programme evaluation. As a Senior Treasury official notes, 'the very fact that the United States could offer over 50 cases of 'Welfare to Work' systems that included rigorous evaluations of strengths and weaknesses was an attraction in itself'. In order to develop an effective search for ideas, the Welfare to Work Unit set up what may be described as a 'Welfare to work Treasury Nexus' that included participants from other issue-related departments of state such as the DfEE, the DSS and the Department of the Environment, Trade and the Regions (DETR). This enabled the unit to draw on the expertise of other key governmental stakeholders.

Contact with Potential Agents of Transfer

During the search process an organization may come across a potential agent of transfer with specialist 'cognitive' and 'elite' mobilization skills (e.g. a policy entrepreneur associated with a powerful epistemic community). In this context, 'cognitive' mobilization refers to the ability of the agent of transfer to develop the necessary political and knowledge resources to satisfy successful policy development. 'Elite' mobilization refers to the ability of the agent of transfer to gain access to knowledge elites and bring their expertise into the transfer network. At this juncture the potential agent of transfer will only be interested in disseminating basic information to the potential client with the aim of seducing them into a dependency relationship. It must be noted that for some agents (e.g. a private sector consultancy such as Ernst and Young), policy transfer is a lucrative business. Hence a significant deal of strategic calculation will go into closing a lead from their part.

From its inception the Welfare to Work Unit established close relations with public organizations in the United States who were responsible for delivering and evaluating Welfare to Work programmes such as the Department of Labor and the United States Office of Personnel Management. In addition, the expertise of several high profile American academics with considerable experience in the Welfare to Work field such as Richard Layard (1997) was also sought. Contact was also made with the architects of 'best practice models' in local experimentation such as 'GAIN' in Riverside, California, 'Florida Wages' and 'Wisconsin Works' (see House of Commons, 1998). As a Treasury official notes, '[t]hese cases were of interest and influence because of their emphasis on work and not training and because they were all demonstrably successful'.

The Emergence of an Information Feeder Network

If the curiosity of the client (in this case the Treasury 'Welfare to Work Nexus') is aroused through preliminary contact the principal agent of transfer will develop an information feeder network in order to increase both the volume and the detail of information. At this stage the agent will be intent on demonstrating the quality of their access to communication and knowledge networks and further opportunity structures for transfer.

The Welfare to Work Unit held several bi-lateral meetings with their American counterparts in order to develop more detailed information on delivery and evaluation issues. As one former official who played a search role in the 'Treasury Welfare to Work Nexus' recalls, '[f]or what seemed like months I spent more time with our American counterparts than with my husband. I stayed in regular contact through email and continue to do so in my new job...[t]he main lessons that we got from the States were about how to join-up services across a devolved structure'. The British team was struck by the quality of research conducted in the United States on Wefare to Work programmes. As the same official observes, '[t]hey are really brilliant at the evidence based evaluation stuff and to be honest we're very poor at it'. This conclusion was also reached at the 530th Wilton Park Conference in New York entitled 'Welfare and Work in Britain and America'. The conference was funded by the Rockefeller, Charles Stewart Mott and Nuffield

Foundations with additional financial assistance from the DfEE, DSS and HM Treasury and was held in July 1998. It represents a classic example of the development of an information feeder network with participants from every level of governance including the transnational level, together with members of think tanks and academics. The conference report concludes that, '[i]n the UK, there is not the same tradition of non-profit research evaluation. It is dependent on the Government, which is not very good at it, and does not always like the results, (see http://www.wiltonpark.org.uk/conferences/).

Cognition, Reception and the Emergence of a Transfer Network

The client will evaluate the information that has been provided through the information feeder network. Cognition and reception will then usually depend on both client and agent of transfer sharing a commitment to a common value system. In this sense policy transfer networks tend to be the preserve of elite activity and involvement in the game is wholly dependent on an agents resources. Table 4.1 provides a snapshot of the key features of the policy transfer network that emerged in relation to the New Deal. An inner circle developed within the 'Treasury-Welfare to Work Nexus', which privileged the competition state's aim 'to rebuild the welfare state around work' (DSS, 1998: 23). This meant emphasizing the bond between welfare rights and responsibilities as an anti-poverty strategy and promoting active labour market policies. For the former, certain lessons would be drawn from the United States and from British welfare traditions, and, for the latter, lessons would be drawn from Australia, Europe and local experiments in the United States.

It is here that differences between welfare traditions became evident and started to play a role. Although the United States and Britain are struggling with the same fundamental underlying challenges, four main differences can be identified. Firstly, the UK approach to Welfare to Work forms part of a comprehensive UK framework of benefit systems, while the United States approach is far more fragmented due to the nature of the federal system. Secondly, the two approaches involve different contexts and different priority groups – in the United States the focus is on lone mothers; in the UK, a broader group is involved, including young long-term unemployed males. Thirdly, the concept of public-private partnerships is far more developed in the United States and hence it is easier to reach small and medium sized enterprises (SMEs) through trade associations. Fourthly, and fundamentally, work is treated as an ethical issue in the United States and as an anti-poverty strategy in the UK. In sum, welfare reformers in the United States believe that the UK already does too much for the jobless and welfare support should be targeted more effectively. The final proposals would be sensitive to these cultural differences.

Table 4.1 The key characteristics of the New Deal policy transfer network

Dimension	Case Study Characteristics
Membership *number of participants*	Very limited, the system has a bias against certain inputs, emphasis on bureaucratic and technocratic elites. An inner circle was coordinated through the 'Welfare to Work' Unit in the Treasury. This included representatives from key departments, US bureaucrats, academics and knowledge institutions.
type of interest	The agents of policy transfer included affected politicians and bureaucrats.
Integration *frequency of interaction*	Within the set time scale, frequent, high quality interaction took place on all matters related to the policy transfer.
continuity	Originally the policy transfer network was an ad-hoc, action orientated network set up with the specific intention of engineering policy change but it still remains in place with a different membership.
consensus	All participants share the basic values of the competition state project although cultural differences exist between UK and US approaches to 'Welfare to Work'.
Resources *distribution of resources (within network)*	All participants hold resources in exchange relationships.
distribution of resources (within organizations	Policy-makers are dependent on the intelligence gathering skills and knowledge resources of the donor organization.
Power	The success of the policy transfer network rested on the ability of the agent of transfer to satisfy the objective policy problem of the client. This was achieved.

At this stage of the policy transfer process policy transfer networks can act as gatekeepers to the decision-making centre and hence the policy agenda may develop a bias against certain inputs. In the case of the New Deal there were four key determinants of the policy agenda – the new welfare ideology of rights and responsibilities; the emphasis on developing processes of market integration; the need to create incentives to keep people off benefits; and, finally, the importance of evidence based reasoning.

Interaction

The agent of transfer will be expected to organize forums for the exchange of ideas between the client and knowledge elites with policy relevant knowledge. These may take the form of representatives of an epistemic community who have similar professional beliefs and standards of judgement and share common policy concerns. It is through these forms of diffusion activity that agents of transfer can act as agenda setters. In the case of the New Deal the establishment of free flowing information systems through an effective information feeder network led to the creation of coherent systems of interaction at an early stage in the process of policy transfer. Hence, the organization of bi-lateral fact-finding missions, conferences and the exchange of programming and evaluation documents occurred quickly and were effectively co-coordinated through the 'Treasury Welfare to Work Nexus'.

Evaluation

Once the client is satisfied with the degree of intelligence gathering that they have engaged in, a process of evaluation will commence that is critical in determining: the objects, degree and, the prerequisites of transfer which will condition the nature of the policy or programme. The New Deal was to be financed through the 'windfall tax' on the privatized utilities to the tune of £4 billion. The final proposals added an element of compulsion to incentivization and were aimed primarily at the young unemployed. It offered four options including subsidized employment and education, and, in line with Labour's intention to increase overall participation in the labour market, the New Deal was also extended to disabled people, carers and single parents. The issue of compulsion, taken for granted in the United States, is now a feature of the New Deal for 18-24 year olds. It is judged to be politically acceptable for this age group, but the impact of compulsion for older age groups is open to discussion, and there is an enduring political reluctance to adopt compulsion for lone mothers. Indeed the imposition of welfare time limits or other policies that might cause severe hardship have not been adequately debated in the UK. As a senior treasury official puts it: '[e]verybody knows that this is about limiting state commitments and marketizing the state. All you have to do is look at the website for the evidence'.

The Formal Decision Stream

In the case of the New Deal there can be little doubt that a favourable economic climate, combined with its fit with the broader competition state project, pushed it to the top of the policy agenda. As one senior Treasury official observes:

> Let's face it if we were suddenly hit with a recession, and one seems likely over the next year or so, much of this would collapse. Why? Because the left is waiting for a chance to reassert itself and Brown has been foolish in resurrecting the language of full employment in a period of economic stability. A recession would provide them with a

set of opportunities to fight for more direct intervention into the economy.

This raises the important question of what happens if the economy goes into recession? Will policies conceived in good times be sustainable in times of economic crisis? It is already possible to identify some implementation problems with New Deal. Firstly, the New Deal for young people has been generously funded for political reasons and has taken a significant proportion of the £4 billion made available from the windfall tax on privatized utilities. The allocation to other strands of the New Deal, such as the sick and disabled and lone parents, has been correspondingly far less. It remains to be seen how effective these elements of the programme can be. Secondly, attempts in the UK to reach SMEs through trade associations have not proved effective. A local approach may be more effective to reach local companies.

In Conclusion: Policy Transfer, Welfare Reform and the Competition State

What does this case study of the emergence and development of a policy transfer network in the New Deal policy arena tell us about the impact of the competition state project on welfare policy development in Britain? Five main conclusions can be drawn from the case study. The policy transfer network approach proves useful in helping us to understand how decision-makers acquire knowledge and how they can act as agents of the competition state. Three important conclusions can be drawn here. First, the timescale which is established to search for policy ideas informs the scope of enquiry and almost inevitably draws policy-makers to accessible exemplars in either the United States, the Commonwealth or the private sector who share a similar commitment to the competition state project. Secondly, multi-level search activity creates a pathology for hybrid forms of cross-national and cross-sectoral policy transfer and consequently policy and programme copying becomes very rare. The New Deal initiative inherited much from the Thatcher and Major governments and represents a paradigm shift in the philosophy of welfarism. The front page slogan on the New York Welfare to Work website sums up this shift in thinking perfectly. Here the slogan 'Welfare to work is a programme that creates independence' is superimposed over the words 'Welfare creates dependence'! Thirdly, the quality of information improved as more sophisticated processes of information gathering developed and further opportunity structures for transfer emerged. Policy transfer thus became an inevitability and begat further policy transfer. In the case of the New Deal, new service delivery approaches have been adopted including one-stop-shops on the Iowa model and the introduction of a single gateway to the benefit system.

Fourthly, an inner circle of policy-making participants emerged who shared a commitment to the common value system of the competition state and in which participation was circumscribed by knowledge resources and organizational capacity. A process of gate-keeping took place in which elite players were selected by the primary agents of policy transfer largely because of their ideological compatibility with the broader competition state project. Indeed it is here that both agents of policy transfer and Treasury officials are seen to be playing a central co-ordinating role in promoting the competition state project and new forms of complex globalization in the attempt to adapt state action to cope more effectively with what they see as global 'realities'.

Fifthly, the battle for the hearts and minds of the British people is a key problem for the competition state for many of its key reforms rest on changing norms and values and challenging the dependency culture of the post-war settlement (e.g. welfare to work, pensions, student loans). These reforms have dramatically symbolized a move away from the norms of labourism (from collective to individual level bargaining, from public to private ownership) and towards consumerist rather than productionist values. In particular, the policy agenda of New Labour attempts to change individual and group attitudes to entrepreneurship whether through welfare to work, pensions policy, student loans, or central bank reform.

Welfare policy has thus been incorporated into the new economic orthodoxy of the competition state through its emphasis on reducing dependency, removing any potential obstacles to the control of inflation and integrating the socially excluded into the labour market. In Brown's words, this calls for 'balanced budgets', 'tight control of interest rates,' and the need to deal with unemployment through the marketplace and not through government intervention.

Chapter 5

Environmental Policy Transfer in Germany and Greece

Stella Ladi

Introduction

Processes of policy-making are increasingly informed by policy exemplars outside the framework of domestic politics. The exchange of ideas, programmes and policies is even more intense between European Union (EU) member states. This has often been described as a process of Europeanization (see Buller, Evans and James, eds., 2002). Terms such as policy transfer, policy learning, lesson drawing, diffusion or emulation have also been used to describe the above phenomenon. Three main theoretical arguments are developed in this chapter. First, it is argued that policy transfer can lead to policy convergence or policy divergence from what is described as the diffusion of 'best practice' models. Inertia is a third possible outcome. The reasons for this can either be endogenous (e.g. the domestic policy environment) or exogenous (e.g. the European and global environments). Secondly, it is argued that the policy transfer process can usefully be analysed through the use of the policy transfer network approach (Evans and Davies, 1999). The approach is utilized in this chapter as a heuristic device for mapping and comparing the reasons for why policy transfer can be successful or unsuccessful in different cases, causing alternatively policy convergence, divergence or indeed inertia. Thirdly, it is argued that the discourses of globalization and Europeanization have an impact upon processes of policy transfer. Here the chapter follows the third wave of the literature on globalization that defines globalization and subsequently Europeanization as multifaceted processes that are both material and ideational (Hay and Marsh, 1999).

In order to explore the above arguments, the chapter provides an empirical investigation of an attempt to transfer an environmental employment programme, *Ecotrans*, from Denmark to Greece and to Germany. The policy transfer process proves to be unsuccessful in Greece and successful in Germany. The policy transfer network approach is used as a lens of enquiry for understanding policy development in the two case studies. The chapter concludes with a comparison of the reasons for convergence, divergence or inertia in the two case studies.

The Policy Transfer Network Approach

Evans and Davies (1999) developed the policy transfer network approach in order to link the policy network approach, especially Marsh and Rhodes's (1992) idea of a policy community, to the concept of epistemic communities (Haas, 1989), as a method for studying the policy transfer phenomenon. The main difference between a policy transfer network and a policy community is that the former places an emphasis on the knowledge resources of agents, while the latter focuses on economic and political interests. The membership of a policy transfer network tends to have more in common with a policy community as the members of the network are expected to be from a range of backgrounds (depending on the policy arena), and are not restricted to possessors of scientific knowledge, as in the case of epistemic communities. A policy transfer network is by its very nature ad-hoc, and is solely concerned with engineering a specific process of policy change via policy transfer (Evans and Davies, 1999).

Evans and Davies (1999) provide an illustrative sequence of the stages in policy development that can but do not always inform the voluntary policy transfer process. They also provide an alternative set of heuristic stages for processes of coercive transfer. The authors do not assume that all the stages of the policy transfer network have to take place or that they take place in the sequence suggested by the framework. It is purely a heuristic model that allows for the rigorous case study analysis of processes of policy transfer. The policy transfer network concept was chosen as the framework to guide this research as it provides the most useful model of policy transfer for evaluating the role of knowledge and power in the policy transfer process. It allows us to organize the case studies, to map the actions of the various agents involved and to compare the process and outcome of policy transfer.

In the remaining sections of this chapter, the policy transfer network approach is used to guide the empirical investigation of an attempt to transfer an environmental employment project from Denmark to Greece and Germany.

Understandingbus and the Transfer of the *Ecotrans* Project

This section explores the process of transferring an environmental employment policy programme from Denmark to Greece and to Germany, namely the *Ecotrans* programme. The prime agent of policy transfer in this case study was a German non-governmental organization (NGO) and knowledge institution, *Understandingbus*, and most of the funding came from the EU. The policy transfer to Piraeus, Greece proved not to be successful while the policy transfer to Dresden, Germany was successful. As the case study takes place at the local and regional levels, an in-depth analysis of the networks that developed provide a rich terrain for evaluating the reasons for policy convergence, divergence or inertia.

The *Headways* research action project on opening employment opportunities for unemployed people in the environmental sector was the starting point for the policy transfer process. *Headways* is a research project that was carried out by 28 partners in the *EVA Network* during 1997 and 1998 and was funded by the Directorate General (DG) V of the EU Commission. EVA stands for Environmentally sustainable projects, Vocational training and Action in the community and involves a network of 28 institutions operating in 10 EU countries with its base in Berlin. It was established in 1994 and one of its founding members was *Understandingbus*. *Understandingbus* undertook this research action in co-operation with the *EVA Network* and under the financial support of the European Commission and in particular of DG V (Grossmann, Umbsen and Furth, 1998). There followed a successful application to DG V of the European Commission for the funding of a project named *Ecotrans*. The project had two main aims: first, to transfer good practice of employment policy in the environment domain from Denmark to Objective 1 regions in Eastern Germany and Greece and to an Objective 2 region in South Yorkshire (UK) in an exemplary way; secondly, to draw some general conclusions concerning the problems faced by transnational transfer projects and to develop and test suitable methods for overcoming these obstacles (*Understandingbus*, 1998: 1).

The programme application to the European Commission clearly stated that the *Ecotrans* project was inspired by the Headways research action project. The logic behind it was that Small and Medium Enterprises (SMEs) can play an important role as job creators in the environmental sector and that training institutions have increasingly started including ecological themes to their training agenda for unemployed people. Headways had shown that bringing together SMEs and non-governmental training institutions is a very effective way for promoting sustainable development. The programme 'Environmental Economics-Competitive Advantages' developed in Viborg in Denmark was selected by Headways as a successful case-study and by *Ecotrans* as a model for transfer in the environmental sector (*Understandingbus*, 1998).

The Policy Transfer Process in Piraeus

The prefecture of Piraeus in Greece was the first target area for the *Ecotrans* project. Piraeus is a port in Athens and it is an area that has experienced major structural changes during the past two decades. The shipping industry, once one of the main areas of economic activity in the region, has declined significantly and it now has a 28 percent unemployment rate, one of the highest in Greece. A shift to service, textiles, tobacco, transport, chemicals, wood, paper and metallurgy sectors has occurred, which has resulted in an urgent need for training programmes. At the same time Piraeus is an area of high traffic congestion and pollution (University of Piraeus, 1999: 35-41).

Processes of globalization and Europeanization both provide an integral part of the discourse informing the Greek political and economic environment. Globalization is seen as a major challenge for the SMEs that have to deal with open markets and competition. Moreover, the modernization of methods of production and market competitiveness are often seen as the way forward for the

SMEs of Piraeus (Piraeus Chamber of SMEs, 2000). It is interesting to note that globalization is not only seen as a problem faced by the SMEs but also as a positive challenge. As Poli Albataki (*author interview*, 18 September 2000), Head of the Small Industry Department in Piraeus's Chamber of SMEs puts it:

> Globalization for the Greek SMEs means competition with more powerful economies, but it also means a challenge for economic development and modernization by taking advantage of the opportunities for policy transfer coming from the EU.

Hence, globalization and Europeanization are processes that are perceived by economic and political actors to be closely linked. Europe is seen as the natural environment for Piraeus for looking for ideas and partnerships in order to deal with its policy problems (University of Piraeus, May 1999). However, environmental awareness does not form part of the political discourse in Piraeus. Indeed, the opposite is true. Although the law concerning the environment and the activities of companies is strict, in reality many companies function illegally and the environment is given a low priority (Grossmann, July 2000: 15).

Table 5.1 summarizes the policy transfer process in Piraeus by using the policy transfer network approach (Evans and Davies, 1999). The first three phases of the policy transfer process, which are described as the recognition, search and contact stages, involved an expert visit that took place in Piraeus in February 1999. The team that participated in the meeting consisted of Uwe Lorenzen from Viborg in Denmark and Peter Umbsen and Arthur Grossmann from *Understandingbus* in Germany. The fact finding visit included meetings with various agents and had as its goal the exploration of the conditions for the introduction of environmental employment projects in Piraeus and the identification of potential participants for the creation of a regional network for the implementation of *Ecotrans*. Public institutions such as the Organization for the Employment of the Working Force (OAED) Piraeus, semi-public organizations such as the University of Piraeus and the Development Company of the Municipalities of Piraeus (ANDIP) and private consultants such as Walter Fissaber and Associates, were among the organizations that were visited by the research team. The results from the visit of experts were encouraging but some problems were encountered. The first positive finding was that several organizations had experience of collaborative European projects. For example, ANDIP had been involved in a programme within Viborg for the exchange of experience on waste management and recycling. A second positive finding was that many of the organizations considered it a good time for projects focusing on employment and training because of the significant unemployment problem being experienced in the region.

There were, however, several problems that were identified at this early stage of the policy transfer process. The first problem concerned the recognition stage of the process. A lack of environmental awareness in the Greek socio-political system was identified. Hence, although some of the potential partners had some experience with environmental projects they all stressed that environmental issues were a low priority in Greece. The second problem that was identified was that the public sector, including organizations such as OAED, is very centralized which

Table 5.1 The emergence and development of a voluntary policy transfer network – The Piraeus Case

1. Problem Recognition – the University of Piraeus and other agencies recognize the severity of the problem of unemployment in the region. There is no consensus on the recognition of the importance of environmental problems.

2. *Search for Solutions* – the regional agents are looking for European programmes that they could apply for and this is why they are open to *Understandingbus's* proposal.

3. *Contact with Potential Agents of Transfer* – regional agents are contacted through the encouragement of *Understandingbus*.

4. *Emergence of Information Feeder Network* – the University of Piraeus participates as a member of the *EVA Network* (European information feeder network). A regional information feeder network does not emerge in Piraeus.

5. *Cognition, Reception and the Emergence of a Transfer Network* – a fact finding visit takes place in Piraeus.

6. *Elite and Cognitive Mobilization* – the Development Workshop organized in Piraeus brings together the regional agents, the Danish partners and *Understandingbus*.

7. *Interaction* – meetings with various agents take place but there is no evidence of productive interaction.

8. *Evaluation* – conflict emerges between the different agents in their attempt to create a regional network. Agreement on the importance of the employment aspect of the project and on living the environmental side out.

9. *Formal decision stream* – a decision is made to implement a programme similar to the Viborg model.

10. *Implementation* – The implementation of the project does not take place.

means that decision-making and implementation processes underpinning the local and regional levels are extremely problematic. A third problem was identified in the overlap of activities between different organizations that made it difficult to select the responsible agent for every activity. Moreover, co-operation between the different organizations was poor. The outcome of the experts visit in Piraeus was that the Greek partners agreed to draw up a list of participants for the regional network.

This may be understood as the phase of policy development involving policy cognition, reception and the emergence of a transfer network. It is interesting to observe at this point that the information feeder network never emerged in a prominent way at the regional level. The information feeder network existed at the European level through the *EVA Network* and the University of Piraeus participated in it but there was no similar activity at the regional level.

In May 1999, the first development workshop was organized in Piraeus. This can be described as the elite and cognitive mobilization stage of policy development. The workshop had a dual purpose. On the first day there was a meeting held for organizations familiar with the *Ecotrans* project that was aimed at finding ways to improve the consulting and training schemes offered to SMEs on the same lines as the Viborg model. On the second day, the *Ecotrans* project was presented to the SMEs in order to ascertain their reaction. The local chambers of commerce and industry supported this activity and invited 400 SMEs. Unfortunately, the turnout was much lower including no more than ten SMEs, possibly because the SMEs in Piraeus are quite small and do not have enough staff or time for meetings that do not lead to direct economic benefits. The ensuing discussion showed that the situation in Piraeus was a difficult one. The multitude of organizations and of programmes for SMEs and the complexity that this causes was once more emphasized. As a result the participants decided that a priority must be placed on co-operation and the possible integration of these organizations. Another outcome of the workshop was the establishment of a list, which identified the most important problems that the SMEs felt they confronted. These included access to funding and technical information, opportunities for consultation about technical and financial aspects, environmental issues and effective vocational training. It was decided that the most important task at that moment was to establish a steering group that would meet regularly and be responsible for the implementation of the *Ecotrans* project.

A follow-up workshop was organized for November 1999 and a working plan was developed. The University of Piraeus was made responsible for developing a proposal about further training for academics and their incorporation into SMEs and ANDIP was charged with providing a proposal about the consulting and training programmes required by SMEs. The supervising team would make suggestions on job placements for unemployed people and outline possible areas of co-operation with OAED, on the improvement of the political framework and on the creation of a regional workshop (University of Piraeus, May 1999). Vassilis Tseledis, the co-ordinator from the University of Piraeus, in an interview evaluating the workshop said that he was satisfied with the outcome given that these organizations had met for the first time and that there was a lack of structures of co-operation in Piraeus (Vassilis Tseledis, Deputy Professor, Department of Maritime Studies, University of Piraeus, *author interview*, 3 August 1999). Indeed, the presence of the Danish and German partners was described as fundamental to the success of the workshop.

A further meeting took place in November 1999, although the Greek partners wanted to postpone it because they did not have any results to present and were afraid of the public impression that this would give. This can be described as the conclusion of the interaction stage in policy development between the agents of transfer and the recipient organizations. An agreement was reached to have an informal meeting. The first thing to observe from this process is that the participants at this meeting differ from the ones that met in May, which suggests that the interaction stage was not productive. The Chamber of Commerce and the Office for Industrial Reform, in the prefecture of Piraeus were represented for the first time. At the same time some agents that played central roles during the May workshop, such as Walter Fissaber consultants and OAED Piraeus were absent. The change of participants caused lack of continuity and inability of implementing decisions already taken. The second observation is that the spectrum of the problems that the Greek partners hoped to tackle through the *Ecotrans* project was far too broad and this was obvious from the beginning of the meeting. For example, they aimed at co-operating with OAED at the regional level and to integrate a variety of regional and national agents into their initiative which would mean fighting against centralization tendencies of the Greek public administration. Unfortunately, aims like these were beyond the scope of *Ecotrans* and were targeting more general structural problems of the Greek political system.

The evaluation stage of the policy transfer of the Viborg model starts here. Because of the failure of the interaction stage, *Understandingbus* tried to establish a more realistic agenda by proposing three themes for discussion: the development of a policy transfer network, the discussion of possible projects for the effective support of SMEs and the development of projects for the effective training and job placement of unemployed graduates. Because of lack of time only the third theme was discussed and the Careers Office of the University of Piraeus presented some proposals. It was agreed that the goal of the project would be to develop training that takes into account the needs of SMEs. To start with, a focus would be placed on the shipping services sector and the environmental dimension was left out of the project. The first actions to be taken would be the gathering of relevant information and the generation of applications to European projects such as Leonardo Da Vinci and Equal for further funding of the policy transfer process from Denmark. The network that was formed consisted of ANDIP, the chambers of commerce, the University of Piraeus and the training centre, Apopsi, and different roles were allocated to them. *Understandingbus* in the evaluation of the meeting said that although the atmosphere was not relaxed and the participants were not very willing to make their ideas public, a project was finally agreed and a network had emerged (Grossmann, July 2000: 27-30). It is easy to observe that the result was far from transferring the *Ecotrans* project itself. So, in the decision stage, a decision was made to continue with the transfer but no implementation stage can be observed.

The outcome of the policy transfer process in Piraeus cannot be described as policy convergence. The Viborg model was not transferred to Piraeus and there is nothing to suggest that this will happen at the moment. In its final report, the University of Piraeus (2000) only identified one area in which the project had been successful; the organization of meetings that brought together SMEs for the first time and introduced them to the idea of networking.

A variety of problems led to the 'failure' to transfer the Viborg model to Piraeus (Grossmann, July 2000: 41-45). First, there were problems related with the Greek political system and the particularities of the Greek society. The centralization of public administration was a major problem. There is no autonomous regional policy which makes the implementation of a regional project very difficult. Arthur Grossmann explains that agencies that were essential for the project simply do not exist in Greece, for example a regional economic promotion department or a regional labour office (Arthur Grossmann and Peter Umbsen, Co-ordinators of the *Ecotrans* Project, *Understandingbus, author interview*, 3 July 2000). Getraud Loewen claims that the decentralization of Greek public administration is the most important task for Greece at the moment (Getraud Loweven, Representative of the Director General V of the European Commission, *author interview*, 7 July 2000). A consequence of centralized public administration is that there is a lack of experience of working within networks in Greece. As far as *Ecotrans* is concerned its main problem is that there is significant competition between the different training agencies so the chances for co-operation are very slim (Grossmann and Umbsen, *author interview*, 2000: ibid). Moreover, SMEs in Piraeus are very small and centrally managed which means that they have limited staff available to participate in networks (Grossmann, *author interview*, July 2000: 44). The SMEs in Piraeus have more basic problems than the SMEs in Viborg. Many of them are unregistered and operate with legal as well as environmental and health and safety problems. There is also a lack of sufficiently trained staff available to participate in projects such as *Ecotrans* and insufficient information on European projects and funding possibilities (Panayiotis Vogas, partner in the SME Toner Artist, *author interview*, 18 September 2000).

A further set of problems was identified with the organization of the *Ecotrans* programme. The development of the programme was constrained by time. The 20-month period allocated to the transference of the Viborg model to Piraeus was not long enough. Because of the factors highlighted above, there was need for more time to develop the network and to search for alternative methods for implementing the Viborg model. There were also budgetary constraints. Because of the lack of staff in the SMEs and at the rest of the agencies involved, there was a need for greater resources to employ temporary staff to run the *Ecotrans* project (Tseledis, 2000: ibid). Finally, there was a problem of co-ordination. The University of Piraeus, the co-ordinator in Piraeus, was not the right kind of organization to run such a project. Although the University is interested in working closely with SMEs in order to improve the training that it offers and the employability of its graduates, it does not have the necessary experience and skills to discharge a co-ordinating role (Grossmann and Umbsen, *author interview*, 2000: ibid). Additionally, the job of co-ordinating the project was directed to only one person, Vassilis Tseledis, who also had many other responsibilities in the University. It is evident that other collaborating organizations should have been involved from the outset in the co-ordination of the project, for example, by participating in the visit in Viborg (Grossmann, 2000: 44).

The Policy Transfer Process in Dresden

The second target area for the *Ecotrans* project was Saxony in East Germany and in particularly Dresden and Zwickau. Dresden is a historical but also a high technology city of 480,000 inhabitants. Its SMEs are not very strong apart from the ones in the chemical sector and the City focuses on attracting large investments. The unemployment rate in the area is quite high (14.7 percent in April 2001) and training is one of its priorities. Zwickau is a district consisting of five regions with a total population of 140,000. The district has a strong industrial sector which is mainly made up of SMEs. The unemployment rate is high and the measures taken up to now have not been effective because of their short-term nature (Grossmann, July 2000: 10-13).

Globalization and Europeanization are part of the discourse within which policy change takes place in East Germany. Sigmar Kuehl, who is the main *Ecotrans* partner in Dresden and Zwickau described globalization as a significant factor informing policy decisions and emphasized the importance of EU funding for implementing the projects. In relation to sustainable development issues Kuehl and Juergen Israel (representative of UNROS, Zwickau) both agreed that they play a much more important role in the German discourse than in other European countries (*author interview*, 7 July 2000). Combining environmental and labour market policies is something that is already working and is viewed as the way forward for the future. This can be described as the recognition stage of the policy transfer network. Table 5.2 summarizes the policy transfer process.

The search, contact and emergence of an information feeder network stages of the policy transfer network involved visits to Dresden and to Zwickau in February 1999 and in March and July 1999. The participants at the Dresden meeting were the representatives from *Understandingbus* and from Viborg, the regional partners and a number of labour and environmental policy-makers. The meeting took the form of a roundtable discussion at which the situation in Dresden was presented. Two main problems were identified. The first problem was that the focus of the Saxon regional government was on large-scale industry and not enough attention was given to SMEs, which meant that it was felt that an effort should be made to convince policy-makers of the importance of SMEs. The second problem relates to the lack of consultants to which the SMEs have easy and inexpensive access.

Despite these problems two major decisions were reached that led to the creation of a transfer network. The first decision that was made was to start the process by transferring the Danish Technological Information Centre (TIC), which is a publicly financed consulting organization to Dresden and Zwickau. The second decision concerned the field of action of *Ecotrans* and it was agreed that it should be broadened to include other areas apart from the environment such as quality management, marketing and information technologies. In Zwickau, the problems identified were quite similar but there was also a worry about the creation and the sustainability of a regional network. A similar decision reached was that the focus of *Ecotrans* should not purely be on the environment but should also include information technology (Grossmann, July 2000: 10-14).

The elite and cognitive mobilization stage of the policy transfer process in Dresden was similar to the Piraeus case study and was crystallized in the organization of a development workshop in July 1999. This took the form of a roundtable discussion and in the first place the SMEs were not invited. The goal of the workshop was to encourage the idea of the existence of an employment and environment network following the Viborg model and to develop a plan of action. The meeting was organized into three phases entitled the 'inspiration', the 'criticism' and the 'fantasy' phases. The 'inspiration' phase consisted of a detailed presentation of the Viborg model. The 'criticism' phase involved a discussion of the advantages and the problems of the implementation of a project like that in Saxony.

Table 5.2   The emergence and development of a voluntary policy transfer network: The Saxony Case

1. Problem Recognition – SBG Dresden and other agencies recognize the severity of the unemployment problem in the region and the possibility of combining environmental with employment solutions.

2. Search for Solutions – the regional agents are looking for European programmes that they could apply for and this is why they are open to *Understandingbus's* proposal.

3. Contact with Potential Agents of Transfer – regional agents are contacted with the encouragement of *Understandingbus*.

4. Emergence of Information Feeder Network – SBG Dresden participates as a member of the *EVA Network* (European information feeder network). A regional information feeder network emerges in Saxony.

5. Cognition, Reception and the Emergence of a Transfer Network – a decision is reached to proceed with the transfer of the Danish TIC. A fact finding visit takes place in Saxony.

6. Elite and Cognitive Mobilization –a development workshop is organized in Saxony bringing together the regional agents, the Danish partners and *Understandingbus*.

7. Interaction – an information meeting for regional SMEs and other actors takes place.

8. Evaluation of options – problems emerge in Zwickau but active interest is shown in Dresden.

9. Formal decision stream – a decision is made to implement a similar programme to the Viborg model in Dresden.

10. Implementation – Study visit of regional agents to Viborg. An implementation phase commences.

A variety of problems were identified during this phase. A problem with local public administration was identified. Important agencies such as the Zwickau employment office did not participate and lacked organizational, networking and promotion skills. In addition, there were funding limitations in local communities and districts. Other problems included the absence of consulting institutions and the incapacity of the SMEs to conduct training and environmental auditing or to build networks because of their day-to-day struggle for survival. In the 'fantasy' phase decisions for the development of regional networks were made. In Zwickau, an agreement was reached to include a network co-ordinator in the budget because of an unsuccessful experience of creating a network in 1994. The conclusion of the meeting was that regional networks should be developed in both Zwickau and Dresden and concrete programmes should be designed in order to approach the authorities and to bid for EU funding (Grossmann, July 2000: 31-35).

In January 2000, the interaction stage of the policy transfer process took place in Dresden in the form of an information meeting for SMEs. In the period between the two meetings efforts were made to find partners for the regional network. The meeting was a success because of a large attendance with the participation of 100 representatives of SMEs, economic groups and training institutions. The Viborg model was for the first time presented to a large audience of user groups and useful contacts were established. On the next day the core participants, the Danish partners and *Understandingbus* had a follow-up meeting that can be described as the evaluation and decision stages of the process of transfer in order to develop an action plan. Several issues for deliberation were identified at this stage including the need to appoint a co-ordinator in Zwickau to run the *Ecotrans* project. In the Dresden region, a decision was reached to continue with the transfer process, to assess various potential players and to approach the SMEs with concrete offers. The Office for Environmental Protection and Employment in the Chemistry Sector (SBG), which was the regional partner and *Understandingbus*, were allocated the responsibility of applying to the EU's Leonardo da Vinci programme in order to continue exchanging experiences with Viborg. The programme was introduced in 1994 with the aim of increasing cooperation among membership states with regard to education and training.

The policy transfer process to Saxony has been described as a success by a variety of agents, including the organizers, the Greek partners and the observers from Barnsley. One of the most important findings identified here was that through the *Ecotrans* project a better understanding of the SMEs and their problems was obtained. The implementation stage can only be partly evaluated due to the limited amount of time that has lapsed since the initiation of the policy. A longitudinal approach will evidently be required at a later date in order to study developments in the *Ecotrans* programme over a 10-year period in order to fully evaluate the process of transfer in the implementation stage of policy development.

Some reference, however, should be made here to potential implementation gaps that may emerge such as the allocation of funding and the absence of effective instruments of policy co-ordination. In Zwickau, for example, although there was a clear interest in the development of a regional network for the support of SMEs, the absence of an Employment Office and the problem of persuading the regional authorities of the importance of *Ecotrans* remain. By the end of the official timetable for the *Ecotrans* project the plan was to persuade the regional authorities to support *Ecotrans*, to set up a counselling centre in the form of a Danish type TIC, and, finally, to bring the SMEs into the network. In Dresden, *Ecotrans* was again a success. The agreement by the end of the official *Ecotrans* period was that a focus should be placed on the training aspect of *Ecotrans* through further studies of the support structures for SMEs and through improving counselling, training and funding services through the continuation of the transfer process from Denmark.

Three projects were identified in order to emulate the Danish model. The first project involved research on the economic situation and needs of the SMEs in order to design the necessary support programmes in accordance with the Viborg model (Grossmann, July 2000: 46-50). This has been concluded. The second project involved the training of Saxony instructors and counsellors in Viborg, supported by Leonardo Da Vinci funding. The focus of the visit was on providing low-level training advice, and needs-oriented educational planning in order to fully incorporate the Danish model (European Commission, 27/3/00). The project was completed in summer 2001. The third project concerned the establishment of a support network for ecologically oriented enterprises in the Dresden area and is on-going. This project involves the co-ordination of a funding mechanism oriented towards the needs of the SMEs, the establishment of what they called the 'one-door principle' for the dissemination of information to the SMEs, the development of a counselling structure in accordance with the Danish TIC model and the linking of economic development to the principle of sustainability (Grossmann, July 2000: 46-50).

In summary, there were two main reasons why it was relatively easy to transfer the *Ecotrans* project to Saxony. First, the Saxony organizations were familiar with the idea of working within a network. Secondly, there existed good co-ordination between and communication with policy-makers. Other factors such as the familiarity of the Saxon partners with environmental issues, the decentralized organization of the public administration in Germany, as well as the urgency of finding new solutions for the training needs of SMEs, also aided the implementation of the *Ecotrans* project in Saxony.

The Outcome of the Ecotrans Project

The transfer of the *Ecotrans* Project shows that policy transfer can lead either to policy convergence, policy divergence or inertia. It also confirms that the reasons for this can either be endogenous (e.g. due to constraints or push factors arising from the domestic policy environment) or exogenous (e.g. due to constraints or push factors arising from the European and global environments). The implementation of the Viborg model in Piraeus was not completed which means that we cannot observe a concrete convergence between Danish and Greek institutions, policies and paradigms. At the same time no policy change occurred to suggest a divergence between the two regions. What can be observed is a transfer of ideas such as the necessity for the Greek public administration to be decentralized or the possibility of creating new jobs in the environmental sector. A convergence between Denmark and Greece may be possible in the long term when these ideas become more deeply embedded but not through the *Ecotrans* project. A possibility for further policy transfer between the two regions is possible now that a network has been created and if the support of *Understandingbus* continues. More evidence of policy convergence can be observed between the target region of East Germany and the Danish model region. The key reason behind the successful policy transfer process in this case was the existence of institutional and policy similarities between Denmark and Germany. For example, institutional arrangements in both countries are relatively similar, with the concept of decentralization playing an important role in the administrative systems of both countries. Moreover, high levels of environmental awareness coupled with common policy styles such as the idea of networking exist in both countries. In addition, *Understandingbus* made a significant contribution to the success of the policy transfer to Dresden. The representatives from *Understandingbus* contend that the geographical proximity between Saxony and Berlin, as well as the common language and their ability to understand the administrative and cultural characteristics of Saxony, meant that they were able to troubleshoot problems effectively during the policy transfer process.

In Conclusion: Do Policy Transfer Networks Matter?

It remains to draw some conclusions with regard to the three theoretical arguments advanced in the introduction to this chapter and to identify some weaknesses in the empirical research that was conducted. First, as the Piraeus case demonstrates, whether policy transfer leads to policy convergence or divergence will depend on the case under study and it cannot be easily observed or predicted. To date, the policy transfer process in Piraeus can best be described as inert, although there is a chance for policy convergence to occur at a later stage. This finding is in line with the third wave literature on globalization, which claims that globalization is a reversible phenomenon that can lead to both convergence and divergence (Hay and Marsh, 1999).

The second theoretical argument that was presented at the outset was that the policy transfer network framework is useful for systematizing the analysis of successful and unsuccessful processes of policy transfer. It can be maintained that the policy transfer network approach is a useful framework when it is used for systematization and comparison. The approach allows us to identify the stage at which the policy transfer process breaks down. However, as Evans and Davies (1999) note, in order, to analyse the reasons for the break down of a process of policy transfer, the approach has to be combined with macro and micro level analysis. For example, the central factor informing the cessation of the policy transfer process in Piraeus was the absence of a cohesive transfer network. A comprehensive explanation of the reasons for the unsuccessful transfer in Piraeus can only be developed if macro and micro level factors are taken into account. For example, the centralization of Greek public administration was one of the main explanatory factors for the non-completion of the policy transfer, but this has to be analysed in conjunction with developments within the policy transfer network.

Some comparative conclusions may also be drawn with regard to the reasons why the policy transfer process produced different outcomes in the cases of Piraeus and Dresden. One set of reasons for why it was so difficult to transfer the Viborg model to Piraeus was related to the centralized nature of the Greek political and administrative system, which leads to a lack of autonomy in regional structures and inexperience in networking. A second set of problems may be identified with regard to specific issues in the Piraeus region, such as the problems experienced by SMEs. Finally, a third set of problems may also be identified with the *Ecotrans* project itself. In particular, time and budget constraints and problems of co-ordination in the Piraeus area. In comparison, the situation in Dresden and Zwickau was far more conducive to policy transfer. The political and administrative system is closer to the Danish model and the belief in combining environmental policy with employment policy, regional structures and mature networking arrangements already existed. Finally, more support was offered by the *Ecotrans* project because of the common language that was shared with the organizers and because of geographical proximity.

In addition, the case study provides an important insight into the role of *Understandingbus*, as an agent of policy transfer. It explains how policy-makers acquire knowledge and also why concrete outcomes failed to emerge from the implementation stage. *Understandingbus* was able to play an influential role during the whole process of policy transfer, apart from in the implementation process where large-scale funding was required. A lack of funds meant that *Understandingbus* and the other partners needed to bid for external funding and this made it much more difficult for the policy transfer process to be completed.

The final theoretical argument that needs to be considered is the contention that discourses of globalization and Europeanization have an impact upon processes of policy transfer. An understanding of the belief systems that agents of transfer hold with regard to globalization and Europeanization is clearly crucial in evaluating the influence of the discourse within which the policy transfer process takes place. While, the central agent of transfer, *Understandingbus*, had a positive approach towards both the European and globalization projects, and, the discourses of globalization and Europeanization were influential in both Germany and Greece, the outcome of the policy transfer process varied. It can thus be concluded that although the ideational sphere is important, it is interwoven with the material sphere and processes of policy transfer can only be successful if the material sphere is also satisfied. The sustainability and vitality of transfer networks rests on the forging of a consensus between policy actors and agents of transfer that a programme has been found that will deal with the problems that they are facing.

Part II

Policy Transfer from Developed to Developing Countries

Chapter 6

Policy Transfer in a Transition State: The Case of Local Government Reform in the Ukraine

Veronica Ivanova and Mark Evans

Introduction

The existing literature on policy transfer has almost exclusively focused on mature policy environments. This chapter attempts to examine the applicability of the policy transfer approach to a state in transition using local government reform in the Ukraine as an example. It contends that policy transfer is not only a useful but also a necessary tool for analyzing states in transition. Furthermore, a model of policy analysis which integrates the policy transfer network (meso-level) approach with macro-level and micro-level analysis offers an effective methodology for analyzing and understanding the dynamics of policy transfer in transition states. At the same time this study argues that the process of policy transfer in transition states and societies should be examined through a 'bottom-up' case study approach. The chapter therefore presents a case study of the role of the Association of Ukrainian Cities (AUC) in facilitating what will be termed 'voluntary but necessary' policy transfers in the transition to democracy. The chapter also explores the linkages between the theory and practice of policy transfer in transition states and should thus prove of interest to both scholars of transition societies, and to practitioners engaged in the process of implementing policy transfer in transitional environments.

The analysis that follows is organized into three parts. Section one undertakes a critical examination of the policy transfer approach in which it emphasizes its limits in less mature policy environments. It then offers a reformulation of the commonly used definition of policy transfer by Dolowitz and Marsh (1996) and investigates the most common forms of policy transfer that are transported to transition states. It then examines the policy transfer environment in a transition society and argues that the multi-level model of policy analysis proposed by Evans and Davies (1999) offers a useful methodology for analyzing and understanding a state in transition. Section two provides an empirical investigation of local government reform in Ukraine using the multi-level model of policy transfer. The chapter ends with a summary of the chapter's key theoretical and empirical conclusions, together with an evaluation of the strengths and weaknesses of the approach and the identification of some important areas for future research.

Policy Transfer in a Transitional Society

The current literature on policy transfer and related concepts is almost exclusively focused on mature policy environments. As Stone (1999: 57), observes, policy transfer is '...discussed predominately in terms of transfer between the UK and the USA'. While Rose (1991) refers to both developing countries and transition societies in his seminal article, his substantive examples are drawn from Western Europe and the United States. This study argues that policy transfer and its analysis is not only a useful area of academic enquiry but a valuable tool for policy-makers engaged in processes of transition. This chapter utilizes the term 'transition societies' instead of 'transition states' to emphasize the empirical observation that policy transfer issues relate to matters beyond government and the public sector. Indeed transition societies, those countries which have emerged from the break-up of the Soviet Union as well as those countries which had communist regimes directed in large part from Moscow, represent a special environment for policy transfer and its analysis.

The whole genitive force for these nation states is the turning away from the path followed by the Soviet Union. As Rose (1991: 14) notes, former '...COMECON nations currently face the difficulty of knowing what they do not want to imitate, namely the Soviet system'. However, as Rose continues on to say, '[they are] less confident about which country offers the best practical lessons for their distinctive circumstance'. The collapse of the Soviet Union has led to an all-pervasive and near-total delegitimising of indigenous policies and policy systems including, importantly, the opportunity for endogenous policy development whether evolutionary or innovative.

Thus policy transformation has inevitably become a necessary feature of transition societies as the whole concept of transition presupposes that existing policies and policy systems must be transformed, even built entirely anew, and indeed this transformation must arise, at least initially, from policy transfer from exogenous sources. Furthermore, as Evans and Davies (1999: 367) note, the nature of these policy transfers requires that the changes be remarkable; they are not merely quotidian, as '...the day to day diffusion of knowledge, intentional or otherwise, [which] are better the subject of organizational analysis or management studies.

The breadth of the transformation of policy structures, policies and policy systems driven by the dissolution of the Soviet system has been dramatic both in terms of its scope and intensity. New nation states based upon the liberal democratic model need, amongst other institutional components, new constitutions, legal systems, legislative and executive functions (national, regional and local), bureaucratic functions and structures, and, the establishment of laws to protect private property and govern public and private relationships.

Simultaneously, old systems have to be removed: the single, omnipotent party system; the centralized economic planning system; the police state apparatus; and, state ownership of virtually all national assets. In addition to these immense indigenous demands for policy transformation, the Washington Consensus and the European Union (EU) are also committed to imposing policy transformation on the Ukraine. Motivated by the fear of nuclear arms, the emigration of Diaspora communities to EU member states, and the political and commercial opportunities that democratization and market transition afford, aid and technical assistance were provided in all transition societies. Crucially, this aid and technical assistance almost always carries with it the requirement for policy transformation. As Brzezinski (in Polokhalo, ed., 1997: 108) contends, above all: '...it is geopolitically essential that the Ukraine succeeds...a critical component of Western strategy has to be the deliberate effort – not only economic, but also political – to consolidate a stable and sovereign Ukraine'.

The Ukraine offers a particularly interesting environment for studying these forces of policy transformation and the resulting policy transfers. Historically the Ukraine has never been an independent state and thus only has a limited history of indigenous policy systems. As it has always been dominated by imperialist rule, Ukraine's policy transformation is a daunting challenge. Moreover, given the West's perception of the geo-political importance of the Ukraine in a post-Soviet world, the pressure to accept coercive forms of policy transfer is unrelenting.

In transition societies generally, and the Ukraine specifically, the scope and intensity of policy transformation reveals the full array of policy transfer elements. Dolowitz and Marsh (1996) develop six broad categories for what is transferred: policies, institutions, ideologies, justifications, attitudes, and negative lessons. All of these categories are to be found in the Ukraine. Similarly all forms of transfer can be identified; both direct and indirect processes of coercive transfer are present. The formal conditions of IMF and World Bank assistance to the Ukraine expressly require both policy change and policy transfer. Other aid programs require with greater or lesser degrees of coercion that Ukrainian governmental or non-governmental organizations undertake both policy change and policy transfer. In general, terms of reference and memoranda of understanding carry direct reference to the obligations of the recipient making it clear that the programs and assistance are not unconditional.

Voluntary policy transfer is also common though it tends to be small scale. Not only are donor countries and agencies prepared to accept requests for technical assistance to facilitate policy transfer, policy units in governmental organizations within transition societies actively seek to engage in rational policy learning. However, the majority of voluntary policy transfers do not involve major policy changes. Rather, most voluntary policy transfers involve private sector groups, businesses and associations and seldom involve foreign actor intermediation (see Stone, 1999). In the public sector, we can frequently witness what we will term 'voluntary but necessary' policy transfer. This may be defined as a situation where the need for policy transfer lies between indirect coercion and the dissatisfaction concept commonly used in the current literature for explaining voluntary transfer.

This is not merely a semantic point. In more mature policy environments, dissatisfaction need not rise to the extreme levels of compulsion encountered in transition societies. As Rose (1991: 11) observes, a '...necessary condition of lesson drawing is that policy makers want to learn something that they do not already know'. In transition societies this desire to learn becomes a genuine need. Policy units are often under such tremendous pressure to find solutions to the problems that they are facing that policy transfers are required, not simply due to the coercive activities of external actors, but because of the enormous endogenous pressure and need for change. At the simplest level the actors within the policy unit are hungry, even starving for policy transfer, and only need to know of the existence of a successful exemplar to embrace policy transfer. It is for this reason that transition societies are so vulnerable to inappropriate forms of policy transfer.

The decision structures, as well as the key actors involved in policy transfer, also conform to those characterized in the literature. Elected officials, bureaucrats, policy entrepreneurs and experts, political parties, pressure groups, and international organizations are all present (see Chapter Two). It should also be noted that a major instrument of policy transfer, at least in the Ukraine, has been the introduction, through processes of policy transfers, of entities that resemble epistemic communities and policy transfer networks; these then in turn become key agents in originating and promoting policy transfer.

Notwithstanding the imperatives for policy transformation and policy transfer, the constraints to successful policy transfer in the policy environment are significant and largely conform to those identified in Chapter Two. These can include: unstable socio-economic environments; technical and resource constraints; the absence of cultural and ideological assimilation; and, conventional implementation gaps. At least two further constraints can be added to this list in transition societies – transferor/transferee asymmetry and nostalgic inertia. The first of these constraints may be likened to the situation in the fable of the blind men and the elephant. If the transferor perceives the 'problem' in terms of the elephant's leg and the transferee perceives the same 'problem' in terms of the trunk of the elephant, the transfer is either not likely to be successful or it will produce wildly different results than those anticipated. The second constraint may be termed 'nostalgic inertia'. This condition arises when the transferee agrees with the substance of the policy transfer, but cannot accept the alteration in form or process required to implement it effectively. In the Ukraine, with its plethora of direct and indirect coercive transfers, these two issues commonly create serious obstacles in processes of policy transfer.

Initially the key sources of policy transfer for transition societies were almost exclusively outside the former Soviet Union. However, in recent times there has been a greater propensity to learn from countries that are experiencing similar problems such as Poland, Hungary and the Czech Republic. The broadening of the search for ideas from Western exemplars to other transition societies has been reflected in the increasingly hybrid character of the form and content of policy transfer. The significant constraints that operate in the learning environment militate against the direct copying of policy programs even in coercive processes of transfer. Here, the adversarial relationship between the donor and the transferee severely limits the degree of transfer. In some cases this limitation produces a transfer wherein the resulting policy change is more beneficial than would be the case with a total transfer, but often the resulting policy change may be significantly or even fatally weakened by these limitations.

Thus, as Stone (1999: 57) notes, there are, '...rich research opportunities in investigating policy transfer across the former socialist states'. However, in order for these processes of policy transfer to be successful, the distinctive character of transition policy environments require a reworking of the 'cultural prejudices' within the current research that Stone identifies.

Applying Policy Transfer Analysis in a Transition State

How, then, might we develop a model of policy transfer that provides useful insights for a society in transition? Policy transfer studies to date have undoubtedly been overly descriptive. Evans and Davies (1999: 361) posit two related questions that must be addressed in policy transfer analysis in order to move beyond mere description of processes of transfer: why does policy transfer occur and how useful is it as an explanation for policy change? It will be argued in this chapter in response to these questions that policy transfer is a necessary condition in transition states arising from the very nature, indeed definition, of transition states as those in which policy transfer is a key dynamic in their policy environment. For example, Bystrytsky (in Polokhalo, ed., 1997: 29) notes that '...the search is now underway for possible models, offshoots, or correlates of West European democracy (civil society and law-governed state) and the norms of civilized and well regulated social existence'. Hence, policy transfer is endemic in transition societies. Indeed, as Nordberg (in Kuzio, ed., 1998: 52) observes, '...the Ukraine's transformation dwarfs in scope any changes being made in the West'. Moreover, as there was no body of knowledge to drawn upon and guide this transformation we must conclude that policy transfer has had a significant impact on the character of policy change in the Ukraine and in other transition societies.

A further question must be added to those posed by Evans and Davies (1999) in order to develop a model of policy transfer that is appropriate to transition societies. If an understanding of policy transfer is so central to any theorization of policy development in a transition society how can we measure and validate its specific contribution? It is thus evident that policy transfer analysis must involve a mapping process that allows us to identify the linkages between 'exogenous inputs' and the 'consideration or implementation of policy changes' in a transition society. As Dolowitz and Marsh (1996: 355) put it, we '...need more work on how and why it happens'. In a mature policy environment with generally well-established policy structures, we do not find the feverish, even chaotic, policy dynamics that characterize a transition state. In mature environments, the policy environment is not so cluttered with actions, events, transferors, transferees, progress, recidivism and general turmoil. In transition societies the signal-to-noise ratio is so low that, without carefully applied analytic techniques, we will find ourselves, in Wolman's words (1992: 33), describing a '...form of policy-making by anecdote rather than by analysis'.

This illustrates the necessity of mapping macro-level problems, pressures and opportunities that characterize the policy environment in a transition state. As noted above, we can determine that the policy environment in transition societies necessitates policy change. We can also identify three forms of compulsion that may impact on governmental actors in any given situation – 'direct coercive' transfer, 'indirect coercive' or 'negotiated' transfer and 'voluntary but necessary' transfer. In addition, we must also consider the behaviour of actors and their response to these macro-level constraints. Intutively, 'direct coercive' transfers will reveal different behavioural norms between transferor and transferee than will 'voluntary but necessary' transfers. Still, it is important at the macro-level analysis to address specifically and accurately how these behavioural norms impact on the process of policy transfer.

Nonetheless we cannot rely on the macro-level approach alone, but must add to our inquiry the study of micro-level processes of policy transfer. However, once this has been completed, we will still need to integrate these two levels of inquiry through the use of meso-level analysis in order to generate knowledge claims that are of genuine explanatory value. Evans and Davies (1999: 370), argue that we must assess '...whether structural processes external to the process of transfer we are looking at have an impact (directly or indirectly) upon the context, strategies, intentions and actions of the agents directly involved'. Hence in this context meso-level analysis refers to the analysis of the relationship between structure and agency and how this affects outcomes of policy transfer. The policy transfer network approach developed by Evans and Davies will be used to accomplish this task. This will allow us to identify the causal pathways that inform policy transfer in a transition society.

The Association of Ukrainian Cities: A Policy Transfer Network for Local Government Reform

This case study is organized into three parts. Part one provides a brief historical overview of local government in the Ukraine and identifies the macro-level pressures, opportunities and legacies that characterize the policy environment in which Ukrainian local government operates. Part two aims to provide an understanding of the role of local government in democratic transition through an examination of the emergence and development of the AUC. It is argued that the AUC, the representative body of Ukrainian local government, may be viewed as a policy transfer network for local government reform. In part two, the case of the AUC as an agent of 'voluntary but necessary' policy transfer is presented. Part three provides a case summary and offers a multi-level explanation of local government reform.

The History of Local Self-Government in the Ukraine

Though the Soviet system pre-supposed three levels of public administration with policy and implementation function – central/national, regional and local – such a division was a mere fiction. The second and third levels merely implemented central dictates (see Avksentyev in Sazonov, ed., 1998: 303). Indeed the defining features of Soviet public administration were its complete subordination to the Party and its hierarchical, 'top-down' structure. The initiation of the reform of the political system in 1988 through perestroika was followed by the break-up of the USSR in 1991 and the eventual collapse of the administrative system. In August 1990, with the encouragement of the Russian President Boris Yeltsin, the former Soviet Republics proclaimed independence one after another. Until 1991, the administration of the Ukraine was fully subordinate to the administration of the USSR and, consequently, this former vassal of Moscow had no institutional experience of taking care of the needs of an independent state. Utilizing Western experience of organizing local self-government became a matter of utmost importance in the post-totalitarian development and state-building processes (Sazonov, ed., 1998: 36).

State building in the Ukraine would prove a daunting task for not only was it necessary to develop a whole new system of public administration but it was also necessary to construct new public infrastructure and develop the human resources and appropriate institutions of governance and forms of public management to deliver on national development goals. Moreover, the key aim of state-building – establishing a legitimate and functioning state – had to be achieved quickly despite the almost complete absence of political stability and consensus. This meant that the reform of the political and economic system had to be undertaken simultaneously.

Despite being short of resources, the government unwillingly started the decentralization process by transferring a range of powers from the capital to the localities. Nordberg (in Kuzio, ed., 1998: 43) observes that '...many of the tasks that were handled by the central government have devolved onto local administration'. These are not necessarily planned changes; the greater role of local government is as much a function of Kiev's lack of funds and inability to collect taxes as it was of organized reform. The process of decentralization has involved considerable re-assignment of spending responsibilities for functions never performed by local governments before, including basic social welfare, housing, education, and health services. However, central governments have retained considerable control over major tax resources, hampering the ability of local government to carry out its new functions.

The term 'local self-government', which had disappeared from the Soviet lexicon after 1917, re-appeared in the Ukraine after the elections to the Supreme Council in 1990 and its subsequent adoption of local government institutions. These two events, for the first time in the history of the Ukraine, had laid down the legal foundation for the re-introduction and dynamic development of local self-government. In 1992, amendments were made to the law on local self-government removing central control and giving the right to local governments '...to arrive by collective means at decisions relating to all questions of local development' (Ukrainian Law on Local Self-Government, 1992). However, these rights existed mostly on paper. In theory, local governments received the right to create their own budgets, but in practice they are heavily dependent on centralized subsidies from Kiev. This financial dependence on central government is impeding the development of local self-government. Several legislative attempts were made to clarify the situation, but they only contributed to the confusion.

The Ukraine's post-independence local governments are failing in a number of areas. For example, the civil service remains underpaid and under trained, and it lacks a clear vision of its role in public management (see Nordberg in Kuzio, ed., 1998: 42). The 1991 poll of local administrators clearly demonstrates the complete misunderstanding of their role. The vast majority of local civil servants identified their main function as '...providing leisure and entertainment for the people' (Boukhalov and Ivannikov, 1995). Among other widely cited problems were corruption, communist nostalgia, and a lack of experience of the role of administration in a free market conditions.

The Ukraine was slow to adopt a new constitution and until 1996 operated under the modified version of the 1978 Soviet Constitution, where there was little provision for the distribution of powers between the centre and periphery. This uncertain political situation and the fight for financial resources ignited conflict between all levels of government – central, regional, and local. Local administrations were often the victims of the political struggle between the President and the Parliament.

The Rise of a Policy Transfer Network for Local Government Reform

In accordance with Evans and Davies's heuristic model for accounting for the emergence and development of policy transfer networks, the following discussion of local government reform in the Ukraine is organized around a discussion of problem recognition, the search for ideas, the establishment of a policy transfer network, policy oriented learning, policy implementation, cognitive mobilization and policy outcomes.

Problem recognition The turbulent political environment described above made it very difficult for local governments to cope with their new powers and responsibilities. Nonetheless, in 1994, for the first time in its history, cities all over the Ukraine held mayoral elections. The newly elected mayors saw the development of effective self-governments as a prerequisite for successful democratic transition, and the consolidation of decentralization processes in the Ukraine. The first key step towards achieving effective local government can be identified with the development of reciprocal relationships between central and local governments and between local governments and citizens to replace the former hierarchical 'top-down' Communist Party control structure. The search for a model of an organization to serve as a link between local and central levels of government was underway.

The search for ideas The mayors had a clear idea of the type of policy structure they needed to achieve their objectives. As Miroslav Pitsyk (*author interview*, 15 April 2000) the Executive Director of the AUC remarks, '[w]e wanted to have an organization capable of accumulating, summarising and analysing the problems and proposals of the cities and then offering their unified position to the national government'. It would be unfair to say that the Ukraine had no precedent of similar municipal associations. In 1913, Kiev held the largest gathering of mayors and municipal officials in the history of the Russian empire and attacked the Tsarist government for its neglect of its cities. The gathering lasted 10 days and finally had to be shut down by gendarmes because it refused to silence its criticism of St. Petersburg, then the capital of Tsarist Russia (Gleason, 1998).

However, mayors in the new Ukrainian state have had to develop a modern forum for developing policy solutions to transition problems. As Pitsyk (ibid.), comments, having studied Western experience, '...we have seen that it is common practice for the associations of cities to come together not just to resolve some isolated problems, but to forward their common interests to the state in order to protect their rights and expand the powers and general competence of local governments'.

The emergence of a policy transfer network In August 1994, a group of mayors from the largest Ukrainian cities met to address the task of re-invigorating the moribund AUC that had originally been created in June 1992. The initial purpose of the AUC was to act as an electoral political action group but it had become dormant after the elections the previous spring. In 1994 it was proposed that the cities should come together to share experience and to strengthen their ability to lobby for favourable policies at the national level, particularly in relation to those policies that would have a financial impact on cities. A major task that was identified at this meeting was the need to establish an effective national organization and a central office in Kiev to coordinate interests and to lobby the centre for local government-friendly policies (The AUC Brochure, 1998).

Thus, the AUC was set up to coordinate the network of cities with the intention of engineering a range of local government policy reforms. The mayors defined the primary goal of the AUC as the development of Ukrainian local self-government in accordance with the *European Charter of Local Self-Governance*. Indeed, AUC experts developed a city charter according to the main principles set out in the charter. The consulting centre organized a seminar for members of the AUC where the model charter was offered to Ukrainian cities as a synthesis of best local government practice. Another important goal of the AUC, according to the statute, was to study and disseminate positive and negative experience of international local government practice (The Statute of the AUC, 1995). This would be the first step in the development of the AUC into a knowledge institution on local government practice.

Policy oriented learning A representative of the United States Agency for International Development (USAID), who was invited to attend the AUCs August

1994 meeting, alerted USAID to this new opportunity to provide technical assistance. The AUC requested specific types of assistance, stressing that the primary need was not for the infusion of foreign financial resources, but the transfer of external knowledge and expertise to local policy-makers and administrators (author interview, Yuri Kushnaryev, former Head of the AUC, May, 1999). An information feeder network was set up where the role of USAID was to provide the AUC with access to information and knowledge of the best local government practices in the West.

The priorities of the first stage of the joint program between USAID and the AUC were defined according to the AUCs request and included: a trip by a group of mayors to the United States to meet with and study the experience of their National Association of Cities; a trip to Amsterdam to participate in the International Union of Local Authorities (IULA) Congress; conferences with local government experts from Europe and the United States; and, the development of policy related resources for the Kiev office in order to allow it to begin to act as a knowledge institution.

Implementation   The AUC presently has 255 city members, an increase of 230 members since its re-launch in 1994. More than a half of the Ukraine's population lives in these cities. Since 1994, it has undertaken a wide range of activities in support of its stated objective of improving and strengthening local self-governance in the Ukraine. The work of the AUC centres on the following areas: the creation of the legal foundations of local self-governance; interaction with national governmental agencies; the promotion of city projects and municipal development programs; the protection of the rights of local government officials; training local staff; and, international co-operation involving the development of bilateral agreements with similar institutions abroad and participation in international and regional institutions (The AUC Brochure, 1998). Table 6.1 provides an overview of the main milestones in the AUC's brief history. It demonstrates the significant influence of the AUC in the process of local government reform.

Another new direction in the AUC's activity is the publication of a thematic collection of standard acts concerning the powers of local self-government bodies in the fields of budget, finance, management of communal property, building, land relations and protection of the environment, education, health care, culture, physical culture and sports, and social protection of the population. The AUC also publishes a magazine *Ukrainske Misto* (Ukrainian City), which acts as a platform for discussing problems in the development of local self-government.

Elite and cognitive mobilization   The AUC is now deliberately engaged in an extensive process of partnership building at the international level with organizations such as the Congress of Local and Regional Governments of the Council of Europe, the USAID, and, the US Information Agency. It has also initiated several co-operative programmes with the Swedish Association of Local Authorities.

Table 6.1 A chronology of the AUC's influence on local government reform in the Ukraine

1996	Through the adoption of the Constitution of the Ukraine a constitutional provision was established for local self-government, together with the basic principles of its powers and functions. The AUC had a significant influence over the development of the new legal provisions for local governance. This culminated in June 1996 with the development of provisions that were much more favourable to processes of decentralization in general and local self-government in particular.
1997	The adoption and implementation of the Law of the Ukraine *On Local Self-Governance*. The AUC was active in lobbying for this law as it further improved the legal basis and practical powers of cities. The AUC helped to draft the law. This law was of particular importance because it led to the effective decentralization of certain powers and competences to the periphery
1998	The AUC was an active participant in the budget formulation process. As a result the portion of the local budget in the consolidated budget of the Ukraine grew from 30 to 36 per cent.
1999-2000	The AUC played a central role in drafting the legislation that forms the basis for local self-government in the Ukraine.
2001	The AUC once again plays an active role in the development of the local government component of the national budget in which the allocation to local governments increased from 36 to 40 per cent.

The AUC has been particularly active in expanding business contacts with similar agencies globally with the aim of sharing experience, developing joint projects and facilitating economic and cultural relationships between cities.

Attracting inward investment to the cities is perceived to be the most urgent problem facing local governments. At the request of its members, the AUC, with the support of USAID consultants (solicited and selected by the AUC), continuously assist cities in preparing specific investment programs related to improving city infrastructure. Several conferences and seminars have been held with the participation of international organizations such as the EU, the World Bank, USAID, TACIS, and others on issues related to attracting investments, reorganizing city infrastructure, financial management. These have included practical training on municipal finance, using financial management software, creating economic planning departments to encourage trade and tourism; and investigating ways to improve services such as transportation (The AUC Information Bulletin N.2, 1998). It is noteworthy that 64 cities are now using the financial analysis models developed by the AUC in co-operation with USAID

(Ukrainian City, 2001).

AUC/USAID-sponsored activities have promoted more open and responsive city government operations, greater public accountability, and increased citizen participation. Open and competitive procurement procedures, budgeting processes, distribution of annual reports, and public hearings have been introduced in a large number of the cities. A zoning manual has also been distributed, which has resulted in the development of zoning rules, enlarged boundaries and planning regulatory schemes in five cities. Ten local governments have received assistance in instituting and implementing computerized titling and registration (The AUC Information Bulletin, No.3, 1998).

The AUC has even developed a series of films about the experience of resolving municipal problems in the Ukrainian cities called *From City to City*. The films have been developed in close co-operation and with the financial assistance of RTI and USAID. Copies of the film have been distributed amongst the membership and a seminar was organized at which participants shared their experience with counterparts from other cities.

Policy outcomes The AUC has acted as a network for: engineering policy transfer; building a local government policy community comprised of mayors, city administrators, local government officials and policy-makers; as well as co-ordinating the activities of all local authorities. In addition to the achievements identified in Table 6.1, the AUC has been successful in establishing: an Academy for Municipal Management; the *Ukrainske Misto* (Ukrainian City) magazine; the Centre for Investments and the Development of Cities; the Association of Municipal Education; the Society of Scientists for the Promotion of Municipal Reform; and, the Congress of Ukrainian Local Self-government (including the AUC, the Ukrainian Association of Local and Regional Authorities and the Association of the Rural, and, Town and City Councils). Many of these reforms have been the product of processes of policy transfer mediated by the AUC, USAID and other external experts. The AUC is now viewed to be the formal representative of the Ukrainian cities in national and international forums.

Case Summary

As the AUC case demonstrates, donor countries and international agencies are not always the main agents of policy transfer in transition societies. Indigenous policy actors are often actively engaged in policy learning from international experience. In the Ukrainian context the needs of the cities were so terribly pressing that no coercive processes, direct or indirect, were necessary to facilitate policy transfer. The cities effectively had no choice but to seek technical assistance from foreign experts. We thus define such a form of policy transfer as 'voluntary but necessary'.

The case study reveals the macro- and micro-level problems, pressures and opportunities that characterize the environmental context within which local government policy transfer networks operate. The first post-independence local governments in the Ukraine found it extremely hard to cope with the further powers and responsibilities conferred upon them. Macro-level pressures from international organizations, as well as the centre, led to increased responsibilities for local government in the areas of economic development, social welfare, housing and education. At the same time that the costs of local government activities increased, the allocation from the global state budget to the local state remained woefully insufficient, thus exacerbating the pressure on local public administrators. Furthermore, several individual attempts by Ukrainian cities to lobby central government for a fairer deal failed. The establishment of the AUC as a policy transfer network was therefore a direct response to the failure of city governments to influence the trajectory of state transformation. The main goal of the network was therefore defined as the reform of Ukrainian local government through '...the evaluation and dissemination of positive experience, the effective implementation of local self-governance in cities and the improvement of city welfare' (The Statute of the AUC, 1995). The establishment of the AUC as a local government policy transfer network began with the growing dissatisfaction of a group of Ukrainian mayors with both central-local relations and the absence of indigenous policy solutions. This precipitated the realization of the necessity to engage in policy transfer from the West. It is evident from the case study, that the AUC conducted a broad search for ideas and did not limit the scope of its learning activity to a small sample of exemplars.

In order to determine the causal relationship between these macro and micro-level forces we now need to examine the relationship between the structures (the policy environment) and the agents, in this case study the AUC and USAID. During the search process the initial contact with an international organization (USAID) was made through the USAID advisor to the mayor of Kharkov. The AUC requested technical assistance with the development of the resources (political, knowledge and material) necessary for the implementation of the transfer program. The need to bring external expertise into the transfer network was considered much more important than obtaining financial resources (author interview with Yuri Kushnaryev, 20 May, 1999). As Vladimir Moroz (AUC Information Bulletin, no. 1, 1998), the ex-President of the AUC remarks, from the very beginning, '...the AUC leadership has strongly stressed the importance of maintaining their relationship with donor organizations on an independent, bilateral and partnership basis'. The AUCs strategic calculation here was that the leadership should avoid developing dependency relationships with donor organizations by maintaining a large degree of financial self-sufficiency through the levying of membership fees and other internal sources of income. The AUC adopted this modus operandi from the beginning and this gave it the autonomy to adopt some programs and decline others. The role allocated to the external agents of policy transfer (USAID and other donor organizations) by the AUC was solely one of providing 'an information feeder' and sources of policy-oriented learning (Evans and Davies, 1999). This allowed the client (the AUC) to evaluate the information provided, filter out unsuitable elements and select policy transfers in a rational way.

There was also an understanding amongst its leadership that the AUC had to find local solutions to local problems wherever possible and this should inform any process of policy transfer. As Kushnaryev (1995) notes, '…there are no ready-made recipes, either in the Ukraine, or elsewhere in the world'. This understanding was demonstrated in attempts by the AUC to develop a procedure for the submission of local government proposals to the national parliament. The AUC had learned of a promising procedure that was used in the Canadian context, however, the Canadian experience was found to be unsuitable for the Ukraine. The AUC was also very interested in adopting German practice, where the Bundestag will not consider a single bill concerning local government until the experts from the Union of German Cities (the German AUC equivalent) examine it. The AUC ultimately decided to develop its own procedure, drawing on German experience (Kushnaryev, 1995: 2).

The AUC has often had to defend its independent position and protect the network from dysfunctional and potentially disruptive inputs from USAID. For example, USAID attempted to get the AUC to initiate a lobbying campaign on a couple of issues of interest to the US government. The USAID consultant even threatened the AUC with withdrawal of further technical assistance unless the AUC agreed. However, the AUC leadership decided that these activities were not in the interest of its members and could be dangerous for the AUC itself. It therefore strongly opposed USAID on these issues and eventually managed to defend its decision. Moreover, in several interviews conducted with members of the AUC leadership for this project, frequent reference has been made to the President of the Ukraine, various political parties, influential business groups and officials seeking the support of the AUC in political disputes or lobbying the AUC to adopt a different course of action. But the AUC has always striven to be independent from both local and foreign forces. The AUC network has insulated itself from the influence of structural processes external to the process of transfer, through its ability to remain financially independent. Hence structural forces appear to have had less of a disruptive impact upon the context, strategies, intentions and actions of the networks actors. The AUC's relative autonomy has clearly had a significant impact on policy outcomes in local government reform.

The density of the AUC network has also played an enabling role. Evans and Davies (1999: 378) argue that '…the process of elite and cognitive mobilization is critical to the success of the transfer network'. The AUC has developed a close-knit policy community of significant density possessing strong mechanisms of self-protection. The AUC has always exhibited a strong sense of commitment to a common value system – the idea of local self-government. Indeed, the influence of the AUC has grown throughout the process of state building in the Ukraine. Notably, this process is taking the form of a struggle between the forces that want to resuscitate the Soviet system, on the one hand, and those who see this country as a law-governed, democratic state with effective local self-government, on the other hand (Kushnaryev, 1995: 2).

The AUC case study demonstrates the importance of the relationship between the internal structure of the policy transfer network and its ability to engage in policy transfer programming. Moreover, the organizational design of this particular network is geared towards developing its role as a knowledge institution and acting as '…a channel for the development of consensual knowledge' (Evans and Davies, 1999: 379). The AUC also became an umbrella organization for the development of policy and epistemic communities of civil servants, local and national government officials, scientists, lawyers and journalists concerned with the problems of local government in the Ukraine. It now serves as an agent of policy transfer striving for best international and local practices. The success of the AUC as a policy transfer network emphasizes the importance of building a national framework to propagate best practice.

In Conclusion: Lesson Drawing from the Case Study

It remains to review the key lessons that can be drawn from the case study for the study of policy transfer. These findings will be presented in three sets of comments – theory and method, empirical observations, and, strengths, weaknesses and further research.

Theory and Method

This chapter has examined the applicability of the policy transfer approach as an understanding of policy development in a state in transition. Having addressed some of the shortcomings of the existing literature with particular reference to its lack of consideration of less mature policy environments, this study has identified the theoretical modifications necessary to improve its analytical utility. We have found that policy transfer is not only a useful but also a necessary approach for understanding a state in transition. This is because it is an empirical regularity in transition societies for exogenous policy inputs to influence endogenous policy development due mainly to the turbulent nature of the policy environment. In a transition society, the vast majority of policy inputs are exogenous in character, as there are few valid sources for indigenous input. However, transforming policy transfer into a tool applicable to transition societies depends largely on employing the multi-level model of policy analysis developed by Evans and Davies (1999), that integrates the policy transfer network approach with macro- and micro-level analysis.

The chapter also found that when policy transfer analysts seek to validate policy transfer in transition societies they need to map both policy outcomes and changes in policy environment structures. The Ukraine does not have well-developed policy structures not does it have useful institutional memory from which to draw lessons. This why one of the key areas of policy transfer lies in the development of appropriate structures of governance and the human resources to deliver on national development goals. The latter is often achieved through civil service reform drawing on successful international exemplars (see Turner and Hulme, 1997).

The case study explored a form of policy transfer which we termed 'voluntary but necessary' as it captures the essence of a structurally determined policy transfer wherein the need for transfer lies between indirect coercion and the dissatisfaction concept commonly used in the literature. It was noted that 'voluntary but necessary' and 'direct' and 'indirect coercive' forms of policy transfer are particularly common in transition states, while truly voluntary policy transfers involving major policy changes in governmental or quasi-governmental organizations are less frequent. Most authentic voluntary policy transfers tend to involve private sector groups, businesses and associations and seldom involve foreign actor intermediation.

Finally, it is also recommended that research into policy transfer in transition societies should focus on 'bottom-up' case studies of 'in-process' policy transfer activities.

Empirical Observations

In order to investigate the claims of the multi-level model of policy transfer analysis an analysis of the role of the AUC as a policy transfer network was conducted. The lessons drawn from the case study are summarized below as well as the framework of variables influencing the capacity of policy transfer network to conceive and implement policy change.

The origin of the network It is argued that in order to ensure that transition societies are insulated from inappropriate policy transfer the driving force for the creation of policy transfer networks should be of indigenous origin.

The density of the network The case study also suggests that the density of the network has a significant impact on the outcome of the process of policy transfer. The close-knit structure of the network provided it with significant autonomy that contributed to the successful outcome of the policy transfer.

Elite and cognitive mobilization The sense of elite commitment to the common value systems and the goals of the transfer program are critical to the success of the network. A policy transfer in a transition society is unlikely to be successful without the full conviction and commitment of all affected parties. This was evident in the case of the AUC.

Resource dependency The independent position of the AUC, which relied entirely on scarce domestic resources, allowed the network to resist dysfunctional exogenous inputs and thus to survive as an effective policy-making structure. Thus, policy transfer networks in transition societies should retain as much independence from exogenous actors and their resources as possible.

The pattern of relationships with donor organizations Independent and partnership relations with donor agencies and the right balance between local and foreign actors within the AUC network were equally important characteristics, which improved its capacity to engineer policy change.

The degree of policy transfer There is a need to avoid the wholesale transfer of particular Western-based programs without due regard for indigenous practices. In transitional societies the effectiveness of policy transfer programs are largely determined by the degree to which the essential components of a national culture are preserved within the policy transfer design and inappropriate foreign content is filtered out in a process of cultural assimilation.

The scope of search activity The AUCs experience demonstrates the benefit of searching widely for ideas across many different exemplars (sectors and countries) rather than relying on the experience of one particular donor. Setting limits on the network's scope of learning activity may severely prejudice its capacity to engineer successful policy change.

The capacity to cct as a knowledge institution The AUC policy transfer network now possesses the capacity to act as an effective knowledge institution. Indeed, it provides an ongoing opportunity structure for policy transfer. At some time in the future, when the need for policy transfer diminishes, this 'permanent' policy transfer network may well evolve into an epistemic community that resembles those in the West.

Strengths, weaknesses and further research

The multi-level model of policy transfer analysis has proved an effective tool for studying and analyzing policy transfer in a transition society. It has helped us to make sense of the myriad of constraints which shape a complex process of policy change in a transitional environment. The study has demonstrated the multi-level explanatory power of the meso-level approach, which provided an explanation of the outcome of the process of transfer by establishing the following relationships between exogenous macro-level factors (economic, political, ideological, technological) and the network; between the network structure and behaviour and the relationship between its individual actors (micro-level); and between the network's structure and the policy outcome.

The policy transfer network approach also proved invaluable in assisting our understanding of the ways in which decision-makers acquire knowledge in a turbulent policy arena that characterizes a transition society. This is of particular importance for the Ukraine, which has to operate in conditions arising from a collapsed state in which all institutional memory is now ideologically unacceptable.

There are, however, obvious limitations in inferring general conclusions through the application of the meso-level approach to just one case study. Further research is required both in terms of developing a greater range of case study investigations of different forms of policy transfer and the range of constraints that condition the success of policy transfer in transitional environments. Further study of the anthropological aspects of these constraints, which we term 'nostalgic inertia', also warrant further elaboration and study. The study has also paid limited attention to the patterns of policy transfer network formation in transition states. Further research should be undertaken to examine the recruitment/exclusion patterns that inform the composition of policy transfer networks as well as internal structural variables such as the competitive struggle between interests, and the balance of strategic resources. This type of analysis can be extended to inform an account of the capacity building, evolution, transformation and ultimately the termination of these networks. Assuming the need to demonstrate the pragmatic value of the study of policy transfer networks in a transitional environment, the effectiveness of particular strategies for building policy networks could be examined further by developing a series of indicators around the themes of resource dependency, participation, transparency, capacity building, sustainability and further policy learning opportunities.

Chapter 7

Policy Transfer in Kyrgyzstan: The Case of General Practice Fundholding

Andrew Street

Introduction

Faced with severe economic crisis following independence from the former Soviet Union, Kyrgyzstan is engaged in widespread structural adjustment reform to transform itself into a market economy. Fundholding has been included among the package of reforms for the health sector. Fundholding was the most innovative aspect of the Thatcherite reforms introduced in the UK National Health Service in the 1990s, the scheme providing general practitioners with financial incentives to contain costs and reduce referral rates. This chapter examines why fundholding was placed on the Kyrgyz policy agenda and the prospects for implementation of the scheme. The case study is analysed using three competing analytical frameworks – rational decision-making, public choice theory, and indirect coercive transfer. It is argued that analytical bias pervades policy transfer analysis for the case study demonstrates that the selection of a particular analytical position pre-determines the conclusions drawn about the process and outcome of policy transfer.

The case study is remarkable in a number of respects. First, to some extent the transfer can be considered voluntary, in that it was the outcome of a joint agreement between the Kyrgyz Ministry of Health and the World Health Organization (WHO). However, there were coercive elements to the development of policy because satisfactory progress on the reform proposals was a condition of subsequent WB and IMF loans. Secondly, the current example differs from many other studies of policy transfer in that it has yet to be fully implemented. By focusing on only those cases where policy transfer can be said to have definitively occurred, the literature is in danger of unnecessarily limiting its scope of analysis. In particular, cases of transfer involving negative lessons (Dolowitz and Marsh, 1996) are underrepresented. Thirdly, in this case study, the agents of transfer were unusual. Those advocating the particular policy were not representatives of the country in which the policy had originated but rather representatives of a third country. Indeed, the policy has since been abandoned in its country of origin.

Finally, alternative explanations can be advanced as to why the particular policy was initially adopted but has yet to be implemented. These provide different lenses with which to view the issues involved in policy transfer.

The chapter is organized in five parts. The next section provides an overview of the literature on policy transfer analysis. Section two briefly sketches the main aspects of the policy in the UK. Section three describes the development of policy in Kyrgyzstan, including the conditions that made reform appear desirable. Section four considers the case study through the application of three analytical frameworks to evaluate progress to date. The final section presents an overview of the chapter's main findings.

Policy Transfer Analysis

Dolowitz and Marsh (1996: 357) define policy transfer as 'the process by which actors borrow policies developed in one setting to develop programmes and policies within another'. This definition, as with Rose's (1991) description of lesson drawing, suggest that policy transfer is generally a voluntary process. However, Dolowitz and Marsh recognise that the process of 'borrowing' may be coercive, such as when a government or a multi-national corporation forces another government to adopt policies that would not otherwise be considered. In practice, it is not always possible to determine whether policy transfer was voluntary or indirectly coercive. The case study described in this chapter provides an example of where it is difficult to draw a clear distinction.

Much of the literature on policy transfer focuses on the nation state, with public officials usually considered the key agents of transfer (Evans and Davies, 1999). Nevertheless, it is recognized that transfer often involves non-state actors or occurs both within and across national boundaries (Dolowitz and Marsh, 1996 and 2000; Evans and Davies, 1999; Rose, 1991). It has been argued that instances of policy transfer are best understood by considering the various actors involved as a 'policy transfer network' drawn from a range of endogenous and exogenous governmental and non-governmental actors (Evans and Davies, 1999). This is the approach adopted in this chapter.

In Rose's description of lesson drawing it is assumed that at least some aspects of the foreign policy are identifiable in the local variant (Rose 1991). However, this excludes instances where policy options are explored but are not implemented. In such cases lessons have been drawn: that of policy rejection. This is closer to the negative lessons described by others (Dolowitz and Marsh, 1996). Cases of non transfer will be under-represented in the literature, if only because there will be less documentary evidence available for analysis. But, as well as redressing this selection bias, analysis of examples of policy rejection may be important in illuminating what constitutes policy transfer rather than lesson learning. As Evans and Davies (1999: 381) put it: '...much of the existing literature rests too much on abstracting alleged perfect fit cases of policy transfer; attention must be paid to the boundary questions, which means in an empirical sense establishing cases which are not examples of policy transfers'.

To maintain that fundholding provides an example of policy rejection is actually premature. The policy of fundholding has not been rejected in Kyrgyzstan. But nor has the policy yet been implemented, except in pilot form in one part of the country. On the face of it, this would appear a serious drawback. However, it is a problem common to many analyses of policy transfer as it is often difficult to determine the point at which policy transfer ends in practice (Stone, 1999). Whether implemented or not, it is still possible to bring the tools of political science to bear in examining the policy process. Moreover, by undertaking the analysis it is possible to identify the prospects for implementation of the fundholding scheme throughout Kyrgyzstan. Before examining why it was considered as a reform option in Kyrgyzstan, the next section describes the fundholding scheme in its country of origin, the UK.

General Practice Fundholding in the UK

Government policies directed at the United Kingdom's National Health Service prior to the 1990s paid little attention to the primary care sector (Bloor and Maynard, 1993). With the appointment of Kenneth Clarke as Secretary of State for Health in 1988, the earlier 'hands-off' approach was to change radically. Clarke sought to tackle increasing pharmaceutical expenditure and to monitor GP activity more systematically. To this end, two major reforms were introduced. First, a new contract was devised for GPs in which their fee structure was revised considerably (Department of Health, 1989b). GP income was linked more closely to their workload with payments introduced for achievement against targets for selected types of activity. Secondly, general practice fundholding was invented. This was an 'add-on' to the far-reaching NHS reforms of 1991 (Secretary of State for Health, 1989), and had its roots in academic discussions in the early 1980s (Marinker, 1984; Maynard, 1986). The rationale for fundholding was to combine budgetary with clinical responsibilities, in the hope that this would encourage GPs to contain costs, use resources more efficiently, and reduce referral rates. It was felt that by linking payments more closely to workload the 'consumer power' of patients would drive improvements in health care delivery:

> The government will introduce a new scheme enabling money to flow with the patient from the GP practice itself. The practices and hospitals, which attract the most custom will receive the most money. Both GPs and hospitals will have a real incentive to put patients first (Secretary of State for Health, 1989: 48).

And,

> The government believes that these changes will give patients more choice and that GPs will have a stronger incentive to improve services to their patients (Department of Health, 1989a).

It was expected that by giving GPs a budget with which to purchase selected services, they would chose to provide care themselves rather than referring patients to the more expensive secondary care sector. By limiting referrals GPs could save money for re-investment in the practice (Secretary of State for Health, 1989).

Initially the scheme allowed participation by general practices with patient lists exceeding 11,000 (Secretary of State for Health, 1989). Such practices could apply for their own budgets from which to purchase a limited list of hospital services, including outpatient services, diagnostic tests and some non-emergency inpatient and day case treatment. Subsequently, the scheme was extended, and fundholders ranged from practices with only 3,000 patients (community fundholders) to schemes involving multiple practices, such as total purchasing pilots (Bloor *et al.*, 2000). By 1996, the fundholding scheme covered over 50 per cent of the population in England.

Many countries monitored the progress of the fundholding scheme, with some considering implementation of their own variant of the UK model (Malcolm, 1993). Kyrgyzstan was one such country.

Health Sector Reform in Kyrgyzstan

Kyrgyzstan gained independence from the former Soviet Union in August 1991. This led to an immediate and continued financial crisis, initially resulting from the loss of macro economic subsidies from Moscow (which represented approximately one third of national income), and since compounded by a deteriorating economy and shrinking tax base. Out of a population of around 4.5 million, the number officially estimated to be in full-time employment has fallen from 1.44 million in 1991 to 0.57 million in 2000 (nsc.bishkek.su/Eng/home/database/index.html, 2000). Many now derive income in an expanding informal economy, limiting the ability of the government to generate revenue.

As with all public programmes, the health system has suffered a significant reduction in funding. Between 1991 and 1994 public expenditure on the health sector was estimated to have fallen by a third in real terms (World Bank, 1995), and by 1995 it consumed only 3.5 per cent of GDP (www.who.int/whr/1999/en/annex1.htm, 2000). Under investment during Soviet times has been exacerbated. Hospital buildings are in a poor state of repair, sanitation is rudimentary, equipment is outmoded, laboratories lack the facilities to perform basic diagnostic tests and pharmacies do not have the ingredients to make generic preparations (McKee *et al.*, 1998; Street and Haycock 1999).

Patients are expected to fund an increasing proportion of their care, the burden of which can be significant. A survey of 2,000 households conducted in 1994 found that, in a fifth of cases, the total cost of illness for one household member exceeded the household's entire monthly income (Abel-Smith and Falkingham, 1995). Patients admitted to hospital are expected to pay for their linen and meals, they generally have to purchase and supply their own medications, and informal payments to clinical staff are not uncommon. The health of the population is deteriorating, as a result both of reduced government expenditure and a decline in nutrition, shelter and hygiene (Manas Programme Unit, 1995). Life expectancy has fallen, particularly in comparison with the improvements made in the mid-1980s associated with the Gorbachev anti-alcohol campaign (Leon *et al.*, 1997). Cardiovascular disease, anaemia, infant diarrhoea and respiratory disease are on the increase (McKee *et al.* 1998). Facing financial hardship and an alarming deterioration in the general health status of the population, exacerbated by minimal funding of preventative and primary care, reform of the health sector was recognized as imperative.

The Kyrgyz government was viewed as the most enthusiastic among central Asian countries in moving toward market reform and, consequently, international donors were favourably disposed to offering foreign aid and advice after the collapse of the Soviet system (McKee *et al.,* 1998). However, immediately after independence donor activities were rarely co-ordinated, leading to duplication, inconsistency and confusion. Moreover, local decision-making expertise was in short supply. Prior to the break-up of the Soviet Union, all decisions of importance were made in Moscow and ministries of health in the Soviet republics were granted very limited discretion (McKee *et al.*, 1998). As such, Kyrgyzstan inherited no '...critical mass of individuals skilled in policy development or implementation' (McKee *et al.*, 1998: 142).

A consistent policy framework was required, in order to co-ordinate local and donor reform efforts. In 1994 the Kyrgyz Ministry of Health signed an agreement with the WHO Regional Office for Europe and formed a team of around 50 local experts to work with representatives from donor agencies in developing a master plan for health care services. Table 7.1 provides an indication of the range of organizations contributing to this formal policy community. This can be considered a policy transfer network; an '...action-oriented phenomenon set up with the specific intention of engineering policy change' (Evans and Davies, 1999: 376).

The result was an ambitious reform programme, the Manas Plan, comprising a set of objectives to be phased in over a ten-year time horizon and a training programme for key staff with responsibility for implementation (Manas Programme Unit, 1995). In the short term, it was recognized that the economy could no longer support the inherited stock of hospitals that locked resources into the acute sector at the expense of public health and primary care. A rationalization plan that added detail to the original Manas programme is currently in the process of implementation (Know How Fund Team, 1996; Street and Haycock, 1999). A health insurance fund, the Kassa, has been created in an effort to secure alternative sources of finance. It is unclear whether this has generated additional income, but it appears to have been successful in promoting change in clinical practice within hospitals.

While progress is evident with regard to these aspects of the Manas programme, reform of the primary care sector has been less obvious. At independence, primary care was poorly developed in Kyrgyzstan. Rural areas were served by a network of

Feldsher and Accoucher Stations (FAPs), staffed by midwives and nurses who offered consultation on health problems and preventive services, but little by way of medical or surgical interventions. Polyclincs served larger populations and employed doctors but offered a limited range of services because of a lack of equipment and skilled clinical staff. Polyclinics tended to act more as referral centres than primary care providers (Borowitz and O'Dougherty, 1997). Rates of referral to the hospital sector were seen as unnecessarily high, but unavoidable in the absence of alternative forms of provision.

Table 7.1   The health policy transfer network in Kyrgyzstan

Kyrgyzstan	Donors
Ministry of Health	WHO Regional Office for Europe
	DANIDA
Manas Programme Unit	Deutshe Gessellschaft fur Technische
> Central level advisors	Zusammernarbeit
> Regional level advisors	Swiss Federal Office for Foreign Economic Assistance
	Swiss Red Cross
	Turkish International Co-operation Agency
Medical Profession	UK Know How Fund
	United Nations Development Programme
	US Agency for International Development
	World Bank

The Manas Plan proposed strengthening polyclinics by transforming them into Rural Primary Health Care Centres (RPHCs) in rural areas and Primary Health Care Groups in urban areas (UPHGs). These were to be staffed by a range of health professionals including general practitioners, nurses, midwives, and paediatricians. It was intended that RPHCs provide a supporting role to FAPs in rural areas and that UPHGS provide a first port of call for the urban population. Over time, it was envisaged that these organizations would operate in a role similar to that of UK fundholding practices:

> In the long-term, as RPHCs and UPHGs as budget-holders contract with autonomous/private hospitals, the patients will be referred to the contracted secondary care providers ... Primary health care providers will also be fundholders and this will ensure them avoiding unnecessary referrals. (Manas Programme Unit, 1996: 81).

To this end a pilot scheme, led by the USAID, was established in the Issyk-Kul region of Kyrgyzstan, supported by a clinical training programme and investment in medical equipment. Practices received a budget from which to purchase specialty consultations, laboratory tests and hospital services. The population was free to select the practice with which it enrolled. As with the UK proposals it was argued that:

The combination of free choice and fundholding creates economic incentives for [fundholders] to provide high quality care for their patients but also to serve as a gatekeeper, reducing referrals for more specialized services such as hospital care (Borowitz and O'Dougherty, 1997: 17).

In the next section, consideration is given to why this policy was adopted and whether it is likely to be successfully transferred.

General Practice Fundholding in Kyrgyzstan

Universal implementation of fundholding in Krygyzstan has not yet occurred. In this section, three alternative theoretical frameworks are applied to investigate why fundholding has not yet been established other than in the pilot region, although plans for implementation in two other regions are time tabled for completion in 2003 (www.imf.org/external/np/pfp/2000/kgz/01/index.htm, accessed March 2000). The three frameworks provide different 'lenses' for examining the problem. In turn these are:

- the 'top-down' rational decision-making model;
- public choice theory; and,
- indirect coercive transfer.

The 'Top-Down' Rational Decision-making Model

Dolowitz and Marsh (1996: 356) note that '…much of the literature on policy transfer assumes that actors involved in transfer are rational and calculating'. This case study can be analysed by making a similar assumption. Two 'rational' explanations can be advanced to explain why fundholding will not be established in Kyrgyzstan. First, the conditions required to make fundholding a success were not realized in Kyrgyzstan. Secondly, new evidence suggests that the incentives introduced by the fundholding scheme have proved less influential than originally anticipated.

As regards the conditions for success, the fundholding project in Kyrgyzstan was ambitious in proposing a substantial structural break from the past organization of primary care. But specific conditions were lacking. Most importantly, there was a lack of trained staff to implement the policy as Kyrgyzstan has no history of general practice. The reform plan indicated that RPHCs and UPHGs would be '…staffed with therapists, paediatricians and, if possible, obstetricians at the initial stage *until general practitioners are made available*' (Manas Programme Unit, 1995: 79, emphasis added). GPs are still being trained as primary care providers and there remain substantial difficulties in encouraging GPs to practice in parts of the country other than the capital city. Fundholding in the UK built on an established tradition of primary care practice, but even then it was not embraced by all GPs. To expect a newly created profession to take on this challenging role in Kyrgyzstan may be overly optimistic.

Another important condition for policy transfer – and implementation – is that all relevant actors are included in the process. The development of the Manas Plan took place within the Ministry of Health with little contact with other government departments. As with other former Soviet republics, the Kyrgyz Ministry of Health is not a particularly strong ministry (McKee *et al.*, 1998). Any aspects of the reform programme with financial implications would have required the approval of the Ministry of Finance. For fundholding to succeed, significant changes would have been required in the way that funding was allocated through the Kyrgyzstan. It was only after the reform programme was published that efforts were made to discuss the ideas with the representatives from the Ministry of Finance.

Moreover, significant reform generally requires substantial investment. For example, the package of health sector reforms introduced in the UK in 1991 resulted in NHS expenditure increasing from 5.7 per cent of GDP in 1990 to 6.7 per cent in 1992. Those running the Issyk-Kul pilot claimed the scheme was a success, however, it was supported by investment in training, medical equipment and an eight-month consumer choice campaign to educate the population about the advantages of the scheme (Borowitz and O'Dougherty, 1997). Hence the question arises as to whether these positive effects were attributable to the scheme itself or to the substantial injection of resources that accompanied it. Given the investment requirements, could Kyrgyzstan afford a general roll-out of the scheme?

With regard to the evidence base, Stone (1999: 54) suggests that '...ideally, decision-makers would look to policy lessons once sufficient evidence had accumulated in order to make valid comparisons'. However, what constitutes sufficient evidence? In the early years of fundholding in the UK, the Conservative government claimed great success for the scheme and a number of empirical studies reported positive findings. For example, a study of fundholding practices in Scotland revealed a significant reduction in referral rates (Howie *et al.*, 1995). Fundholders also began to diversify their practices by providing new services (e.g. physiotherapy) and developing specialist outreach clinics (Corney, 1994). A comparison of fundholding and non-fundholding practices in Lincolnshire found that the former achieved better cervical cytology uptake, child health and pre-school surveillance and undertook higher amounts of minor surgery (Baines and Whynes, 1996). But other studies contradicted these conclusions. A comparative study of practices in the Oxford region found no evidence that hospital referrals were influenced by budget holding (Coulter and Bradlow, 1993). In a follow-up study it was found that, three years into the scheme, NHS referral rates by General Practice Fundholding had actually increased slightly (Surender *et al.*, 1995). Hence the UK evidence is equivocal about the incentive effects of fundholding.

Even if reductions in referral rates were evident, questions were raised in the UK about whether they could be attributed to fundholding at all. Fundholding was a voluntary scheme and it may be that those practices that participated would have been successful anyway. In an examination of the possibility of selection bias, it was concluded that '...practices obtaining fundholding status in the early waves were those most capable of achieving success as officially assessed' (Baines and Whynes, 1996: 137). Moreover, innovations were not exclusive to fundholding practices. Practices were reviewing prescribing protocols and investing in new facilities long before fundholding was introduced (Corney, 1994). Following a review of the scheme, the NAO concluded that fundholders made relatively modest changes to patient benefits and may not have provided sufficient improvements to justify their higher cost (Audit Commission, 1996). When it came to power, the Labour government (NHS Executive, 1997: 33) announced it was to abandon fundholding:

> Despite its limitations, many innovative GPs and their fund managers have used the fundholding scheme to sharpen the responsiveness of some hospital services and to extend the range of services available in their own surgeries. But the fundholding scheme has also proved bureaucratic and costly. It has allowed development to take place in a fragmented way, outside a coherent strategic plan. It has artificially separated responsibility for emergency and planned care, and given advantage to some patients at the expense of others.

If they had taken stock of the conflicting evidence emanating from the UK research community and the withdrawal of official support for the scheme, policy-makers in Kyrgyzstan would have been less likely to continue promoting the transfer of fundholding to their country. Failure to implement this aspect of the reform programme could be viewed as a rational response to new evidence.

Public Choice Theory

The 'top-down' model assumes that policy objectives are complementary to the motivations of the bureaucrats and other agents involved in the policy process. This assumption may not be satisfied in practice, leading to a failure of policy implementation (Sabatier, 1986). Public choice theory is based on the assumption that bureaucrats are motivated primarily by self-interest. This possibility has been recognized in the policy transfer literature: '...others may adopt lessons for symbolic purposes or as a strategic device to secure political support rather than as a result of improved understanding' (Stone, 1999: 56). Similarly, in an analysis of the transfer of legislation for the disabled, Lightfoot (1999: 39) argues that '...policy makers will only introduce programs consistent with their own values unless their goal is to sabotage a program'. If organizational and private motivations do not coincide, the public choice model may be more illuminating than the 'top-down' model.

The aim of the reform plan, as expressed by the Minister of Health of the Kyrgyz Republic, was to '...develop a consistent health care reform policy and strategies to be able to ensure improvement in the health status of the population' (Manas Programme Unit, 1995: foreword). But suppose the national experts working in the Manas Programme Unit were not primarily motivated by this objective. In a country with high and rising unemployment it is reasonable to suggest that job security is important to bureaucrats. It is therefore possible to construct a more complex utility function that illustrates that if job security is important, it may lead to a failure to implement organizational policy.

An obvious way for a policy advisor to enhance job security is to be recognized as an important source of expertise on a specific topic. By putting a topic on the policy agenda and by building knowledge in the area, individuals are able to strengthen their claims to be valuable members of staff. Those policy advisors working in the Manas Programme Unit were able to do just this. By helping to write the reform plan they enjoyed a degree of control about what topics were included as reform options. By virtue of their membership of the Manas Programme Unit they had access to information resources not available to other members of the policy community or the general public that would allow them to strengthen their knowledge base. For example, members of the Manas Programme Unit were often included on foreign study tours that were sponsored by donor agencies and were designed to transfer Western policy ideas by building local expertise.

Hence, the greater the knowledge possessed by policy advisors, the greater the information asymmetry between advisor and politician. Information asymmetry can be widened in the advisor's favour by placing more complex initiatives on the policy agenda, but this will also limit the chances of successful implementation (Dolowitz and Marsh, 1996). But even problems that arise in the process of transfer can be to the advantage of the advisor, who would benefit from procrastination. Indeed, the implementation of the policy has the potential to undermine the advisor's power base on two counts. First, knowledge gained from elsewhere would be relegated in importance compared to the lessons arising from local implementation, with the local knowledge base becoming more diffuse. Secondly, the policy might not succeed. The policy advisor would be in danger of being blamed for any failure of implementation.

If bureaucrats were interested in job security, public choice theory would predict that advisors would select options for reform that are complex and have little chance of immediate implementation. General practice fundholding fits the bill in this regard. This interpretation of events would suggest that it was proposed not because it was felt that it would enhance the health of the population, but because it held the promise of improving tenure for those employed by the Manas programme.

A similar argument can be constructed to explain why fundholding received the support of the medical profession. Faced with the threat of redundancies from the hospital sector, expansion of the medical profession into primary care provision was an appealing strategy. This meant encroaching on the activities that, traditionally, had been undertaken by FAPs. However, FAPs were regarded unfavourably by the medical establishment, because they employed nurses and midwives, rather than doctors. As such, they fitted uncomfortably in a medically dominated view of the health system. Whilst not as powerful as organized medicine in many Western countries (McKee *et al.*, 1998), the medical profession occupies an elite position in the health sector in Kyrgyzstan. This position is preserved through a number of arrangements. First, most medical students are trained at the Kyrgyz State Medical Academy. This allows the profession to ensure that similar values are passed on to successive generations of graduates. Secondly, there is no independent managerial cadre in the health sector. Doctors fill all management posts, including that of the hospital chief executive, who is referred to as the 'Chief Doctor'. There is no local group able to challenge the power enjoyed by the profession, although a Centre for Health Management was established in 1997 to rectify this problem in the long term. Finally, donor representatives typically visit the same people when undertaking situational analyses and when developing proposals for reform. The profession is able to control both the local agenda and donor perceptions of what solutions might be deemed acceptable. The failure to ensure broad representation from the health care community when developing the local 'epistemic community' is likely to result in the exclusion of various interests and options from the policy agenda. If those working in FAPs had been involved in the policy network, it may be that alternatives to the fundholding model would have been recommended.

Indirect Coercive Transfer

The preceding discussion considers the Kyrgyz health sector as largely autonomous. But this ignores the broader policy context and the motivations of the donor agencies offering support to Kyrgyzstan. This section explores the possibility that fundholding was an example of indirect coercive transfer (Dolowitz and Marsh, 1996).

Those proposals that make it onto the policy agenda are likely to be consistent with the prevailing ideologies of influential policy actors. Much of the reform process in Kyrgyzstan is driven by the need for support from the WB and the IMF, both of which are encouraging Kyrgyzstan to liberalize its economy. This is evidenced by the Kyrgyz government's request for financial support from the IMF, outlined in the Memorandum of Economic and Financial Policies. This describes a programme of:

> Macro-economic support and structural reform in order to launch an economic recovery driven by the private sector ... The principal goal of the program will be to continue our efforts to lay the basis for sustainable economic growth and establish a fully-fledged market economy (www.imf.org/external/np/loi/2000/kg/01/index.htm, 2000).

Similarly, the ideological stance of donor agencies will be influential in framing domestic policy options. Market based solutions pervade the strategies promoted by USAID, which has funded a range of projects in Kyrgyzstan, including fundholding and the mass privatization project that resulted in some 1,000 enterprises being transferred from state control. (www.info.usaid.gov/ countries/kg/kyr.htm, 2000).

USAID is explicit about the type of social stabilization policies it would recommend for implementation, 'USAID efforts focus on health and housing with the aim of introducing market-based approaches that increase individual choice and rely when possible on the private sector (www.info.usaid.gov/ pubs/cp98/eni/countries/kg.htm, 2000). This suggests that it is unlikely that public sector solutions would be entertained or promoted by USAID. If, in addition to

Policy Transfer in Global Perspective

improving the welfare of the Kyrgyz people, USAID has a secondary agenda, such as promoting US interests in the region, this ideological stance would be understandable. USAID emphasized this point in its 1998 Congressional budget presentation:

> There is an interest to work with reformers in Kyrgyzstan to build and sustain a democratic and market-oriented country that could serve as an example to neighbouring countries that seem less committed to these values
> (www.info.usaid.gov/pubs/cp98/eni/countries/kg.htm, 2000).

Opening up the region for US companies is also likely to be an important motivation behind US aid policy. Supported in its application by USAID, Kyrgyzstan was the first Confederation of Independent States country to join the World Trade Organization (WTO), becoming a member in 1998. The WTO exists to promote free trade and has been criticized for advocating the privatization of traditional public services (Price *et al.*, 1999). In its preparation for the WTO ministerial meeting in 1998, the US Coalition of Service Industries recommended that the General Agreement on Trade in Services (GATS) be revised to provide greater opportunities for US health care service suppliers to penetrate overseas markets. The Coalition's objectives were to encourage more privatization, to promote pro-competitive regulatory reform, and to obtain liberalization. The public sector was viewed as the major barrier to US expansion in foreign health care markets:

> Historically, health care services in many foreign countries have largely been the responsibility of the public sector. This public ownership of health care has made it difficult for US private sector providers to market in foreign countries
> (www.uscsi.org/services_2000_ustr_federal.htm, 2000).

This, then, provides the third explanation for the presence of fundholding on the Kyrgyz policy agenda: the model accords with the ideological stance of USAID. But market-based solutions may not deliver the benefits claimed by their proponents. USAID was highly enthusiastic about the potential benefits of its privatization programme:

> Specific beneficiaries include the hundreds of thousands of citizens of Kyrgyzstan who own shares in newly privatized government enterprises and stand to gain if these new firms increase in value or pay out dividends. Aspiring entrepreneurs stand to benefit from a more comprehensive and more transparent legal environment. The entire population stands to gain from a market-based economic system that creates employment, increases incomes, lowers prices, and expands individual choice
> (www.info.usaid.gov/pubs/cp98/eni/countries/kg.htm, 2000).

There is no recognition that holding shares is risky or that the benefits are unlikely to be distributed evenly among the population. In particular, market strategies are likely to worsen the position of the poorest members of society. Indeed, to date, macro-economic reform has failed to deliver tangible benefits to the majority of the Kyrgyz population, as the United Nations Development Programme comments:

> Macro-economic stabilization ... did not translate into an improvement in living standards for most people. The price of transitions has turned out to be high, and a significant part of Kyrgyzstani has become poorer (www.undp.bishkek.su/english/country.html, 2000).

Similarly, fundholding may fail to improve the health of the Kyrgyz population and it is unlikely that increased consumer choice will encourage efficient behaviour by fundholders. It is more probable that competition among fundholders will take the form of 'cream skimming', whereby people with a high risk of incurring future medical expenditures will be discouraged from enrolling with the fundholding groups. This discouragement may be through explicit or more subtle means (Newhouse, 1982). The regional administrations may attempt to limit the incentives for such action by setting budgets using a capitation formula that makes some adjustment for individual risk. But because fundholders are likely to be better informed about their (prospective) patient's health than the regional authorities, this will prove an imperfect corrective mechanism. The danger is that a significant proportion of the population will find it difficult to enrol, in the same way that many will be excluded from the health insurance programme also being promoted by USAID. The fact that 20 per cent of the population in Issyk-kul have failed to enrol (www.info.usaid.gov/pubs/cp98/eni/countries/kg.htm, 2000) ought to be a cause for concern, particularly as these citizens are likely to be among the most socially disadvantaged.

This type of behaviour is precisely what is observed in the US health insurance market and what motivated the US government to embark on its major public health insurance programmes for the elderly (Medicare) and the poor (Medicaid) in the 1960s. As a result of these programmes, the public sector plays a major role in the US health care market, accounting for 47 per cent of total US health care expenditure (http://www.who.int/whr/1999/en/annex1.htm, 2000). For USAID to argue for the pre-eminence of market-based solutions is not only to ignore the adverse consequences for universal health care provision but also to overlook the fact that, even in the US, the public sector has been forced to expand its role in the finance and provision of health care to correct the inequities and inefficiencies of the private health care market.

In Conclusion: Policy Transfer as Political Strategy

Why was fundholding considered as a reform option for Kyrgyzstan? Quite possibly it was included in the reform plan more to suggest completeness rather than as a realistic option for implementation. The reform plan attempted to be all encompassing, covering issues such as the rationalization of the hospital sector, alternative sources of financing, and revised central-local relations. To omit discussion of the primary care sector would have been remiss. Fundholding was tagged onto the broader agenda simply because it was in vogue in the UK and USAID, in particular, was keen on the policy because of its emphasis on consumer choice. However, the extent to which policy-makers in Kyrgyzstan agreed with fundholding as an appropriate policy option can be questioned. In view of their difficult economic situation, the Kyrgyz were reliant on the support of external agencies and would have been under pressure to develop a reform plan that reflected donor perceptions of the situation and way forward. Lacking an established 'epistemic community', the Kyrgyz lacked a knowledge base from which to reject donor suggestions.

If the objectives of policy had been more sharply articulated, alternative instruments of reform may have been considered. The potential to reduce referrals was seen as the main problem to be addressed, but the population was probably more concerned about the access to basic medical treatment. Effort may have been better spent responding directly to the health care needs of the population, for example by financing courses of antibiotics to treat tuberculosis rather than by the current practice of hospitalizing patients for extended periods. In view of this, the government's promise to provide '...sufficient funding for control and prevention of various diseases and for widespread vaccinations for children' (www.imf.org/external/np/pfp/2000/kgz/01/index.htm, 2000) is welcome.

The policy agenda was also limited at an early stage by the composition of the policy transfer network. This was comprised of donor agencies, some of which were explicit about their ideological support for the introduction of market-based mechanisms to the health sector. Local representation was dominated by the medical profession, which would have welcomed private sector initiatives because of the employment and income generating opportunities these promised. If the policy network had been widened to include those already working in the primary care sector or the general public it is likely that a different set of problems and reform options would have been identified. In the future, the network may be widened. Broader representation may be secured following the creation of a Centre for Health Management, as a result of USAID's assistance in helping to establish a nursing association, and through efforts, sponsored by USAID and UNDP, to encourage greater citizen participation in the democratic process.

What does the preceding discussion add to the policy transfer literature? Four main contributions can be identified. First, at first sight it seems that the reform programme as a whole was undertaken voluntarily by the Kyrgyz, albeit in collaboration with external donor agencies, in response to severe economic crisis. But, having invited external assistance, it is less clear whether specific policy proposals were entered into voluntarily. Fundholding may have been voluntarily adopted if it was believed that it would be the best strategy to promote the health of the population or because local bureaucrats and doctors felt it would best advance their own interests. But the policy choice also reflected indirect coercive pressures by the USAID pushing an ideological agenda. In practice it is likely that voluntary and indirect coercive transfer merged in this instance. It may well be that this is the norm, particularly when donor agencies are part of the transfer network. After all, transfer is more likely to be successful if coercing agents convince the policy transfer network that the transfer is in their interests or if the alternatives are perceived to be less palatable.

Secondly, the case study suggests that the problem of delimiting the domain of policy transfer may not unduly damage the possibility of analysis. Selection bias has been identified as a key weakness in the policy transfer literature because 'perfect fit' cases are more likely to be the subject of investigation (Evans and Davies, 1999). The policy examined in this chapter has yet to be fully implemented, although there are plans to extend the programme to the Bishkek and Chui regions. But despite the fact that implementation has not yet occurred, the chapter demonstrates that it is possible to examine the process of policy transfer, if not the final outcome.

Thirdly, a crucial message emanating from this study is that the interpretation placed on examples of policy transfer may depend on the perspective adopted by the analyst. This has important ramifications for policy transfer analysis because it raises the prospect of analytical bias. Most examples of policy transfer assume a rational model of policy making (Dolowitz and Marsh, 1996). In this case, the rational model would predict policy rejection. However, the policy may be implemented if ideology rather than evidence drives the process. The analytical position may predetermine the conclusions that are drawn from empirical analysis about the nature of the process and outcome of policy transfer.

Finally, the case study suggests that the subject matter of policy transfer does not require its own theoretical basis distinct from the remainder of political science. It has been argued that '...policy transfer analysts do not have the benefit of a common idiom or a unified theoretical or methodological discourse from which lessons can be drawn and hypotheses developed' (Evans and Davies, 1999: 361). But a unified theoretical framework may undermine understanding of policy transfer if different theoretical perspectives have the potential to offer different insights into the political process.

Chapter 8

Transferring Higher Education Policies to Mexico: The Case of the Technological Universities

Pedro Flores-Crespo

Introduction

This chapter evaluates higher educational policy change in Mexico using the policy transfer framework. It is organized into three parts. In the first part it will be shown that because of its intrinsic characteristics, education policy can function either as a channel or a means for moving ideas from one place to another as objects of transfer. It is precisely in this context that education has become the subject of unprecedented international cooperation and is consequently a fertile policy arena for the study of policy transfer. External assistance in the educational sector has also led to a system of entangled relations between the governments of less developed nations, international agencies and financial organizations. As a consequence of the economic crises experienced by Latin American countries, some states are facing the dilemma of either remaining the main providers of educational services or embarking upon reforms in which state intervention is restrained and public funding limited. Such reforms meet significant political resistance as education in countries such as Mexico has historically proved the key vehicle for social and economic development. Indeed, several Mexican scholars subscribe to the view that the 1990s university reforms were imposed by financial international agencies such as the WB, the IMF or OECD (see, for example, Marín, 1998 and González-Casanova, 2001). Even though the influential role of such organizations should not be underestimated, it is equally important for policy analysts to pay careful attention to the role of national actors. For these above reasons, it is argued that education policy in Mexico represents a fertile policy arena for investigating the policy transfer approach.

The second part of this chapter observes that the Mexican government created a vocational-oriented model of tertiary education by emulating the model of the Institute Universitaire de Technologie in France. In the development and implementation of the Mexican Technological Universities (hereafter referred to as UTs) the imperatives of the global epoch as well as the social purposes of educational policy sought to be reconciled. As the vocational courses of the UTs responded to the needs of local employers, it was expected that vocationally oriented education reform would help to stimulate regional economic development in some of the relatively poor areas of Mexico. It was also claimed that short course programmes could dramatically reduce the opportunity cost of studying and that the practical orientation of the curriculum would facilitate the transition from school to work. The creation of the UTs has certainly enhanced the quality of life of many individuals (see Flores-Crespo, 2002a and b), notwithstanding the structural inequalities in Mexico, which still limit the effectiveness of education policy as an instrument of development. In contrast with France, a much lower number of young people in Mexico successfully complete their technical studies. Moreover, drop-out rates seem to vary in accordance with regional income disparities in Mexico, and, sadly, in some cases, the naïve attitudes of some UT students are associated with their socially and culturally deprived background.

The third part of the chapter explores the implementation lessons that can be drawn from Mexican experience for other countries that share similar development problems. It will be argued that if policy-makers and practitioners really wish to make education relevant for development they need to conceptualize education within a broader perspective and thus introduce reform that will maximize the potential of knowledge for development purposes.

Understanding Education Policy in Mexico

To venture into the study of policy transfer with education as a subject of analysis involves several intellectual challenges. Owing to its capacity to help knowledge dissemination, education can be used as a *means* of transferring particular ideas from one place to another, but it can also be the *object* of transfer through the introduction of new pedagogical practices or educational reforms. This dual character of education can be investigated simultaneously within the policy transfer process. The most recent investment policies in education help to illustrate this claim. The WB and the influential financial leader George Soros have recently committed themselves to fund The New Economic School of Moscow (NES), which aims to help 'Russia and the other members of the Commonwealth of Independent States (CIS) develop all aspects of modern economics – education, academic research, policy analysis, and the training of professionals' (*Transition*, 2001: 6). The NES was founded in 1992 and it is the first non-state graduate school in Russia. While the Bank is investing US$250,000 a year for at least the next three years into the budget of the NES, Soros is providing US$350,000 a year for the next five years. Hence, the knowledge provided by the NES constitutes a way of diffusing 'modern' education practices and pedagogy in economics within a former socialist state that is historically biased towards Marxist ideas. Of course, this is not to say that students are subjects determined to act by following a particular ideology, as this assumption neglects the critical capacity of individuals to learn and to deal critically with their own reality (see Freire, 1993 and 1996).

Analyzing education reform through the study of policy transfer predisposes policy analysts to investigate international cooperation and external assistance in the educational sector. According to Phillip Coombs (1985: 287), there was a remarkable growth in inter-country educational cooperation in the immediate post-war years:

> Hundreds of governmental, intergovernmental, and nongovernmental organizations the world over became involved in cooperative educational activities, especially in connection with student and faculty exchanges and with material and technical assistance to Third World countries to spur educational and other forms of development.

As a consequence of the economic crises of the 1980s, this unprecedented upsurge of international cooperation in education created a new complexity of relations between developing countries and international organizations. Faced with rising international interest rates, hyperinflation, recession, and debt crisis, Latin American countries were left in a state of economic disarray (Torres and Puiggrós, 1997). To overcome this situation, international agencies such as the IMF and the WB exhorted governments in the region to adopt structural adjustment policies (Samoff, 1994). These policy recommendations included the reduction of government expenditure, currency devaluations, reduction in import tariffs, and an increase in public and private savings. These measures were aimed at reducing drastically the participation of the state in economic and social affairs and shifting industrial and agricultural production toward exports.

As the role of the state contracted, concerns emerged regarding the future of public education. This was more evident in Latin America where the nation-state has traditionally played an active role in extending, through education, social benefits to vast sectors of the population. Mass schooling, for example, was viewed as a means of building a responsible citizen, a skilled labour force and also of increasing social mobility. This was particularly evident in Mexico where education was one of the 'pillars of the social policy of the post-revolutionary administrations' (OECD, 1997: 29). For example, the total number of students in the educational system rose from 1.3 million in 1930 to more than 30 million in 2000 (PNE, 2001). The 'hand of the state' was undoubtedly crucial to this extraordinary period of growth.

It is also worth noting that Article 3 of the Mexican Constitution establishes that education policy should be designed '...to develop harmoniously all the faculties of human beings, fostering a love of the homeland, awareness of international solidarity, independence and justice' (OECD, 1997: 33). This Article also states that '...all kinds of education provided by the state will be free'. Hence when a policy analyst engages in the study of policy transfer in Mexico, it is necessary to bear in mind two key issues. First, it is the notion of the 'conditioned' state that helps us to understand the contradictions in public policy formation. Secondly, as Torres and Puiggrós (1997: 21) observe the institutional identity of the state is bound up in its role as a promoter of development and social change. Hence, the globalizing elements of education reform represent a challenge to the traditional development role of the Mexican state and provide a source of tension as the 'hollowing out of the state' progresses (see Latapí 1996, 1997, 1998 and

2000). If the state loses its role as the main promoter of educational provision and alternative private delivery systems undertake this responsibility, it is very likely that education will become an increasingly politically sensitive issue for policy transfer analyses.

When a group of international experts commissioned by the OECD visited Mexico with the aim of gathering information for the *Review of National Policies for Education,* they were '...struck by how quickly any debate or initiative affecting higher education turned political' (OECD, 1997: 139). Though they recognized that this was not exclusive to Mexico, they noted that '...several factors seem to have contributed to this process of politicization' (ibid: 140). According to Torres and Puiggrós (1997: 11), apart from its unquestionable contribution to social development, Mexico's educational system has also been '...dependent on the consolidation of the corporatist state as a mode of governance and political legitimation'. This point is supported by some authors who argue that the astronomic growth in higher education, which was much higher than the rate of population growth during the 1970s, was a useful strategy used by the Mexican government to co-opt dissident students and teachers of previous decades (see Vaughan, 1975; Torres, 1991; Ordorika, 1996). As a result of the frenetic expansion of the 1970s a period of 'improvization' emerged because academic structures and the role of teachers were not redefined as the disproportionate growth in student enrolment and teachers' recruitment took place (OECD, 1997: 139-140).

In addition, some public universities became political arenas in which student activists proclaimed that the prime role of the university was not to provide education but to change society. For Levy (1994: 260), various university groups have 'powerfully' affected policies and, in so doing, '...they often block innovation ardently pursued by other sectors of the university'. Levy's observation highlights the recurrent tension between two distinct conceptions of university reform. One has been labelled the 'modernist' perspective and the other the 'populist' perspective. Ornelas and Post (1992) argue that the former includes the efficient integration of graduates into the labour force with the purpose of meeting the needs of the economy (or the needs of employers). The 'modernist' perspective embraces greater student competition for university places based on standardized examinations and it is suggested that the direct cost of studying should be paid by the direct beneficiaries of university education rather than by the state. Hence, they argue for 'top-up' tuition fees. In contrast, the 'populist' perspective seeks broader social change as a result of university reform. Its proponents emphasize 'social classes, not individuals, as the clientele of the university' (Ornelas and Post, 1992: 279). Populist reformers generally reject any increase in tuition fees and favour the widest possible access to the education system. This leftist reform project aims at establishing the university system as an instrument of popular struggle and emphasizes the importance of broadening the role of students, professors and workers in university governance.

It is argued in this chapter that ideological polarization can lead to irrational policy-making. Drawing constructive lessons from successful exemplars in the international domain can be a wholly rational approach to policy-making as long as the non-indigenous lessons that are drawn are culturally compatible with the indigenous context. For example, if a university succeeds in making higher education accessible to the masses by drawing constructive lessons from other overseas institutions then this is to be applauded. For instance, some Scottish universities organize summer access schemes '…to help youngsters for whom university would otherwise be an unattainable goal'. These schemes consist of short orientation courses to introduce disciplines to students as well as to allow them to become familiar with facilities and life on campus (*The Guardian Education*, 16 July 2002).

A set of observations should be highlighted from this brief introduction to education policy in Mexico to provide an understanding of the policy environment. First, the education policy arena is both a site of significant state transformation in which the traditional role of the state is being challenged and a site of struggle between populists and modernizers. Secondly, an open-minded approach should be adopted in studying policy transfer within the educational sector. As stated above, it is necessary to bear in mind the dual role of education as a *means* and as an *object* of development within policy transfer processes. Furthermore, it is crucial to adopt rational policy analysis when reviewing the policy recommendations of international agencies and their possible outcomes as the inappropriate transfer of education policy can have a devastating impact on educational facilities in less advanced nations. Finally, as Will Hutton and Anthony Giddens (2001) put it, as everything seems in question in a globalizing world, it is necessary to adopt an imaginative, reflexive approach to public policy rather than conforming to old dogmas.

Transferring Modernization: The Mexican Technological Universities

The case of the Technological Universities constitutes an interesting example of policy transfer in the education policy arena. The main aims of the policy were twofold: first to respond effectively to the economic challenges of globalization; and, secondly, to broaden educational opportunities for citizens in the relatively poor regions of Mexico. The following section considers why Mexican policy-makers engaged in policy transfer.

Why Policy Transfer? Globalization and Higher Education

During the administration of President Carlos Salinas (1989-1994), modernization was the main element of the national development strategy. Moreover, within this strategy education policy was viewed as a key instrument of economic reconstruction for shifting Mexico from one state of development to another. According to the National Development Programme, 1989-1994, the transformation of education constituted an '…indispensable condition for modernizing the country' (PND, 1989: 102). Significant changes were therefore implemented in the educational sector, modifying both the broader aims of higher education and the institutional organization of the university sector. Scholars noted that the traditional concern for expansion and universal consumption was substituted with a concern for quality and efficiency (Ordorika, 1996). Hence, an emphasis was placed on the introduction of planning and coordination instruments, as well as teaching quality assessment exercises and outcomes-oriented schemes to inform the distribution of public funding (Rodríguez, 2002). The content of public discourse emphasized the contribution of higher education policy to economic development as it was increasingly argued that global economic competitiveness rested on the knowledge and skill of the workforce (Brown, 2001). Hence, the content of the curriculum was transformed in order to produce a virtuous cycle between schooling and the economy. In sum, technical education was regarded as a key policy instrument for achieving higher rates of economic growth in Mexico. As the OECD (1997: 179) reported:

> The effectiveness of a modern economy depends to a considerable extent on its technicians and middle managers: within the North American economic area, the development of these intermediate qualifications may in the medium term represent Mexico's opportunity. In particular, trained technicians and middle managers are better suited to the needs and capacities of smaller enterprises which represent the bulk of the Mexican economy.

The Secretariat of Public Education therefore decided that the development of technical education would help to bridge the technological gap that exists between advanced countries and Mexico (SEP, 1991). Hence, with the technical assistance of Professor Phillip Coombs, the secretary of public education, scanned the education reforms which had been introduced in countries experiencing high economic growth such as the United States, Germany, Great Britain, France and Japan. It was found that the *Institute Universitaire de Technologie* (IUTs) in France was '...the most adequate' option for adaptation in the Mexican context (CGUT, 2000a: 10).

Despite the disillusionment in the 1970s with manpower forecasting due to its over-rigid view (Blaug, 1974), and its ambiguous methodology (Hinchliffe, 1987, Lorey, 1993); it was thought that the potential of Mexico's economic growth depended on matching the education supply with the future demand for professionals (Reséndiz, 1998). This presumption was evidenced with data from the International Standard Classification of Education (ISCED) developed by UNESCO, which showed that Mexico lacked technically qualified workers in comparison with developed countries (see Table 8.1). As the former sub-secretary of higher education in Mexico, Daniel Reséndiz (1998) observes, the creation of the UTs provided a new cohort of professionals with 'intermediate' qualifications.

It is worth noting that the ISCED classifies higher education programmes into three levels. *Level 5* refers to academic programmes leading to an award not eqūivalent to a first university degree. This is sub-divided into two ('A' and 'B') sublevels. The former comprises of programmes that are largely theoretically based and are intended to provide sufficient qualification for gaining entry into advanced research programmes and professions with high skills requirements. The latter includes programmes that are generally more occupationally specific than ISCED '5A' programmes. It is precisely in this latter category where the UT's educational model falls. *Level 6* programmes consist of those leading to a first university degree or an equivalent qualification. While *Level 7* includes programmes leading to a postgraduate university degree or equivalent qualification (UNESCO, 1997). Table 8.1 supports Reséndiz's observations, but also shows that, if Mexico wishes to catch up with the economic pattern of advanced nations, it needs to train professionals not only at ISCED *Level 6*, but also at levels six and seven.

France, the nation that Mexican policy-makers have used as a reference point for developing its higher education model, registers the highest proportion of workers holding *Level 7* ISCEDs (18 per cent). This is clearly at odds with the Mexican government's focus on investing more in *Level '5B'* than levels six and seven. The former sub-secretary of higher education scientific research explains that the stock of highly qualified personnel is outstripping the actual requirements of Mexico's labour structure (Reséndiz, 1998). Thus, in order to avoid social and political conflicts and regressive economic effects (i.e. over-training, and/or brain drain), adjustments on the supply side have to be introduced. Nevertheless, gearing human resources towards specific needs in the labour market also reveals the limited capacity of an economic system for providing valuable employment opportunities for highly skilled professionals. This highlights the importance of conducting structural changes not only in the education sector but also within the whole economic system of a less advanced nation.

Searching for Solutions

The creation of the UTs can be defined as a case of 'negotiated transfer' in response to economic interdependence, externalities, perceptions of the performance of other nations, and the impact of technological change. Negotiated transfer occurs through the voluntary agency of politicians and policy-makers who devise transfer strategies when they perceive that their country is falling behind its neighbours or competitors. In the case of the UTs, policy change may be understood as a consequence of both a changing macro-economic environment affecting educational systems and a voluntary process of policy learning. It should be stressed that Mexican policy-makers were proactive in responding to global changes in educational systems. They actively sought to draw lessons from French educational experience. However, although the French educational system possesses some remarkable qualities that are often a source of inspiration and emulation, the Mexican government failed to explain why it adopted the *Institutes Universitaire de Technologie* (IUTs) model, if, as the SEP recognised, similar characteristics were found in other educational systems. The US, Japan, Germany and Great Britain, have all created higher education institutions where intensive courses (of two or three years in length) of this type are taught. Indeed they all have courses with: well-equipped laboratories; strong links with industry and business; entrance examinations; and, highly qualified teachers. Moreover, these colleges have allowed students the opportunity to pursue further studies such as bachelor degrees (SEP, 1991). Given this, why did the Mexican government adopt the IUT model?

Table 8.1   The employment structure in Mexico in comparison with a sample of developed countries

Type of qualification	ISCED level	Percentage of population employed in the formal economy			
		Mexico	*Italy*	*Switzerland*	*France*
Directors & professionals	6 & 7	3.7	10	17	18
Intermediate occupations	5	3.2	15	17	16
Operators & technicians	3	10.6	35	30	31
Low skilled technicians & workmen	2	82.5	40	36	35

Source: Reséndiz, 1998: 60.

The answer lies in the historical influence of the French system. According to Tünnermann (1996), when Latin American universities were reformed in the eighteenth century, they followed the Napoleonic model of education. This imported model consisted basically of substituting universities with professional schools and concentrating scientific research in institutes and academies. At that time it was thought that the cultural and professional training of the bourgeoisie within special institutes would ensure both the unity and the political stability of the state (Tünnermann, 1996: 21). Latin American elites clearly had a fascination in this period for all things French. At the end of the nineteenth and the beginning of the twentieth centuries, the positivism of the French sociologist, Auguste Comte, arrived in Mexico thanks to a Mexican political and intellectual elite who had travelled to Europe to study undergraduate and postgraduate courses. Subsequently, a positivist approach was introduced as a mode of teaching in all Mexican universities (Pallán *et al.* 1995: 14). It is worth noting that political actors primarily promoted the imposition of the positivist approach on the Mexican education system. International financial institutions or other international organizations had yet to emerge. Hence, historically national actors have been no strangers to transferring policies voluntarily. It is also worth noting that the education secretary who proposed the transportation of the UT model to Mexico studied in France. Hence it is possible to identify a continuous exchange of ideas between Mexican policy-makers and their French counterparts. In sum, policy transfer historically begets policy transfer contemporaneously.

Defining the Public Policy Problem

There are more cross-cultural influences in the world than is typically acknowledged by those alarmed by the prospect of cultural subversion (Sen, 1999). However, recognizing this trend does not preclude evaluating the limitations of applying non-indigenous policies from developed countries in less developed countries such as Mexico. Attempting to catch up with economic development in advanced nations through human capital formation raises big questions concerning the way in which structural inequalities in developing countries can be addressed. Vocational-oriented models of higher education can certainly play a key role in the formation of skills for competing in a global economy, but it is necessary to pay primary attention to how knowledge can enrich the lives of human beings. Although President Vicente Fox has ranked Mexico's economy ninth in the world (*La Jornada*, 22 July 2002), only one in five Mexicans aged 19-23 are enrolled in a university programme (PNE, 2001). Moreover, despite the relative increase in higher education enrolment during the last decade there has been a significant increase in people excluded from provision. According to the *Observatorio Ciudadano de la Educación* (a citizen's education watchdog), while in 1990 there were 6.7 million persons without access to university education, by 2000, this number had increased to nearly 8 million (OCE, 2000a). This statistic reveals a serious problem of inequity. What barriers are preventing young people from entering public or private higher education institutions? In order to explain this, it is necessary to pay careful attention to both the severe economic restrictions that most Mexicans face and the controversial public policies that have been formulated to finance public education (Márquez, 1999).

Between 1984 and 1996 household incomes in Mexico have fallen considerably (OCE, 2000b). In the aftermath of the economic collapse of 1995, almost two million jobs were lost and real wages in manufacturing fell by almost 40 per cent (Faux and Mishel, 2001). At the same time public expenditure in advanced levels of higher education has decreased significantly. From 1994 to 1998, public expenditure per student in the upper secondary and higher education levels fell by 25 per cent and 46.3 per cent, respectively (OCE, 2000c). The development of these policies was strongly predicated on the WB's thesis that public subsidization at the advanced education level is regressive because university students in this sector normally come from richer households (WB, 1994). Hence to make-up for the reduction of public funds it was proposed that this cohort should be charged for higher education services (see Barnés, 1999). This policy was clearly unwise at a time when Mexico needed to increase its proportion of highly qualified citizens (Ruiz, 1997).

The high drop-out rate from the higher education system in Mexico was also an issue of great concern. The SEP (1991) reported that the graduation rate in Mexican universities was only 50 per cent. High drop-out rates are normally attributable to economic problems. As the OECD (1997: 169), notes, '...young people cannot assume the cost of their studies or have to work at the same time in order to pay their way, this merely exposes the unfairness of the system'. However, students also experience problems with traditional teaching and learning methods:

> ... students find it difficult to adapt to the demands placed upon them, this must raise doubts either about the admissions procedure or about teaching methods. Another cause may be that, for some of the population, especially those of more modest origins the prospect of such lengthy studies is discouraging, which brings us back to the lack of differentiation in course lengths (Ibid).

It is important to bear in mind that all these inequities do not follow a homogenous pattern. Educational, economic and social disadvantages tend to reflect the deep regional disparity that has characterised Mexico's historical development. In educational terms, for instance, the consumption of higher education is very uneven across the Mexican republic. While the richer states such as Nuevo León or Mexico City have enrolment rates for first degrees of over 25 per cent, the poorest states such as Oaxaca, Chiapas, or Hidalgo have rates of less than 15 per cent (ANUIES, 2000). This means that a young person aged between 20-24 who lives in an affluent region has more chance of coping with tertiary studies than a student in a relatively deprived zone. Moreover, this disparity is broadened by the regional migration of skilled professionals from poor areas to affluent regions (ANUIES, 2000). Hence, special attention needs to be paid to the development of education policy instruments that can help to offset structural inequalities.

Implementing Technological Universities in Mexico

The national aspiration of achieving higher rates of economic growth combined with the urgent need to diversify tertiary education and to meet the educational needs of citizens from the most deprived regions of Mexico encouraged policy-makers to engage in policy transfer. They sought a solution that would deal with both the imperatives of a global economy and the structural inequalities it facilitates. According to the SEP, technological universities are state-government decentralized public bodies that offer two-year programmes leading to a higher university technician qualification. It follows that their aim is to encourage young people to remain in their place of origin and subsequently take up work there, thus contributing to the development of that region (SEP, 2000).

The UTs were an attractive model to the Mexican government for three main reasons. First, it was expected that as the relationship between the UTs and industry became closer, curriculum design would be informed by the needs of local enterprises and would thus be sustainable. Secondly, it was also considered that through privileging practical learning over theoretical knowledge the transition from school to work would be easier for people living in relatively poor areas. Thirdly, it was argued that short academic courses would reduce significantly the opportunity costs of studying, contributing to an increase in graduation rates. In comparison with the other options for higher education, the growth of the UTs' system has been very ambitious (OCE, 2000e). Table 8.2 shows that in relative terms enrolment in UTs has increased by almost 45 per cent, while that of the technological institutes and autonomous universities has been less than 3 and 4 per cent, respectively. Despite this, the number of young people enrolled represents only 1.5 per cent of total enrolment in the higher education system.

Table 8.2   Enrolment in Mexican higher education by sector and type of institution, 1998-2000

Institutions	1998-1999 thousands	1999-2000 thousands	Change (No.)	Change (%)
Public sector	1315.6	1367.1	51.5	3.9
Autonomous universities	816.2	862.0	31.6	3.8
Technological institutes	202.7	273.6	7.2	2.7
Technological universities	20.6	29.8	9.2	44.7
Teacher training schools	144.2	137.1	-5.1	-3.6
Others (e.g. military & naval colleges)	133.9	64.6	8.6	15.4
Private sector	522.3	595.7	73.4	14.1
Total	1837.9	1962.8	124.9	6.8

Source: SEP, 1999 and 2000.

It is evident that the UTs' system has been promoted enthusiastically. While in 1991 only three UTs were created, in 2000 the Mexican government embarked upon the creation of forty-four new educational institutions covering 24 states in the republic. In the 2000-2001 academic year 40,000 students were enrolled, an increase of 34 per cent from the previous year. Since its creation in 1991, the UT system has registered a positive growth in student enrolment. However, it is equally important to note that there is a gap between the official student enrolment and the maximum student capacity in such higher education systems (CGUT, 2000a, b).

The number of places available in the UT system has considerably exceeded demand over time. While in the 1997/98 academic year almost 30,000 places were available in the UT system, by 2000/01, this number had risen to 40,000 places. This trend necessitates some thinking about what measures should be implemented to cope with the evident under-utilization of the UTs' infrastructure. If young people from relatively disadvantaged regions are charged for studying in the UT, as the SEP initially proposed, will it be possible to attract a higher number of youngsters to these universities? This seems unlikely as structural inequalities in Mexico are reproduced in its educational system. For example, drop-out rates vary from 4.2 per cent to 29.4 per cent by UT, which reflects economic regional disparities. According to the CGUT, drop-outs are caused basically by the poor academic background of students and by their limited economic capacity to afford monthly university tuition fees (CGUT, 2000: 21). Graduation rates in the UT system have fallen over time too. While in 1993 62 per cent of students finished their studies successfully, by 2000 this proportion had fallen to 52.7 per cent (CGUT, 2000a). Sadly, this indicator is also significantly lower than that expected by the SEP (80 per cent). This highlights again, the fact that vocational-oriented models of tertiary education should be seen as a key component of a more comprehensive and equitable social policy. However, a realistic vision of what education can do for development within the relatively poor areas of Mexico must be adopted. This discussion of the structural inequalities that characterize the Mexican education system allows for the identification of cultural differences between the UT model and the IUTs in France, which are reflected in the emergence of implementation gaps.

It is expected that as the macro conditions in both nations differ greatly, their respective technical models of higher education will also work differently. Table 8.3 presents some economic and social indicators that help us to contrast the situation in Mexico, as a 'borrower' of education policy, with France, as the 'donor' of the UT model. Even though GDP per capita has increased considerably in Mexico from 1990 to 1999, the minimum wage also fell dramatically. In contrast, in France, the minimum wage doubled in the same period. Moreover, in 1999, a French worker spent less time in his or her job than their Mexican counterparts. This demonstrates that they have the spare time to pursue part-time study. Indeed these statistics provide prima facie evidence that the economic conditions in France seem to be contributing to improvements in the living standard of the people. The capacity of people to live the kind of lives that people have reason to value has to be incorporated, as Amartya Sen (1999) argues, in a broader concept of development which contrasts with narrower views of development that centre on the growth of gross national product, the rise in personal incomes, or with social modernization.

As Table 8.3 reveals, there has been a remarkable increase in the proportion of young people entering university in France, despite the fact that annual government expenditure per student is considerably higher than in Mexico (US$7,177 and US$4,519, respectively). It seems that as France has grown economically, it has also developed an inclusive education system. While in 1990 only 20 per cent of youngsters entered the French higher education system, by 1999 the percentage had risen to 50 per cent. In Mexico, only 20 per cent of young people aged 20-24 entered higher education in 2000.

These inequalities are captured in the Human Development Index (HDI) of both nations. The HDI of Mexico has registered a greater decline than that of France. Coincidentally, this has occurred since the government adopted a modernization strategy.

Table 8.3   Macro economic and social indicators in Mexico and France

	Mexico		France	
	1990	1999	1990	1999
Real GDP per capita (US$)	4,624	8,297	13,961	22,897
Minimum wage (US$)	1,343	768	6,053	12,072
Average hours worked per week	43	45	40	39
Annual expenditure per student in all tertiary education (US$)	-	4,519	-	7,177
Gross enrolment ratio in tertiary education	14	20	25	51
Human development index	0.876	0.790	0.974	0.924

Within such vastly different policy environments, it is not surprising that the IUT system has performed more efficiently than their UT counterparts. In 1990, the French IUTs registered graduation rates of 67 per cent for those students enrolled in a manufacturing-related course and 71 per cent for those who studied a programme related to the tertiary sector of the economy (Villa and Flores-Crespo, 2002). In contrast, the graduation rate in the university system of Mexico was 50 per cent when the UTs were created in 1991 (SEP, 1991), but by 2000 it still remained at the same level (PNE, 2001). Although the graduation rate in the UT system was slightly above the national mean (53 per cent and 50 per cent, respectively), it remained significantly lower that those reported by the French IUTs of 67 per cent and 71 per cent. In sum, more young people in France successfully complete their technical courses than in Mexico.

'Fairness' is also an issue that is highlighted when the UT system has been the subject of international assessments (see CGUT, 2000a). Since 1996, leading international experts such as Rector Claude Pair (France), Dr. John R. Mallea (Canada) and Dr Martin Carnoy (USA), amongst others, have recommended the implementation of institutional mechanisms to protect students from academic failure and dropping-out. These have included: the creation of scholarship schemes; the reduction of class sizes; and, the development of personal career development strategies with the purpose of integrating students into the labour market. In some UTs an association between the persistence of naïve attitudes to the job market and the low socio-economic backgrounds of students has been identified. For example, according to the Director of the Alumni department of the UT of Tula, Mr Miguel Cruz, local employers generally recognize that the academic qualifications of the UT graduates are relevant, yet, when young people are interviewed for an occupation, '...they do not know how to express themselves' (Flores-Crepo, 2002a, b). The inability of students to communicate effectively has proved to be a bigger handicap than educational planners had imagined when they created the UTs. In order to address this problem, the UT of Tula has organized extra curricular activities to empower its students and its graduates. 'Interpersonal Skills' workshops are conducted by Mr Cruz every Saturday with the aim of raising the self-esteem of young people as well as advising them on how to deal with difficulties that arise in the workplace. It is evident that attempts to adapt the curriculum to the needs of the productive sector has not facilitated an easy transition from school to work in the Tula region (Flores-Crespo, 2002a). Extensive institutional changes and remedial strategies were also required. This is an important lesson to be learned by policy-makers in other developing countries that are facing similar problems.

It would be wrong, however, to give the impression that IUTs have been an unmitigated success. Bureaucratic innovations have been persistently recommended for the system of the French institutes (Villa and Flores-Crespo, 2002). In 1994, the review of the *Cour des Comptes* highlighted the need to improve accounting and administrative procedures and coordination between the IUTs and departments in the Ministry of Education. It was also proposed that greater decision-making capacity should be devolved to rectors who participate in academic groups and that greater coordination was needed between the IUTs and universities.

Most UT graduates in Mexico, like their counterparts in France, wish to continue their studies at tertiary level as a traditional university degree is held in higher esteem in the job market than a UT qualification. According to local employers, UT graduates lack analytical skills and in-depth knowledge of specific subjects, thus it is very difficult for a technically trained person to occupy a white-collar position (Flores-Crespo, 2002a). Hence effective institutional cooperation is required to bring the UTs and other higher education systems into a fruitful association. However, this has been very slow to happen. It was not until eight years after the creation of the UTs, that a cooperation agreement was signed with the Office of the Technological Institutes (ITs) to allow students to upgrade their technical qualifications to a higher degree (engineer or bachelor). Despite this agreement, it can be argued that in the most deprived regions such as Tula, mechanisms to upgrade technical qualifications are not available. This has meant that the opportunities for self-improvement through the education system remain severely restricted. Hence the bureaucratic innovations that have been persistently recommended for the French institutes should also be implemented in Mexican UTs.

As the UT system is growing exponentially and becoming gradually more complex, it will be necessary to respond efficiently to future challenges to vocational-oriented models of higher education as they emerge. It is therefore only rational that a continuous process of policy learning is established with appropriate exemplars.

In Conclusion: Voluntary Policy Transfer in a 'Runaway' World

This case study illustrates the importance of developing a multi-level explanation of policy change in the Mexican education sector. The policy transfer framework provides a useful approach in this regard. The negotiated policy transfer of the UTs may be viewed partly as a response to the imperatives of globalization (WB, 2000), and, partly as a response to poor performance at the micro-level. This policy transfer was founded on the flawed premise that UTs could be used as an effective tool of development. The French IUT system was identified as the appropriate model for transfer to the Mexican context. This was because historical ties between the Mexican and French education system created an opportunity structure for further transfer. Yet paradoxically, the Mexican state also dramatically reduced public funds to tertiary education during the period of reform provoking severe contradictions between policy systems and precipitating popular political resistance. Much of this resistance was founded on the assumption that modernization strategies have challenged the traditional role of the state in offsetting structural inequalities thus exacerbating social cleavages. In hindsight there has been little evidence that inequalities and poverty in Mexico could have been alleviated during the last twenty years (see Cortés, *et al.*, 2002 and Boltvinik, 2000). This calls into question the way in which educational policy has been developed and implemented. In sum, the thesis that vocationally oriented higher education systems can function as an instrument of economic growth, needs to be re-examined.

Nonetheless, in a 'runaway world' (Giddens, 2002) where cross-cultural influences are increasingly common and progressive, it would be irrational to ignore foreign experiences in the development of indigenous public policy processes. However, policy learning must work with the grain of indigenous policy systems and be compatible with social norms, values and behaviour.

Chapter 9

Public Management and Policy Transfer in South-East Asia

Richard Common

Introduction

The overall aim of this chapter is to challenge the notion that New Public Management (NPM) is being globalized – in other words, that the package of administrative reforms developed in the Anglo-American democracies is being disseminated around the world. As Lynn (1998: 232) observes, 'one of the most provocative questions raised by the NPM is the extent to which a convergence, a kind of isomorphism, of administrative forms is occurring across nations and cultures'. The key purpose of this research is to expose the weaknesses of globalization studies that assume homogeneity in policy development across all countries. In order to achieve this primary aim, it seemed obvious to identify potential research sites outside the core group of countries in the OECD. Hence the impact of NPM was analysed in relation to three governments in South-East Asia – Hong Kong, Malaysia and Singapore.

As an international reform movement, NPM appears to be driven by policy transfer activity. An analysis of reform programmes in individual governments should therefore reveal the extent to which the NPM canon has been transferred. NPM is regarded in some quarters as a new global 'paradigm' for public administration (see Massey, 1997), and, its' potential for global diffusion has been recognized by authors such as Christopher Hood (1991), and others (see Dunleavy, 1994). Due to space constraints, this chapter will not engage in a broad ranging discussion of the merits and demerits of NPM, it will rather focus on its transportation from one administrative jurisdiction to another.

In order to comprehend why NPM appears to have international appeal, a multi-level policy transfer framework was deployed. This is presented briefly in the first section of the chapter. The theoretical discussion is combined with an analysis of some of the key methodological problems confronted in data collection, not least the difficulty of proving that policy transfer has actually occurred. The chapter then systematically applies the framework to each case study. The focus here is on the extent to which policy transfer can explain administrative reform in each case. It is concluded that it is apparent that the global diffusion of public policy is easily observed but the transfer of NPM is a far from straightforward process and its impact is often minimal or reduced to rhetoric.

Theory and Method

Because of the sheer scope of the task tackled here it is not possible to include a comprehensive theoretical and methodological treatment of the issues at stake. Please see Common (1999a, 1999b and 2001), for a broader elaboration. The analytical framework used in this research consists of three overlapping elements: a model of administrative change, policy transfer analysis as a method for analysing an observable and measurable process and NPM as public policy output to be observed. These analytical models were applied to each case study. First, a model of administrative change was developed to understand the wider pressures facing governments when considering the transfer of reforms. As Evans and Davies (1999: 14) argue:

> ...in order to comprehend the nature of policy transfer it is crucial that we contextualise social and political action within the structured context in which it takes place. We must assess whether processes external to the process of transfer we are looking at have an impact (directly or indirectly) upon the contexts and the strategies, intentions and actions of the agents directly involved.

Secondly, the Dolowitz and Marsh model (1996) was also utilized to understand why and how policy transfer occurs. And, thirdly, a NPM checklist was developed consisting of a range of policies, programmes, institutions and instruments that can be used to identify whether policy transfer has taken place at the micro-level of administrative organizational change.

This multi-level approach to the study of policy transfer emphasizes the importance of investigating the administrative and cultural context within which a particular policy is being transplanted. The appearance of NPM reform is thus wholly dependent on the range of variables in the causal model of administrative change that either facilitate or obstruct the potential transfer of policy. Many variables act in combination, but here I have attempted to disentangle them in order to facilitate a systematic comparison of the selected range of countries.

The Case Studies

Selecting Hong Kong, Malaysia and Singapore as the case study sample for this research might at first sight appear to be a recipe for unpromising results, given their geographic distance from the core NPM reforming countries in Europe and North America. However, the claim that NPM is being 'globalized' precludes that discussion. If we are investigating a phenomenon that has claims to being globalized, then NPM should appear in dramatically different settings. The choice of these three countries strikes a balance between difference and similarity. The governments of the three countries share the English language as a language of government and geographic proximity, while strong cultural and societal differences remain. Perceptions of similarity between Hong Kong and Singapore, for example, have also fostered the notion of rivalry between the two states. At the same time the potential exists for policy transfer between the countries as well as from the core NPM group of countries in the OECD.

A further similarity between the three countries is that they have all been colonized and influenced by Britain, and this acts as a historical setting variable. They are different, however, in that since gaining independence from Britain they have followed very different political, economic and social trajectories. Their political systems are different from the OECD or the Anglo-Saxon core group of NPM countries. If the differences were to prove substantial, it is possible that the research may produce three separate sets of statements that contribute little to the general theory on policy transfer. However, the similarity between the three, as a result of the colonial imprint, is such that the countries will retain a permeability to ideas being developed in Britain in particular, and the West more generally. As Seeliger (1996: 302) observes, any similarity is useful in elucidating 'how the limited number of differences in political structures and processes affect the timing and degree of policy change, or pinpoint certain mechanisms of policy transfer and policy learning'.

Establishing a Time Frame for Analysis

We can only account for policy transfer if we observe changes over time. Although it is possible to research with some accuracy when transfer actually occurred by looking for where and when particular policies are implemented, a time frame needs to be established to frame the study. Developments between 1988 and 1998 were therefore considered as 1988 was the year *Improving Management in Government* was published in the UK. This signified the intensification of the scope and intensity of NPM reform both in New Zealand and elsewhere. This time frame also allows for the diffusion of *Government Management*, the New Zealand Treasury's briefing documents to the incoming government of 1987, which is regarded as the 'manifesto' of NPM (Boston *et al* 1996: 3, Nagel 1997: 351).

Administrative Change in Comparative Perspective

A model of administrative change was developed 'for analyzing the crucial attributes of social and economic systems that may make them amenable to transplantation' (Peters 1996: 25). It encompasses global, regional, domestic and elite level structural variables that may help to explain administrative reform. As policy transfer is treated as a discrete process, it can be argued that transfer can only be facilitated through the impact of structural variables. Thus the model identifies structural processes, posited as independent variables, that may explain, or otherwise, the adoption of NPM in the selected range of governments.

The model of administrative change used in the research was developed from an Asian perspective, although it incorporates the variables usually ascribed to the appearance of NPM in western liberal democracies. Hence, when viewed from a comparative perspective, we can make some assessment of the varying importance of these variables when accounting for administrative change. In particular, it was useful to identify those factors that render states susceptible to the transfer of NPM. These variables are presented in Table 9.1 in a comparative analysis of administrative change in the three countries. A 'yes' denotes that the determinant affected administrative reform and vice versa for a 'no'. 'Not articulated' (N/A) means that no strong evidence was found either way.

It is extremely difficult to quantify the impact of globalization on public administration, but initiatives identified in Malaysia and Singapore have been attributed to the demands of economic globalization. One difficulty of evaluating the impact of globalization is the differences between countries in terms of the speed of reform initiatives. While much of Hong Kong's administrative system was effectively frozen by the Basic Law and uncertainty over the transition, Malaysia responded to the economic influence of Japan in the 1980s and went through a reform cycle in the early 1990s, while Singapore waited until the mid-1990s. For Hong Kong, the biggest challenge that faced the territory was reunification with China, and this factor alone usurped other considerations and effectively insulated the bureaucracy from reform from 1990 onwards. Hong Kong also proved to be the exception in terms of economic development. This is explained by its purported support for limited government, although the expansion of social policy from the late 1960s was a response to addressing the problems brought about by economic expansion. There is also strong evidence to suggest that changing societal expectations, along with governments seeking to legitimate their role in a rapidly changing domestic environment, also help to explain the appearance of NPM. Administrative reform was used to bolster the legitimacy of government in the absence of genuinely pluralist democracies. Demands from a better educated and more mobile and outward looking society also prompted calls for reform.

It is noteworthy, however, that none of the governments justified reform on the grounds of New Right ideology. Furthermore, the persistence of the colonial imprint in the form of a strong bureaucracy coupled with the post-colonial movement towards indigenization were formidable obstacles to the adoption of NPM. The durability of post-colonial bureaucracies allied to indigenous management cultures were powerful forces for conservatism.

Political globalization appears to be irrelevant to the three countries. Substantial democratization will not occur in the foreseeable future, nor is cultural homogenization likely to occur. It is economic development that has served to enhance the colonial structures of public administration in all three countries, which still retain the features of the developmental state. The drive for economic development has energized the political systems of Malaysia and Singapore.

Table 9.1 Modelling administrative change

Form of change	Hong Kong	Malaysia	Singapore
1st order variables			
Globalization	N/A	Yes	Yes
Level of development	N/A	Yes	Yes
Changing Societal Expectations	Yes	Yes	Yes
Legitimacy/symbolism	Yes	Yes	Yes
Ideology	No	No	No
Colonial Imprint	No	No	No
Indigenization	No	No	No
2nd order variables			
Tax Consciousness	No	No	No
Civil Service Capacity	Yes	Yes	Yes
Fiscal Crisis	Yes	Yes	Yes
Individualism	No	No	No
Managerialism	No	No	No
Egalitarian Social conditions	No	Yes	Yes
Western/Internationalization	Yes	Yes	Yes
Economic change elsewhere	Yes	Yes	N/A
International Organizations	No	Yes (past)	Yes (past)

Although this is important for the Hong Kong government, the fact that it has never been an 'independent' state and has practiced limited intervention, means that the impact of economic development on its administrative system has been diminished. Moreover, more egalitarian social conditions, which supposedly parallel economic development, only had a marginal impact on public administration in Singapore and Malaysia as both countries had to manage inter-ethnic relationships.

All three countries stressed the need for a sound civil service system and as the level of corruption compared favourably with international standards NPM could be given priority. Furthermore, the importance of cost containment following the fiscal crisis in the mid-1980s helped to focus thinking about public administration and this accounted for the first raft of NPM initiatives, particularly public sector reform in Hong Kong. There is little evidence, however, of the presence of several variables that account for administrative change in the West such as the relationship between political ideology, tax consciousness, rising individualism, and managerialism. The limited importance ascribed to individualism and consumerism supports Ridley's (1996: 18) view that, 'where society is not as "modern" (e.g. more deferential, clientelistic or rural), the marketization of public administration and new public managers seem less evident...'. Although only

Malaysia has a significant rural population, the cultural variables of deference and clientalism apply to this group of countries. Furthermore, although individualism is of significant cultural importance in the West while the East is more communitarian, Chen (1995) warns that we should be wary of making generalizations based on this dichotomy alone.

However, the differences are such that many NPM-type reforms may be rendered unfeasible in the Asia-Pacific. Some exceptions were found such as the encouragement of public consultation in Singapore, which seems to reflect a middle-class sentiment that wants individualized rather than 'mass' treatment from government (Chen, 1997). On the basis of these observations NPM should be confined to the urbanized West, with Singapore regarded as an exceptional case. Furthermore, in relation to Western notions of individualism and consumerism, there was a lack of managerialism (at least in the Western sense) in these countries. This may partly be ascribed to the persistence of 'rule-governed hierarchies' which 'may, in fact, 'fit' much more readily with the cultural norms of Asian countries than do the principles of NPM' (Brewer, 1998: 9). In addition, as Root (1996: 159), points out, 'the effectiveness of modern management techniques...is deterred by the persistence of traditional notions of social status and paternalism'. In sum, a backlash against the dominance of the American model of business management theory appears to have begun in Asia. Paradoxically, while the colonial imprint on the bureaucracy has been preserved and maintained, local organizational cultures have also been enhanced and strengthened. Hofstede's (1980) study shows, for instance, how Asian countries (including Hong Kong and Singapore) display more 'power distance' in hierarchical settings than in core NPM countries such as New Zealand and the UK. The consequence of which is the 'classic' colonial bureaucracy.

The application of the model of administrative change suggests that these countries should have no interest in learning about NPM-type reforms, and if they did, they would face insurmountable obstacles to the transfer of NPM. However, the appearance of NPM may depend on the need for dominant elites to legitimise their activities through the symbolic use of administrative 'reform'.

Building the capacity of the civil service was of crucial importance in all three case studies and was the subject of much reform effort. The drive against corruption had largely been conducted before the time frame utilized in this research. Fiscal crises, or at least a perception of crisis, certainly helped to trigger reforms in the 1980s, especially in Hong Kong and Malaysia. However, the reining in of big government, which prompted calls for reform from the early 1970s onwards in the West, was simply not applicable in the Asia-Pacific region. Moreover, governments in the region did not sustain large welfare states. Hood's (1995: 106) notion that 'small government states' provide less of a motive for politicians to engage in the type of cost cutting measures suggested by NPM certainly applies to Hong Kong and Singapore. Exposure and travel to the West and its ideas by the elites, particularly those who received an education in the West, was also of some significance. Economic changes elsewhere, especially within the region and Japan in particular, had some influence during the 1980s.

The variables of administrative change prove, in many cases, to be highly resilient to the NPM (for example, post-colonial administrative systems) or are too weak to have sufficient explanatory power (for example, neo-liberal political ideologies). However, by using policy transfer analysis the weakness of the globalization thesis was further exposed by the selectivity and the superficiality of many of the policy adoptions observed across the three countries.

New Public Management and Policy Transfer in Hong Kong

1989 saw the publication of *Public Sector Reform* (PSR) (Finance Branch, 1989) in Hong Kong, which had many similarities with the UK's 'Next Steps' initiative. Initially, PSR focused on financial management reform, in the same way as the Financial Management Initiative (FMI) in the UK from 1982 to 1987. In addition, the notion of 'trading funds' appeared to copy the UK's 1973 Trading Funds Act. More generally, both NPM in the UK and PSR in Hong Kong appear to share the same intellectual antecedents, especially as it became difficult for policy-makers in Hong Kong to ignore international trends in public management including NPM and privatization.

PSR was more of a case of direct coercive transfer than it first appears. In the 1980s, Hong Kong had a series of secondments from the UK Civil Service. This was considered to be good for the secondees, as work in Hong Kong was more challenging in terms of policy development due to the fusion of administration and politics. One such secondee from the UK Treasury was Robert Wright who arrived in 1986 to join the Finance Branch. Wright was a key architect of the PSR document although he knew little about Hong Kong. However, his Treasury experience meant that he was fully versed in the Thatcherite brand of NPM. Wright worked in the Finance and Civil Service branches and focused on financial and human resource issues at the micro-level. Another contributor to PSR was Colin Sankey, who had been a career civil servant in the Hong Kong government since 1974. The British firm of consultants, Coopers and Lybrand, also worked on PSR.

Wright missed the fact that the executive agency model already existed to some degree in Hong Kong, in the form of small policy branches that worked well in the Hong Kong context. Wright also seemed unaware that culturally, the notion of the Finance Branch confronting departments would not be welcomed in Hong Kong. The culture did not reward people who would say 'no' to spending departments. Furthermore, senior civil servants are more mobile in Hong Kong than their UK counterparts, so the notion of 'capture', a key public choice tenet of 'Next Steps', was not applicable to the Hong Kong context. The Hong Kong government was extremely conscious of the UK Next Steps initiative yet the academic commentary on PSR appears unaware that PSR was an experiment in NPM conducted by ex-patriate officials.

Administrative reform continued to be modelled on Britain after the arrival of Chris Patten in 1992, especially the notion of a 'service culture' and the introduction of the Performance Pledges (PPs), a corollary of the UK Citizen's Charter. However, PPs were not an exact copy of Citizen's Charters because they did not include compensation schemes, sanctions on government departments or performance-related pay schemes. Indeed Sankey (1988) describes PPs as a 'simplified' version of the Citizen's Charter. PPs had a symbolic importance within the service culture Patten was trying to introduce. Huque *et al* (1998: 119) suggest that PPs are manager driven and do not empower 'the consumer as the NPM ethos suggests'. Rather it is the bureaucracy that is empowered by enhancing its managerial autonomy. They were also a 'cultural imposition' as traditionally, Hong Kong public servants enjoy holding power over the public. Patten had set the example by allowing the public to win appeals against the bureaucracy, which was considered unusual in Hong Kong. However, the top-down nature of PPs, driven by performance standards, ensured their widespread implementation.

PPs were more of an adaptation rather than a direct coercive transfer. Since Sankey's appointment as Head of the Efficiency Unit in January 1996, he was visited once by the UK Efficiency Unit, and he made one reciprocal visit, but only after PPs were announced in 1992. The responsibility was Patten's. There is some evidence that Hong Kong looked to the work of the Deregulation Unit in the UK (Tsang, 1997) and Patten helped develop trading funds, an idea imported from the UK and introduced in the PSR report. The *Management of Public Finances* document (Finance Branch 1995) also advocated the kind of financial delegation that occurred under the UK Next Steps initiative. Like the UK Treasury, it was expected that its Hong Kong counterpart, the Finance Branch, 'should focus more attention on strategic performance issues...and that more authority for financial management should be delegated to policy branches and departments'. The notion of framework agreements (Efficiency Unit, 1995) appears to copy the Framework documents between ministers and Chief Executives in the UK. However, what was lacking was a structural change consistent with 'agencification' and there was no suggestion that executive units concerned with identifiable business areas be 'hived off' from government departments.

Although the executive agency model has been mooted in Hong Kong, since reunification with China in 1997 it has remained little more than a proposal. As well as the UK, New Zealand and Canada also served as a model for putting agencies at arm's length, as well as establishing trading funds. Although, according to Sankey, nothing substantial has been adapted from Canada. Australia, the US and Singapore were also cited as potential models. In particular, the Target-Based Management Process (TMP), announced in 1997, promised to delivery strategic policy objectives across departmental boundaries. Sankey describes TMP as 'managing for results'. New Zealand also influenced TMP when Hong Kong's Finance Secretary, Donald Tsang, sent a delegation to New Zealand in 1996 to look at its reform programme, led by the then Secretary to the Treasury, K.C. Kwong. The visit proved the catalyst to the establishment of TMP. Furthermore, calls for a system of accrual accounting rather than the preparation of budgets on a cash basis have been made on the basis that 'Hong Kong should learn from New Zealand' (HKDF Policy Committee, 1998). Although it appears that until 1997, the UK had set the pattern for reform in Hong Kong, there was no question of coercion. Cheung (1996: 43), however, remains sceptical about the role of policy transfer in the case of Hong Kong. He notes that NPM provided external legitimation for administrative change in the absence of political legitimation:

> By embarking on a reform programme that looks like an overseas reform movement, the local initiative can gain an added degree of acceptance and can downplay whatever political and bureaucratic implications that may arise from the reform.

For example, following the release of *Civil Service Into the 21st Century* (Civil Service Bureau, 1999), the Secretary of the Civil Service, Law Woon-Kwong, pointed out that similar schemes to introduce performance contracts and incentives for civil servants had been introduced in the US and Australia (Hon and No, 1999: 6).

Table 9.2 applies the policy transfer model to administrative change in Hong Kong. There were three key, interrelated motivations for the transfer of NPM. The first is power of NPM as a legitimizing discourse for administrative change. This motivation is related to the political context that underpinned the pending reunification with China. As the key political institution in Hong Kong, the civil service was anxious to emphasize its legitimacy as the transition approached in 1997, and afterwards in the absence of full democratic reform. The perceptions also surrounding Hong Kong as an Asian financial powerhouse in competition with the other 'Asian Tigers', especially Singapore, meant that the government had to demonstrate its appetite for current reform ideas.

Bureaucrats from within and outside the Hong Kong government transferred the NPM rhetoric in the PSR document from the UK. It is clear that the Hong Kong government wished to emulate 'Next Steps' without necessarily copying it. Consultants also contributed to the PSR document and added managerialist credibility. On the other hand, Patten attempted to transfer a number of NPM programmes from the UK during his tenure as Governor but initiatives such as PPs could only be adapted to the Hong Kong context. Following its transition to a Strategic Administrative Region (SAR) status in 1997, the Hong Kong government was no longer obliged to look to Britain. The bureaucrats had a free rein to learn from elsewhere at a time when New Zealand was becoming a powerful global exemplar of public sector reform. It is not surprising therefore that TMP was adapted to Hong Kong from New Zealand.

New Public Management and Policy Transfer in Malaysia

In Malaysia, there is a reluctance to acknowledge policy transfer, from both the West and neighbouring countries, particularly in Singapore. Halim Shafie regarded policy transfer as being particularly difficult in the Malaysian context.

Table 9.2   Policy transfer and public sector reform in Hong Kong

Why engage in transfer?	Who conducts the transfer?	What was the degree of transfer?
• *To legitimate conclusions already reached (voluntary)*	• *Bureaucrats (Sankey, Tsang, Wright etc.)*	• *Adaptation/ Emulation and Inspiration*
• *Political context (China)*	• *Consultants (Coopers and Lybrand)*	• *Adaptation/ Emulation*
• *International perceptions*	• *Political Appointee (Patten)*	• *Adaptation/ Emulation*

What is transferred?	Where from?
• *NPM rhetoric in PSR*	• *UK*
• *PPs, Efficiency Unit, Trading Funds*	• *UK*
• *TMP*	• *New Zealand*

This is due to federal government and strong central control: 'our political structure and history does not allow full implementation of these (NPM) ideas' (*author interview*, Dr Halim Shafie, Director, National Institute of Public Administration (NTAN), February 1999). Despite the British legacy, Malaysia looked to the US in the early years of independence, rather than the UK. The Ford Foundation sponsored the consultants that introduced the Performance Program Budgeting System (PPBS) in 1969-70. These 'reforms' can arguably be regarded as coercive transfers from North America. In the case of PPBS, it was assumed that the benefits 'would be automatically reaped' once the system was installed.

As Canadian consultants were largely responsible for the implementation of PPBS, problems soon emerged due to the consultants' lack of sensitivity to the Malaysian context (Doh, 1994: 127). Despite these initial setbacks, PPBS proved remarkably durable, surviving until 1990 when it was recast as the Modified Budgeting System (MBS). As this only 'modified' PPBS, it could be argued that MBS remains a policy transfer from Canada. Tan Sri Ali, the Chief Secretary to the Government (*author interview*, Malaysia, February 1999) and Ahmad Sarji (*author interview*, former Chief Secretary to the Government, 1990-96, Malaysia, February 1999) both stated that PPBS was the only reform to come from abroad as Canada is a federation, like Malaysia. The New Zealand model was rejected on the grounds that it would require splitting politics from administration, which was not considered appropriate to Malaysia (*author interview*, Dr. Mohamed Shahar bin Sidek, Deputy Director General, Malaysian Administrative Modernization and Information Technology Unit [MAMPU], February 1999).

Policy transfer is more evident in Malaysia in terms of economic policy. The

'Look East' policy statement which, appeared in December 1981, explicitly invoked Japanese management methods and ethics as a means of improving Malaysia's economic development. The Prime Minister (Mahathir 1983: 276) declared that his 'Look East' policy involved 'emulating the rapidly developing countries of the East in an effort to develop Malaysia', with Japan held up as the prime exemplar. As a consequence, it was to Japan and South Korea that administrators and students were sent to learn management skills and techniques. In particular, 'Look East' intended to highlight group rather than individual based benefits that were observed in the success of Japan and South Korea. However, following the policy learning of 'Look East' came the policy transfer of 'Malaysia Incorporated' in 1983, a concept similar to 'Japan Incorporated'. 'Malaysia Incorporated' emulated the Japanese MITI model of economic development. The main ramification of this for public administration was that Malaysia was to be regarded as a company, or a 'corporate nation'. Sarji was cited by the *Malaysia Business Times* (8 February 1994) as saying that 'Malaysia Incorporated' was not an exact copy of the Japanese model, adding without irony that in Malaysia there is no exodus of retiring senior civil servants to the private sector, as in Japan.

Within the time frame established for this research, there is limited evidence of further policy transfer of NPM-type reforms from 1988 onwards. The Client's Charter, announced in 1993, appears to be a faithful copy of Britain's Citizen Charter than Hong Kong's PPs. For instance, there is a procedure for compensating an aggrieved public service user; but there is no direct evidence of transfer. Indeed Root (1996) refers to it as the *Citizen's* Charter rather than the Client's Charter and, Osborne and Plastrik (1997: 239) claim that Malaysia adapted the Citizen's Charter from the UK, although they provide no evidence. Sidek, however, claims that the private sector rather than the British initiative inspired the Charter (*author interview*, Sidek, op. cit.).

Although many of the other reforms conform to the NPM model, evidence of transfer was not forthcoming either in documents or interviews. None of the Circulars on Administrative Reform make any reference to developments elsewhere. Although Sarji (1996: 172) was aware of the similarity of the Charter to that of the UK and New South Wales's 'Guarantee of Service' in Australia, he did not admit to having actively learnt from those two countries. Before deciding to go ahead with ISO 9000 for the Malaysia public service, Sarji consulted both the Secretary General of ISO and Sir Robin Butler, his UK counterpart, about the experience of other countries in implementing ISO (Sarji 1996: 290-293). However, it can be extrapolated from the writings and reported speeches of Prime Minister Mahathir and former Chief Secretary to the Government Sarji that they were the agents of policy transfer given their exposure to and appetite for reform ideas that were in currency in the West. Clearly, Sarji in particular, is a member of the NPM epistemic community (as former Chief Secretary to the Government and President of CAPAM).

Table 9.3 applies the policy transfer model to administrative change in Malaysia. As a developing country, Malaysia has sought to modernize its system of public administration. Following rapid economic development in the 1980s, the political leadership became dissatisfied with the public service. Problems were also perceived by a new generation of senior bureaucrats who were becoming exposed to the discourse of NPM. The three examples presented in Table 9.3 reflect the transfer of a diverse range of policies. As MBS was a revised version of PPBS, it was a policy adaptation from Canada. The Look East policy aimed to emulate certain East Asian countries and resulted in some administrative reforms such as Japanese economic management techniques, but this was unrelated to NPM. By the 1990s, once appointed as Chief Secretary to the Government, Sarji became a key agent of policy transfer who subscribed to the policy agenda of the NPM epistemic community. The circulars on administrative reforms, issued between 1991 and 1996, are a series of NPM adaptations from the NPM epistemic community. However, this highlights a problem with the policy transfer model. It assumes that in cases of cross-national transfer, an exporter of policy ideas can be identified; usually another country. In the case of Malaysia, it was clear that Sarji was learning about NPM from a wide range of sources. Even in-depth research interviews cannot fully reveal the true extent of where individuals learn about policy innovations.

Table 9.3   Policy transfer and public sector reform in Malaysia

Why engage in transfer?	Who conducts the transfer?	What was the degree of transfer?
• *Dissatisfaction (voluntary)*	• *Bureaucrats (Sarji, INTAN)*	• *Adaptation/ Emulation*
• *Dissatisfaction (voluntary)*	• *Politicians (Mahathir)*	• *Adaptation/ Emulation*
• *International perceptions*	• *Bureaucrats (Sarji)*	• *Adaptation/ Emulation*

What is transferred?	Where from?
• *MBS*	• *Canada*
• *'Look East' QCCs*	• *Japan, Korea and Taiwan*
• *NPM ideas and rhetoric*	• *NPM policy community*

New Public Management and Policy Transfer in Singapore

Given Singapore's policy learning imperative, it is not surprising that many of these reforms, as well as others introduced before the advent of NPM, are examples of policy transfer. As in the case of Malaysia, Singapore inherited line-item budgeting and its financial management system from the British but began to experiment with PPBS in 1974. PPBS had been extended to the entire government by 1978 but there were fewer implementation problems than those faced by Malaysia (Doh, 1994). The Block Vote Budget Allocation System replaced PPBS in 1989 and marked the introduction of managerialism in the Singaporean public service (Jones, 1999: 8). Japan also influenced the development of new management techniques such as Work Improvement Teams (WITs) and Quality Control, but it is not clear how much was actually transferred from Japan. As a degree of cultural congruence between countries is required for transfer to take place, methods associated with Japanese management culture would appear more easily transferable to Singapore than those techniques developed in the West.

The first transfer was the establishment of the Service Improvement Unit (SIU) in 1991, as part of a broader quality management initiative. The SIU resembles a combination of both the UK's Efficiency Unit and Citizen's Charter Unit, yet Singapore has preferred a more 'organic' approach to service quality standards. Although Singapore looked at the UK Charter Mark initiative in particular, it was decided that it was better for the public sector to compete with the private sector for Quality Awards in the Business Excellence scheme. As in Malaysia, all public service departments are encouraged to apply for ISO 9000 certification.

The clearest case of policy transfer to Singapore is the adoption of the executive agency model from New Zealand. Although there is some evidence that it was also based on some policy learning from Queensland, Australia and the UK (*author interview*, Ong Ye Kung, Director, Prime Minister's Office, December 1998). NPM has clearly influenced the permanent secretaries who have been the architects of the new initiatives; although they steer clear of adapting models wholesale and are quite careful about using the language or rhetoric of NPM. Administrative reform in New Zealand first came to the attention of the Finance Minister, Richard Hu, in 1992, following the visit of a New Zealand minister. A three-member Finance Ministry team then visited New Zealand to study the reforms first hand. The first appearance of the concept 'budgeting for results' (BFR) was announced at a Finance Ministry seminar in July 1994.

Although Singapore has looked to New Zealand as a model for public sector reforms since 1993, there were three omissions in its adoption of executive agencies. First, there was no accompanying freedom of information laws for citizens. Secondly, Singapore's chief executives are not employed on short-term contracts. And, thirdly, there are no contracts between permanent secretaries and ministers. In addition, target-setting was not implemented from the top-down, as in the UK, as it was felt that this should be the preserve of Chief Executive Officers in ministries and statutory boards rather than being left to the minister and his or her team. In contrast to BFR, PS 21 is considered a 'home-grown' reform initiative. Introduced in May 1995, the objectives of PS 21 (PS21 Office 1995: 3) are to nurture an attitude of service excellence in meeting the needs of the public with high standards of quality and courtesy; and, to foster an environment which induces and welcomes continuous change for greater efficiency and cost-effectiveness by employing modern management tools and techniques while paying attention to the morale and welfare of public servants.

PS 21 consolidates and extends an existing number of schemes and represents the human resource management thrust of Singapore's administrative reforms. Although the NPM canon appears to have influenced this reform, unlike BFR it is claimed that PS 21 was generated by the senior bureaucracy rather than at ministerial level. Conceptually, PS 21 relies on public servants being responsive to their clients, whereas BFR is aimed at improving the efficiency of government by making it more accountable to the political leadership (*author interview*, Lucy Tay, Prime Minister's Office, Public Service Division, December 1998). Hence as Table 9.4 reveals, it is difficult to ascribe PS 21 to any particular overseas initiative. It appears that it was the general discourse surrounding NPM that was absorbed by the senior bureaucracy given Singapore's penchant for policy learning. Thus, it is unlikely that PS 21 is completely home grown.

The partial adoption of the NPM model in Singapore may be characterized as a process of voluntary policy transfer, which helped to legitimate conclusions already reached by the elite about the need to modernize Singapore's public service. Table 9.4 reveals the clearest case of policy transfer in this study, the adoption of BFR from New Zealand, which has proved to be an attractive exemplar for many countries in terms of NPM.

Table 9.4   Policy transfer and public sector reform in Singapore

Why engage in transfer?	Who conducts the transfer?	What was the degree of transfer?
• *Legitimate conclusions already reached (voluntary)*	• *Bureaucrats (Public Service Division)*	• *Emulation/Adaptation*
• *Legitimate conclusions already reached (voluntary)*	• *Politicians (Richard Hu)*	• *Emulation/Adaptation*

What is transferred?	Where from?
• *NPM rhetoric in PS 21*	• *NPM policy community*
• *BFR*	• *New Zealand*

Comparing Policy Transfer Activity

This chapter has shown that NPM has been transferred to Hong Kong, Malaysia and Singapore to legitimate the political programmes of dominant elites. Table 9.5 applies Dolowitz and Marsh's policy transfer model across the three countries.

The 'heuristic functions' or the rhetoric of NPM provides a motive for the voluntary transfer of NPM. The only exception is Hong Kong, which for much of the period was still a British colony, so there was an element of coercion in the transfer of NPM in this instance. Moreover, policy transfer activity was constrained pending the transition to SAR of China status after 1997. Hence, the autonomy of the Hong Kong government to engage in policy learning was circumscribed by its colonial status. This independence was further compromised by the Basic Law, which preserved the colonial system. Thus, Hong Kong presents a fairly unique case in the global context. Malaysia and Singapore's independence, however, has allowed them to engage in policy transfer activity in response to demands to improve the performance of their public services.

Perceptions are important here, as one of the primary reasons for policy transfer is when decision-makers begin to worry that their country may lose out to competitors elsewhere (Dolowitz and Marsh, 1998: 41). In the case of Malaysia and Singapore, the main motive appeared to be economic competition from within the Asia-Pacific region in particular and the demands of economic globalization in general.

The international consensus or epistemic community that has built up around NPM has served to intensify these perceptions of best practice. With the exception of Patten imposing PPs on the Hong Kong government, none of the transfer activity falls into the category of 'coercion'.

Identifying the actors involved in the transfer policy process proved to be a difficult task, but it generally involved senior bureaucrats, supported by elected officials. Senior bureaucrats, such as Sankey in Hong Kong, Sarji in Malaysia, and Guan in Singapore, all had access to the NPM epistemic community. Thus, NPM rhetoric as well as ideas and best practices generated through the networking activities of senior bureaucrats allowed the circulation of NPM to all three countries. The availability of key texts such as 'Reinventing Government', undoubtedly reinforced this process. Thus, not only programmes from individual countries such as New Zealand came under scrutiny, but international organizations such as the OECD acted as 'stores of information to be drawn upon' (Dolowitz and Marsh, 1998: 51). The bureaucratic nature of all three governments helped to facilitate the relatively rapid infusion of ideas from other countries and the international community into the policy formulation process.

In Conclusion: Policy Transfer and the Politics of Administrative Change

As Table 9.5 illustrates, administrative change is not just about reforming management processes, it is accompanied by political change as NPM involves political impacts that alter power relationships in the public sector.

Hence, public sector reform appears to be more important to elites than simply changing or 'banishing bureaucracy'. This is not to deny that the publication of PSR in 1989 in Hong Kong, the range of initiatives introduced in Malaysia beginning with MBS in 1990, and BFR in Singapore in 1995 all marked serious attempts at changing the management processes in the civil services of the respective countries. However, these reforms need to be understood within the context of wider pressures on the public sector and have the aim of convincing external audiences that the behaviour of the bureaucracy is commensurate with the expectations of society at large and the business community in particular. Hence, over-arching initiatives such as *Vision 2020* in Malaysia in 1991, *Serving the Community* in Hong Kong and *PS 21* in Singapore, both announced in 1995, encompassed both change and rhetoric. Vision 2020, for instance, was supposed to herald a new 'paradigm' in the management of Malaysia's public services yet the old 'paradigm' of a centralized and hierarchical bureaucracy persists.

Table 9.5   Applying the policy transfer analysis model

	Why engage in transfer?	Who conducts the transfer?	What was the degree of transfer?
Hong Kong	• *Legitimacy and coercive (colonial)*	• *Colonial, post colonial, bureaucratic elite*	• *Emulation and adaptation*
Malaysia	• *Legitimacy and perceptual*	• *Bureaucratic elite*	• *Emulation and adaptation*
Singapore	• *Legitimacy, pragmatism and perceptual*	• *Political elite*	• *Emulation and adaptation*

	What was transferred?	Where from?
Hong Kong	• *Rhetoric and programmes*	• *UK*
Malaysia	• *Rhetoric and programmes*	• *Canada, NPM epistemic community*
Singapore	• *Rhetoric and programmes*	• *New Zealand*

The first conclusion from this research is that the globalization of NPM is perhaps too easy an assumption to make simply on the basis that the three countries have initiated top-down reforms in a similar fashion to those in the 'core' countries of the OECD. Moreover, because these three cases involve highly centralized political systems, including federal Malaysia, there is more opportunity for policy-makers to adopt NPM from a single reference point. Although the administrative inertia that characterizes these post-colonial systems means that administrative reform is inevitably top-down, senior politicians and bureaucrats can quickly proclaim the 'success' of particular initiatives to both domestic and international audiences. NPM thus appears to be a global movement that is easily observed, but for any reform to be sustained a sense of ownership is required by both public servants and users. In Singapore, *PS 21* was regarded as an example of a successful administrative reform as it attempts to respond to citizens' demands and institutionalizes the reform process within the bureaucracy. Although the transfer of NPM rhetoric helped to justify decisions already reached by senior bureaucrats, the insistence by officials that *PS 21* was an indigenous response rather than an imitation from abroad, gave the officials a sense of ownership over the reform. Although NPM might appear to be easy to detect, only when its impact is tangible to both public servants and users the world over can we claim it as a global phenomenon.

Secondly, despite the evidence to support the role of policy transfer on administrative change in the three governments, there was no firm pattern of influence. The influence of Britain remains strong in all three cases, but policy-makers have also looked to Australia (Hong Kong), New Zealand (Singapore) and Canada (Malaysia) to learn about policies and programmes. Although the transfer of NPM rhetoric appears to be taking place in the region, it is what is *not* transferred that undermines those who would claim that we are witnessing an international convergence in public management. For instance, there was an overall reluctance to implement performance contracts, which had the potential to undermine hierarchical chains of command. More generally, none of the countries observed were willing to implement radical structural changes to their administrative systems, nor were they willing to 'marketize' large areas of public sector activity. There is no simple convergence on the NPM model taking place in these three countries, although NPM has increased the range of options available to policy-makers considering administrative reform. Public management reform efforts in the Anglo-American countries continue to appear to be the most attractive exemplars to these three countries yet there is a growing recognition that Western-style management is unsuited to Asian government, and this may lead to the development of an Asian-style public management in the near future.

Thirdly, the notion that the transfer of NPM results in an increasing number of 'inappropriate' policy adoptions that are unsuited to local political, cultural, social, economic and administrative contexts, now appears false. If the values underpinning NPM (rationality, individualism and dynamism) are considered Western, then we might expect NPM to be inappropriate to the context of these countries. Yet the discourse of NPM has considerable rhetorical impact, which means that changes in bureaucratic practice do not have to correspond completely with indigenous practices. Conversely, no individual public sector organization will display all the characteristics of the full adoption of the NPM model as systems of public administration are embedded within their own particular political socio-economic contexts. This explains why the transfer activity that takes place involves a process of policy adaptation, such as PPs in Hong Kong and BFR in Singapore. At a rhetorical level, the attractiveness of the NPM model is that it suggests what administrative reform can accomplish.

Fourthly, the case study evidence highlights the emergence of influential epistemic communities that are a consequence of globalization. Policy learning is conducted through a wide range of mechanisms. In the case of administrative change, the powerful rhetoric of NPM is mediated through the epistemic community. Members of an epistemic community will learn from one another in international forums and then pass lessons and advice on to organizations over which they have considerable influence. Sarji in Malaysia, Sankey in Hong Kong and Hu and Lim in Singapore represent members of such a community. The key difficulty of empirical verification in this study is that even when these key agents of policy transfer were interviewed, it was difficult, if not impossible, to establish what was learnt from whom. Furthermore, the availability of publications, the activities of international organizations and its agents of policy transfer; officials and politicians sent on visits, secondments, study placements and tours; and interaction with academics and conferences, are among the other transmission mechanisms of policy learning. At the meso-level at least, a key problem encountered by the research was assessing the impact of these various mechanisms as primary data obtained by publications and speeches and so forth become obscured by jargon and declamatory statements.

There are both strengths and weaknesses associated with the multi-level framework employed in this research. First, in the model of administrative change, globalization was treated as an independent variable that determined both NPM and policy transfer. In other words, globalization was identified as making individual countries more amenable to transplantation. However, developing a model of administrative change inevitably invites debate about what other variables should also be included to avoid the mobilization of bias in research findings. This problem was also encountered with the NPM model. Secondly, the policy transfer model has proved to be problematic due to the methodological challenges it presents. In particular, the 'recall' problem begs the question: can people in an interview situation remember exactly where or from who they absorbed a particular idea? Most people are conscious of influences but after a period of time it becomes difficult to ascribe ideas or concepts to particular publications, places or persons. As an integrated approach, it was possible to use the qualitative interviews to substantiate aspects of the model of administrative change and identify links between the different levels of analysis. For instance, it was clear from the interviews that economic globalization encouraged Singapore to engage in policy learning and to adopt models of administrative change from abroad.

Finally, the chapter opens up a fresh avenue of debate in policy analysis. If we are witnessing the 'globalization' of public policy, we should be concerned that policy-makers are convinced that access to information can substitute for domestic policy innovation. In other words, policy borrowing becomes the 'easy option'. In the case of health care policy, Marmor (1997: 348), calls policy learning 'the World Cup' fallacy due to:

> ...the notion that cross-national learning is like picking the best soccer team. The task is to find the best model (technique, system, payment policy) from around the world and transplant it elsewhere. This approach is, of course, foolish. No institution, policy, or program is transplantable in this simplistic way. Yet there continues to be a 'market' for one-size-fits-all reforms that continues to attract articles, speeches and, most of all, conferences on the state of medical care.

It is this global market for ideas that continues to flourish as governments go shopping to satisfy their sponsors back home. In Hong Kong, Malaysia and Singapore, although some of the products from this market have been bought, they have been adapted to suit local tastes and preferences. Much of this is the same as the global restaurant chains that have penetrated Hong Kong such as McDonald's and Pizza Hut, where one can find Chinese and Japanese style dishes side by side with Western fare. On the evidence presented here, there is no coherent global paradigm being systematically transplanted across the world. Bureaucracy itself is proving to be highly resilient and has emerged from the latest wave of NPM relatively unscathed.

Part III

Policy Transfer from Developed Countries

Chapter 10

Policy Transfer and the Developing Country Experience Gap: Taking a Southern Perspective

Anthony Nedley

Introduction

The generic term policy transfer encompasses a host of concepts describing the process of moving policies, programmes, ideas or institutions from one time and space to another. Studies of this temporal and spatial transfer of policy knowledge present us with many varied forms from voluntary lesson drawing (Rose, 1991) to coercive negotiated policy development (Dolowitz and Marsh, 2000). The policy transfer literature describes, almost uniformly, a lateral ring of voluntary North-North policy information 'exchange' (Wolman, 1992; Bennett, 1991; Robertson, 1991) that is broken only by the 'export' of policy solutions, North-South, or 'down' to the developing nations. What the literature lacks is any focused reference to South-North traffic, from the developing to the developed nations, of policy influence. This chapter asserts that by failing to acknowledge that policy entrepreneurs in the North may have something to learn from successful programmes already underway in the South, policy transfer search activity is wholly irrational.

My central argument is that to date policy transfer analysis has evolved in a vacuum of its own making that exhibits myopic tendencies by failing to see the full extent of knowledge available to it. Furthermore, the exclusion by Northern policy-makers of developing country experience suggests an unhealthy inability or unwillingness to access what 'the-other-half' knows. This approach inhibits the opportunity for genuine global dialogue and, in turn, confines both policy learning and transfer. The chapter challenges the short sightedness of the contemporary policy transfer literature and contributes to it an additional Southern perspective. It also provides an example of the potential for lesson drawing from the South through comparative analysis of two case studies showing similarities in approach to health sector reform – one in England and one in Tanzania. The first case study provides an insight into policy change affecting health sector reforms in the UK. The Labour Government's flagship programme, Health Action Zones, attempts to introduce collaborative approaches to primary health care, which emphasize partnerships between local communities, health professionals, local government and the private and voluntary sectors. The second case study explores an example of a collaborative health programme in Tanzania, Community Based Health Care, which has been effective for the past decade. The chapter then proceeds to a consideration of the opportunities and obstacles to South-North policy learning. The chapter will begin, however, with a critical review of the lesson drawing approach, which will provide an organizing framework for the ensuing analysis.

The importance of this project lies in attempting to provide a more balanced learning environment between salient programmes in both hemispheres. The objective is to open up the literature to potentially fertile areas of research in developing countries, and through this to promote fresh lesson drawing opportunities for policy-makers in developed countries.

The Lesson-Drawing Approach

According to Rose (1991) lesson drawing addresses the question 'under what circumstances and to what extent can a programme that is effective in one place transfer to another?' For Rose, the important features of this process are the circumstances surrounding the learning of lessons from other sources, the extent to which they are taken up and, crucially, the effect they may have incorporated into a new policy environment. It is these features of the process of transfer that provide a useful perspective from which to analyse the potential for South-North transfer. Other authors readily assimilate Rose's definition into their own work as it usefully describes 'an action oriented intentional activity' (Evans and Davies, 1999: 4) that also allows for the drawing of negative lessons (Dolowitz and Marsh, 1996: 344). Stone (1999: 52) also identifies with this 'emphasis on cognition and the redefinition of interests based on new knowledge which affects the fundamental beliefs and ideas behind policy approaches'.

A useful method for defining a subject is to observe what it is not. Rose asserts that lesson drawing is not merely about 'singling out examples of present success elsewhere'; or about 'what politicians think ought to be done', nor is it about 'an innovation per se' or 'reasoning from first principles'. He defines a lesson as 'an action oriented conclusion about a programme or programmes in operation elsewhere' (1991: 4-8). This is a definition that confirms its practical utility in the area of comparative politics. Lesson drawing is not pre-determined to transfer policy per se, it also allows for the learning of negative lessons or what not to transfer. This form of 'prospective evaluation' provides the opportunity to appraise programmes, ideas and potential solutions to domestic problems from afar, prior to incorporating them into the domestic policy environment (Rose, 1991). A concern for the transferability of a programme and the 'intentional' character of the process of learning are of major importance. However, the mere transportation of ideas from one context to the next, regardless of the extent to which the old idea may fit with the new experience, does not, in itself, constitute a lesson drawn (Evans and Davies, 1999: 4).

Who Draws Lessons?

Dolowitz and Marsh (1996: 345-5) list several types of agent that are involved in policy transfer processes: elected officials; political parties; bureaucrats; pressure groups; policy entrepreneurs/experts; and, supra-national institutions. The role of policy entrepreneurs is particularly relevant to this study as they advocate the exchange of lessons and concern themselves with special subjects that lead, through a network of contacts, to sources of ideas for new programmes. Of equal importance is the exchange of ideas promoted through supra-national organizations such as the EU and international organizations such as the World Bank or the OECD.

However, as described earlier, these institutions involve themselves for the most part in exchanging or 'pushing' policy and ideas between either the economically 'developed' states of the Northern Hemisphere or down to the developing nations of the Southern Hemisphere. Their inability or unwillingness to appreciate and promote learning upwards from the developing world reflects the imposition of self-imposed parameters to their learning environment, which in turn weakens their capacity to draw potentially significant lessons. Rose attempts to brush off this weakness by suggesting that: 'subjective identification is more important than geographic propinquity in directing search. Neighbours are not necessarily friends' (1991: 14). Such an explanation however, merely illustrates further the degree of short sightedness inherent in the current analysis of the policy transfer process and an apparent unwillingness to broaden the scope for learning to a truly global scale.

The proactive drawing of policy lessons from developing country experience requires agents of transfer to remain more independent and operate in less formal, non-governmental circles, than those identified above. Stone (1996) identifies think tanks as policy entrepreneurs that offer prime examples of non-governmental mechanisms for the dissemination of policy ideas. Their capacities include: the ability to collate and distribute information; advocate ideas that may be considered, beyond the mainstream of government thinking; and, the promotion of national and international networking on policy oriented issues.

Think tanks are perhaps most readily defined by their particular role. Unlike government sponsored or academic-based entities such as policy units or task forces, that may carry out specific research and be subject to agreed terms of understanding, think tanks often act independently, researching and advocating on behalf of their members for ideological reasons on a not-for-profit basis. As Stone observes, (1996: 3 & 23), '...they are outside the public sector and have a significant degree of autonomy from corporate and other interests.' Think tanks are at their most effective in the role of transferring '...the ideas and ideologies, the rationalizations and legitimations for adopting a particular course of action and ...draw[ing] attention to developments overseas'. Several examples of UK-based think tanks emerge as being particularly relevant to the dynamics behind learning from developing country experience including the International Institute for Environment and Development (IIED), the Institute for Development Studies (IDS) at the University of Sussex and the Nuffield Institute for Health Policy

Research. For the purposes of this chapter, the list of actors engaged in lesson drawing can be further extended to include the role played by members of non-governmental organizations (NGOs).

Why Engage in Lesson Drawing?

Rose argues that the key stimulus to spark a search for lessons is political dissatisfaction. Dissatisfaction '...occurs when routine is disrupted and policy-makers can no longer operate on the assumption that what was satisfactory before is still satisfactory'. External events can stimulate dissatisfaction, for example, the Blair government's reaction to the growth of public awareness of long patient waiting lists for NHS services, provoked a range of health care reforms and corresponding increases in public expenditure in 2000 in the UK. Sometimes the stimulus to learn becomes an imperative as in the public health cases of response to epidemics such as AIDS, where, as Stone (1999: 53) emphasises, 'lesson drawing could assist decision-makers to respond more quickly or appropriately to crises'. At such time, Rose (1991: 10-13) asserts, 'policy-makers must then search further afield'.

Dissatisfaction can be spread internally merely to prompt political change or to discredit a particular programme for political gain. Opposition politicians who 'have a vested interest in generating dissatisfaction with the current programmes of government' will create an atmosphere of unrest by emphasizing programme failure. Robertson (1991: 55) supports these assertions when he writes that: '... lesson drawing is not politically neutral. The value of lessons lies in their power to bias policy choice'. Lesson drawing is thus further utilized as '...an instrument of power to gain leverage in political conflicts' (Robertson, 1991). Lessons can be manipulated, either in support of or to provide ammunition against, programmes that have been identified as prospective candidates for transfer. When dissatisfaction with the status quo has reached such a pitch as to spark the search for new lessons amongst policy-makers and other agents of change, the political environment can become charged with the frenetic energy of lesson drawing and certain policy options will gain new currency. However, '...advocates of a momentarily unwanted programme need not abandon their idea; they can adopt a patient stance, waiting for the winds of political fortune to shift...' (Rose, 1991: 13).

How are Lessons Drawn?

Rose proposes a simple three-step approach to drawing lessons. The first step involves finding 'fresh ideas' from a broad trawl of information relating to programmes that appear to be solving problems in other places or countries. At this stage, policy-makers are merely interested in identifying knowledge that may eventually prove transferable, and not in importing any detailed programme designs.

The second step utilizes this information to construct generalized 'conceptual model[s]' of each programme under consideration, that can be used to examine the programme's functions and further the exploration for a desirable transfer fit with the importing country. The emphasis at this stage is to derive, from a thorough examination of the model, what makes a particular programme tick, its obvious strengths and less-obvious weaknesses, in a particular place under particular conditions. There is no reliance built up regarding the degree of transferability and hence much time may be spent constructing and examining non-transferable models.

The third step seeks to draw comparisons between the 'foreign' models and the identified problem in the importing country that led to the information search in the first place. It is at this stage that the intricacies of potential transfer can be investigated. Are conditions comparable? Do the similarities outweigh the differences? Will the import of such a programme satisfy public opinion? Can the programme be resourced sufficiently? (Rose, 1991: 20-21).

From Where are Lessons Drawn?

Lesson drawing concerns itself with programmes, their development and policy change, in the political arena. As Rose (1991: 6) notes, '...whereas the goals of government are the primary concern of elected politicians, the everyday activities of government concern programmes, the instruments by which these ends may be secured.' As 'instruments of public policy', programmes provide us with more tangible manifestations of political hopes and policy schemes. It is because programmes vary around the world, evolving out of peculiar blends of environmental, economic and social constituent parts and maturing at different rates, that they lend themselves so well to the concept of lesson drawing. They are concrete examples of political whim and wishful thinking. For the purposes of the arguments advanced in this chapter, lesson drawing between programmes, North and South, represents fertile ground for redressing the imbalance created by the one-dimensional nature of transfer processes described in the literature.

This chapter has defined some of the operational parameters implied by the conceptual framework of lesson drawing, it has argued that the lesson drawing framework has the most utility for investigating the current North-North constraints that operate on policy learning.

Health Action Zones: A UK Case Study

Following the Labour party victory in the May 1997 general election, the new Secretary of State for Health, Frank Dobson, formally announced the establishment of Health Action Zones (HAZs) with the aim of targeting:

> ...a number of areas where we believe the health of local people can be improved by better integrated arrangements for treatment and care. Areas where there are pockets of intense deprivation, problems with unemployment, crime – all of which are acute and hopelessly tangled up with poor health, housing and education. (Frank Dobson, Secretary

of State for Health, Speech to the NHS Confederation, 25 June 1997).

In stating the HAZ aim in such bold rhetoric, Dobson was committing the majority of England's Health Authorities to engage with such unfamiliar territories, methodologies and tools as social exclusion, collaborative and partnership approaches, community participation and holistic systems thinking. That neither the Health Authorities, local or national government nor local communities had much, if any, experience of working in such ways did not dampen the enthusiasm for this new way forward. All those involved, from the Minister to the layperson, would need to learn new lessons along the chosen route. The HAZ approach was to be process-oriented with participants expected to incorporate and exploit new knowledge as and when they came across it. To further complicate the learning process there existed few opportunities for lesson drawing from similar institutional and public change programmes from either past UK policy or within the usual policy-sharing environment of economically and socially similar states of North America, Scandinavia and Europe. The HAZs would need to substantially widen their lesson drawing net and re-think their approach to policy-making.

Defining Health Action Zones

HAZs represent a flagship element of the Labour Government's modernization agenda. They are seven-year multi-agency programmes between the NHS, local government, voluntary and private sectors and community groups. The principal aim of HAZs is to tackle inequalities in health in the most deprived areas of England through health and social care service modernization programmes. By spreading the HAZ approach beyond the traditional confines of institution-based medical support, opportunities to address other interdependent and wider determinants of health such as housing, education, employment and urban regeneration become apparent.

The first eleven HAZs commenced in April 1998 followed by a second wave of fourteen in April 1999. These twenty-six zones were selected on a needs-based criteria established from a range of health, health care and deprivation indicators. HAZs now cover more than fifty percent of the population living in deprived areas in England, involve thirty-four Health Authorities, seventy-three Local Authorities and cover over thirteen million people. HAZs differ in complexity and size, covering single to multiple Authorities with populations ranging from just under 200,000 up to 1.4 million. They also vary in their local characteristics; consequently each one addresses different health as well as service priorities. More than two hundred work programmes within the HAZ structure have been initiated centred on six key areas of health and social care services, community empowerment, strategic development and partnerships, health problems, population and the wider determinants of health (Sands, HAZ Briefing Paper, NHSE, 2000).

The HAZ programme is designed to overcome the internal politics of competition with its emphasis on developing an integrated approach to local health and social care economies. Such a pioneering approach throws up new challenges as NHS organizations, Local Authorities and other local stakeholders are urged to co-operate in an atmosphere of mutual interdependence. As Maddock (1999: 1-10) puts it, '...such change is difficult and dependent on proactive parties overcoming intransigent structures and building positive relationships with people they may have previously been hostile to...'. HAZs are encouraged to adopt a 'whole systems' approach to identifying and engaging in partnership with a wide range of stakeholders who are interested in reducing health inequalities. Facilitators within the programme train personnel in the use of large group intervention techniques for engaging and involving disparate groups of stakeholders.

The HAZ programme is underpinned by seven key principles:

- equity in resource allocation and access to services;
- empowering front-line staff and developing flexible organizations;
- a person-centred service approach;
- engaging communities;
- an evidence based approach to service planning and delivery;
- partnership working; and,
- taking a whole systems approach engaging stakeholders across the local care system.

The Department of Health works with HAZs and other government departments to pilot initiatives for implementing 'joined-up' government. Several HAZs have developed a single strategic plan that sets out priorities and targets for agencies operating in a local area. The plan also serves as the main instrument of accountability to central government. As progress on reducing health inequalities depends on the commitment and involvement of other local delivery agencies, this is an important area for HAZs. This is also an example of central-local partnership as central government develops policy ideas with local delivery agencies (Sands, NHSE: 2000).

Initial assessments indicate that HAZs are attempting to set interim targets to achieve long-term goals. Other emerging indicators suggest that HAZs are beginning to work in different ways than before and, crucially, more closely with other partners whilst genuinely seeking to involve communities in decision-making (Judge, 1999).

Evidence of Pre-Health Action Zone Community Involvement in Health Issues

There was some evidence prior to the establishment of the HAZ programme of governmental awareness of community involvement in health issues. Smithies (1992), a consultant to the 1992 Standing Conference *HealthGain* in Dublin, described the impetus for community involvement in the new health authority role as having come from a blend of national policy and community development practice. She cites the fact of the UK being a signatory to the World Health Organization's (WHO) *Health For All* project, and adoption of the key principles of community participation and empowerment as an international influencing factor. On the domestic front, a raft of NHS policy guidance documents including such titles as *Working for Patients, Local Voices* and *The Health of The Nation*, have been launched since 1990. They invariably attempt to establish the credentials of strengthening consumer choice and moving beyond consultation to direct community involvement in the promotion of good health practice. *The Patients Charter* explored the area of the rights and responsibilities of health service users, purchasers and providers. Smithies (1992: 10) astutely identifies the new role for Health Authorities as: no longer owning or managing services; measuring and monitoring the health needs of their community and understanding the economic, social and cultural backgrounds to those needs; identifying priorities for action in promoting health and changing the pattern of services provided in response to health problems; and finding ways of creating those changes within the community and through negotiations with provider units

These developments appeared at first sight to symbolize a radical change in the role of health authorities towards a community owned and managed health service. In reality, however, it remained largely rhetorical and incoherent, with very few major changes in this direction actually occurring until some policy consistency was gained with the advent of the HAZ programme.

Implementing the Health Action Zone Programme

Community involvement and partnership working are central to HAZ philosophy. However, although there is some history of local action in most zones, progress in these key areas has been patchy. Those zones that have a history of community development projects and interaction between the local authority and community or self-help groups, even where the projects themselves have ceased to exist, are observed to have the higher levels of community involvement in the HAZ. As Maddock (1999: 4) observes: '...community development projects, funded in the late 1970's, have demonstrated 'value for money' by their legacy of voluntary and community action networks...these local connections continue to survive'. In other locations though, community participation in HAZ initiatives is described as minimal. Similarly, the involvement of the voluntary sector has been somewhat piecemeal, which appears mainly due to the lack of a coherent interface between it and local communities. Lack of funds to stimulate collaborative primary care projects has also hindered progress in this area. The main problems appear to be associated with a lack of dialogue and programme facilitation, as communities are expected to participate in HAZ programmes but fail to see how and where they fit in the new structure or what added value they can provide to existing health care provision.

Even where local community groups are formed and functioning, the mechanisms enabling their effective involvement in HAZ initiatives may not have been established yet. Communities may have much to say but either they do not yet know how to articulate their input or the HAZ entity remains ill-equipped to listen. For at least two decades community development practitioners in developing countries have been engaged in 're-learning' how to establish efficient communication between and within communities and between communities and state social service providers. Methods such as Participatory Learning and Action (PLA), an umbrella term for a wide range of approaches including Participatory Learning Methods and Participatory Action Research, have been introduced. These methodologies enable communities to define their needs on their own terms, thus overcoming the usual bureaucratic obstacles and administrative confinements to communication. PLA employs a broad range of communication 'tools' – diagrams, role play, interviews, theatre, video etc. – designed to encourage people to clarify and prioritize their planning, implementation and evaluation of community projects. Common to all of these methodologies is the promotion of interactive learning, shared knowledge, flexible-yet-structured analysis and the opportunity for mobilizing local people for joint action.

The use of PLA methods in the UK community participation context is relatively new and untried. Where it has been attempted, it has met the same pitfalls as those experienced in the early days of its elaboration in the developing world. Connold and Rowley (1999) describe an attempt at using Participatory Rural Appraisal (PRA) techniques – part of the range of PLA methodologies – with a local, semi-urban community in Reading, Berkshire. The appraisal was requested by the local Parish Council in order to gain a better understanding of the problems experienced by local housing estates and some suggestions of how to tackle them. Several limitations to the appraisal soon became apparent: local people, due to their mobility and work demands actually did not seem to have the requisite in-depth local knowledge. Local people appeared to have little time to spare, either for their neighbours or for engaging in the appraisal.

Of greater relevance to this chapter is the attempt at using PRA methods in a health sector setting. In one such approach – to assess the provision of palliative care services in Bradford and Keighley Districts – a team comprising nurses, health educators, health programme auditors and representatives of the voluntary sector, met with a wide range of health service users and providers. All involved agreed that the PRA tools used in the assessment had helped to generate a lot of useful detailed information in a short space of time, all of which enlarged the perspectives of both patients and health professionals. At the same time though, all involved similarly agreed that their initial objectives had been far too ambitious and a narrower focus, perhaps on one particular service, would have provided more realistic outcomes for subsequent action (Jones, 1996).

This case study shows that those involved with the HAZ programme – whether community participant or health professional – have much to learn regarding collaborative approaches to health systems. This message has been repeatedly stressed by Health Ministers and facilitators alike, learning at all levels will play a large and central role in the success or failure of the programme. Nonetheless, the commitment to the process is there. Health Action Zones have a proposed programme duration of seven years, with an initial expiry date of 2006. This timeframe acknowledges the need for longer-term planning and experiential learning within the HAZ process: both fundamental requirements in any genuinely collaborative project involving community participation. The case provides indicative evidence of the challenges facing any approach to collaborative social service delivery. For those involved in the HAZs, a key problem arises: the absence of a comparable programme from which lessons can be drawn and solutions to problems developed. The following section introduces another collaborative approach to primary health care; one which has been established for over twelve years in a developing country setting. When considered on its merits against its Southern Hemisphere origins, the case provides several important lessons for UK policy-makers and practitioners engaged in health sector reform.

Health Sector Reform in Tanzania

In this section a case study is analysed that explores the experience of a health programme in a developing country. The case study presents an example of policy change that was brought about partly as a response to local needs but also in recognition of the limitations of national economic resources. The programme shares many of the community participation and partnership elements exhibited in HAZ programmes. Of equal importance to the lesson drawing potential that straightforward comparative analysis of the two cases may yield, is an awareness of the emerging global or cross-national dimension to policy learning that developing country programme experience can provide.

The International Health Policy Context

Before focusing on the Tanzanian case, it is necessary to set the national scene within the broader, changing international health policy context, especially where it impacts on developing countries. Post-war economic policy up to the 1980s supported state control of public sector development, arguing that market forces were inadequate in developing economies. The neo-liberal analysis of the 1980s advocated structural adjustment, prompted by the failure of central governance to promote the interests of their populations and inefficiency of public sector programmes. Bi-lateral and multi-lateral international aid programmes that had expanded to support state control now spread their technical and financial inputs to non-state beneficiaries. At the same time, the WB and IMF introduced conditionalities, such as political and economic reforms, as part of their loan agreements with developing country governments. Economic adjustment programmes began to bite on social service budgets with profound negative effects on the health sector, brought on by the introduction of private health provision, user-charges and cost-sharing (Walt and Gilson, 1994).

A growing awareness of the links between poverty and poor health by social scientists began to challenge the dominant orthodoxy that medical science, in the hands of professionals, would triumph internationally. Although breakthroughs in containing and even eradicating some major diseases were impressive, the shift away from centralized provision to more socially inclusive primary health care programmes was inevitable. The shift was partly fuelled due to the recognition of international donors that health programmes required not only medical expertise but also transparency and accountability in terms of acknowledging the values, culture, morale and sense of involvement of the population at large.

In their search for new policy solutions, donors promoted decentralization policies to remove control from central, distant authorities; service delivery through non-governmental organizations which were perceived to be closer to local communities and which might instil a greater sense of democracy; and 'Good Governance' which included reform within smaller bureaucracies...and greater accountability (Walt and Gilson, 1994: 356).

The National Health Policy Context

Tanzania, like many other post-colonial nations, has for many years followed the UK's NHS model of health service delivery. The UK approach, which has been universally applauded over the past 50 years, championed tax-based financing and institutionalized primary medical care. NHS reforms over the past twenty years have introduced a broad spectrum of changes, including: a managed-systems format which sought to gain greater economies, efficiencies and effectiveness (1980s) and, over much of the 1990s, the advent of 'contracting out' and increased autonomy from state control through the establishment of hospital trusts. The thrust of most recent reforms, however, herald more socially inclusive policies for the new millennium. These are designed to aid collaborative methods of primary health care delivery in a multi-actor, multi-disciplinary way that relies heavily on the participation of the public and non-government organizations for its future success (Collins *et al*, 1999). It is in this latter approach that Tanzanian health sector reforms can be said to have stolen a lead on their Northern counterpart, by opting over a decade ago for community-based initiatives in collaboration with the recognized financial power, ideological purpose and development skills of non-governmental organizations.

Proposals for reforming the Tanzanian health sector combine moves towards decentralization with cost sharing and privatization. International donor agencies play a large part in funding preventive and primary health care, with project funds being channelled either through government budgets or, more commonly, directly to NGOs running health programmes. Fee paying for health provision is becoming more commonplace (Mackintosh, 1997). In line with a broad policy objective of '...improving the health and well-being of all Tanzanians, with a focus on those most at risk, and to encourage the health system to be more responsive to the needs of the people...' (Government of Tanzania, 1994 cited in Robinson, 1998), eight specific policy objectives were identified:

- the reduction of infant and maternal morbidity and mortality through provision of adequate and equitable maternal and child health services;
- the promotion of nutrition;
- the control of communicable diseases;
- ensuring availability and accessibility of health services to all in urban and rural

areas;
- movement towards self-sufficiency in manpower;
- sensitization of the community to common preventable health problems through building capabilities and genuine community involvement;
- the promotion of awareness in government and the community that health [problems can only be adequately solved through multi-sectoral co-operation; and,
- the creation of awareness through family health promotion that the responsibility for one's health rests squarely with the individual as an integral part of the family.

The policy insisted that these objectives must be achieved through '... co-ordinated action by all concerned: health and health related sectors, local authorities, industry, NGOs and voluntary agencies, the media and the community at large' (Government of Tanzania, 1994, cited in Robinson, 1998).

In order to implement this policy commitment – considered by some national observers as being somewhat progressive and even radical – the government of Tanzania promoted the use of a health 'tool kit'. This included: District Health Planning Guidelines, a Health Management Information System, Environmental Sanitation Guidelines, Health Education Guidelines and Community Based Health Care Guidelines (Robinson, 1998). It is the origins and implementation of the latter element of the kit that is of most interest to this study.

Tanzania's Community Based Health Care Policy (CBHC)

CBHC was developed in 1988 by the Kenya-based African Medical Research Foundation (AMREF), in close collaboration with the Tanzanian Ministry of Health. It was designed to complement an existing and more formal, institution based approach to health care. The latter, with its standardized processes operating within a highly qualified and centralized medical framework, remains the favoured health care system of the economically stable nations of the Northern Hemisphere. Tanzania's CBHC, however, acknowledges not only the limits to centralized infrastructures in terms of reaching the poor but also the primary role of community organization in a developing country situation, and plays to its strengths. CBHC also recognizes the linkages between the social and economic conditions that epitomise poor health and poverty – low or no monetary income, lack of access to jobs, information and market opportunities, poor quality water, sanitation, housing, environment and education – and attempts to address them in a holistic manner. Of equal importance is the recognition that if the community is to address the problems associated with poor health it must be empowered and enabled to do so.

At the root of community action in CBHC is an awareness that chronic ill-health in an individual snowballs into a household problem to a community and state problem. In this way the continuum – from individual liability to public commitment – is forged. Communities also understand that externally-imposed solutions to their problems often fail simply because they are inappropriate for the local environment, derived as they are at the institutional level and imported into the community without prior consultation.

An important part of CBHC is the desire to learn experientially and to engage all actors in genuine dialogue that disseminates new information through networking. It is, in international donor parlance, a 'process-project'; learning as it goes. Networking is central to CBHC philosophy and extends from concerned individual members of the community up to senior government officials at ward, district and regional levels. Village Health Committees, teachers and government extension service staff from a range of sectors including water, agriculture and social services all engage in the CBHC process. Networking at the 'top end' is usually the role of the NGO involved in the process that will have extensive contacts with other relevant NGOs, government departments and the international donor community – both multi and bi-lateral. This creates a flow of information and a knowledge base that is of great importance, especially where other communities or NGOs may wish to replicate the CBHC in other geographic areas. It also serves as a monitoring and review mechanism for maintaining standards over time.

CBHC came about primarily as a rejection of the standardized health package being promoted by the WHO and readily adopted and disseminated by the Tanzanian health system. The package, common to most developing countries, promotes health on an institution-led basis with clear distinctions made between the technical superiority of the doctor and the passive role of the patient. The WHO health package, however, failed to accommodate local needs providing the impetus for more appropriate community-based and learner-centred approaches.

The Role and Importance of Non-Governmental Organizations in Community Based Health Care Policy

CBHC, as a concept, was largely developed by NGOs, often as one element within a comprehensive integrated development programme that works with communities to develop several sectors – education, health, food and income security – simultaneously. Depending on the wealth of development experience and funds available, the NGO concerned will occasionally act as a facilitator, engaging and enabling a constructive dialogue between the community and relevant government social service departments. This facilitation role may be as basic as providing transport, accommodation costs and a venue for both parties to meet and discuss their options for collaboration. Although often overlooked in the wider scheme of things, such simple, low-cost assistance helps to overcome one of the major barriers to social progress in the developing world; lack of access. Neither the community nor government representatives have adequate budgets that allow for the luxury of face-to-face dialogue. Lack of contact between the two inevitably breed mistrust, false assumptions and even fear which further entrenches the polarity of each side's position.

When dialogue is secured, the NGO may often play an intermediary role, to further reduce the potential for conflict born out of misunderstanding, as government and community adapt to each other's negotiating positions and air each other's grievances. Further NGO support is provided in terms of information resources and the payment of fees to cover the cost of hiring consultants on specific issues. The promotion of best practice in CBHC is 'pushed' through NGO networks and promoted through related human resource development projects such as the training of health education trainers, midwives and HIV/AIDS personnel.

In the context of CBHC, an NGO is usually a non-government, non-private-sector agency, working on a not-for-profit basis to facilitate the promotion of primary health care in a given geographic area. Most NGOs receive funds from donor sources external to the country in which they work. Large-scale international development NGOs such as Oxfam or Save the Children Fund, have evolved a range of funds to support their overseas work. This encompasses public and private donations as well as actively seeking project funds from international donors based on the submission of detailed proposals. Funds are channelled to resident developing country programmes and distributed down to community level, often through national NGOs, according to plans drawn up in collaboration with government and community representatives. Checks and balances are built into the system of fund distribution and range, in this example; from UK Charity Commission reviews of stated NGO policy and actual project implementation, to external and internal agency financial and programme audits. National governments of developing countries also enforce codes of conduct for local and international NGOs operating within their sovereign territory.

Non-Governmental Organizations, Community and Government Collaboration

Collaboration between communities and NGOs is not uncommon in aid-dependent countries, where it can often mitigate against the pressures from externally imposed structural adjustment programmes aimed at controlling or reducing public expenditure totals (Mackintosh, 1997). The financial input is also relatively substantial. When considered collectively, the funds of medium to large size NGOs represent a large proportion of most developing countries' expenditure on health. The WB's World Development Report (2000) estimated that combined NGO financial inputs to health programmes in developing countries were worth almost twenty-five per cent of total external donations. Such funds are increasingly targeted away from centrally controlled programme budgets and towards autonomous or semi-autonomous projects where individual agencies believe they can derive more value for money, avoid government manipulation and monitor outcomes more effectively.

In the case of CBHC, however, co-operating NGOs have worked closely with government representatives in the design and implementation stages. Efforts to ensure the longer-term sustainability of the programme are strengthened through training programmes for government staff on such topics as organizational development, the project management cycle and community participation approaches. It is also commonplace for government staff to join NGOs either on secondment from a relevant ministry or as full time staff. They bring with them valuable knowledge of how government functions and empathetic contacts in high places that can further lubricate the CBHC process.

This case highlights the potential role of non-governmental actors in processes of policy development and implementation. It enables policy thinking along more horizontal and socially inclusive lines. There are several opportunities for the HAZ programme in the UK to learn from the CBHC model in Tanzania. These will now be explored together with the identification of the potential constraints to learning and an assessment of how these might be overcome.

Learning Opportunities

What are the most appropriate elements of developing country experience that could be prospectively evaluated for future transfer to the UK? In their comparative paper on UK health sector reform, Collins *et al* (1999) identify four learning opportunities: the policy-making process itself; the focus on primary care; the political shift from competitive to collaborative delivery strategies and priority-setting within the NHS. The first three of these are directly relevant to the central argument of this chapter and are further examined in the light of the information revealed within the case studies and from other sources.

Opening up the Health Policy-making Process

Health sector policy in the UK over most of the last twenty years has been largely characterized by a 'closed-shop' mentality informed by a narrow range of influences that were ideologically close to the policy-makers themselves. Such a confined approach to policy-making led to the exclusion of those whose links with and knowledge of practical health issues – Doctors, Nurses, other health professionals and NHS users – would have provided the most pertinent inputs and could have led to the consideration of a broader range of policy options (Collins *et al*, 1999 p. 3). Despite the rhetoric of collaboration and some early indications of increased community participation, as revealed in the HAZ case study, the lack of a genuine consultative dialogue with key stakeholders persists. The Labour government continues to create policy within a limited network of technocrats and trusted policy informers in the apparent rush to satisfy an electorate sold on pre-election promises of the abolition of NHS internal markets.

There are alternatives to the relatively closed process described above. Several commentators (Chambers, 1983; Ong and Humphries, 1994; Popay and Williams, 1994; Rice *et al*, 1994), assert that the way forward towards more inclusive, democratic and realistic policy-making is to acknowledge and utilize the community perspective as a guiding principle for setting health care priorities and determining policy. A rethink of the relationship between decision-makers and users is required that makes citizens integral to the policy process (see Parsons, 1995: 541-2). This participative approach to policy-making is central to the philosophy guiding the CBHC programme in the Tanzania case study and is echoed in the progressive health policies of other developing countries.

Brazil provides a pertinent example of inclusive, open policy-making that went in to the development of its acclaimed 'Unified Health System'. This system promotes the principles of universality, equity, decentralization, integrated care, popular participation and public financing. The policy-making approach incorporates an exhaustive network of Health Councils, Health Conferences, representative bodies and intergovernmental commissions. Smaller municipal and state health conferences, drawing on approximately one hundred thousand delegates, meet throughout the country to discuss their health system. Their findings go on to inform a quadrennial national Heath Conference that feeds directly into and guides policy-making. As Collins *et al* (1999) observe, there are clearly opportunities here for UK policy-makers to gain '...new perspectives and ideas about negotiation, legitimacy and [the] potential for more open policy-making in the NHS'.

Asserting the Role of Primary Health Care

During the past twenty of its fifty years in existence, NHS decision-makers have concentrated their energies almost exclusively on structural aspects of service delivery. Moving from general management trends to managed competition and a range of provisions that include contracting-out, fund-holding and greater autonomy than ever before for newly created health trusts. Throughout this period, though subsumed within the eagerness to adopt the new public management ideals discussed by Richard Common in the previous chapter, the delivery of primary medical care was the dominant ethos. It was the issues of universal access to this type of care in the UK that first attracted a host of other countries – both developed and developing – to aspire to a similar model. In contrast, during the 1980s and 1990s many developing countries (India, Brazil, Tanzania etc.) were inspired by the outcome of a 1978 WHO conference that pronounced universal primary health care as a fundamental human right. The subtle replacement of the term 'medical' with 'health' was to lay the foundations of most progressive health care policies in the developing world; policies that the developed world is only now beginning to contemplate.

Article V1 of what became known as the *Alma Ata Declaration* provided a template for moving the new thinking on health care forward:

> Primary health care is essential health care based on practical, scientifically sound and socially acceptable methods and technology made universally acceptable to individuals and families in the community through their full participation, and at a cost that the community and country can afford to maintain at every stage of their development in the spirit of self-reliance and self-determination. (WHO, 1978).

Further articles called for improved co-ordination between relevant sectors and common support in the areas of education, housing, public works and industry, in an early recognition of the interlinked nature of the social causes of poor health.

The role of governments in formulating national policies and plans of action, as part of a comprehensive national health strategy in co-ordination with these various sectors, was made explicit.

Prior to the *Alma Ata Declaration*, Tanzania had attempted to emulate many aspects of the UK primary medical care model but with minimal success due mainly to the shortage of trained health professionals, and an under-resourced health service infrastructure. The CBHC case study exemplifies the move away from medical to health care and the benefits to developing countries of shifting the ownership and maintenance of a health system away from central control and towards a more sustainable community level. Other developing countries readily adópted primary health care strategies, evolving their own blend of appropriate technologies and community-based initiatives. The Chinese 'barefoot doctor' approach reduces reliance on cost-ineffective doctors, placing more emphasis on the skills of less trained but more locally informed nurses and medical assistants, thus enlarging the geographical scope of health care. This initiative has found favour in many African countries (Tanzania, Zaire, Lesotho, Zimbabwe etc.). A similar approach, and again very common in Africa, is the training of village or community health workers (V/CHWs). This latter initiative works most effectively when the V/CHW is selected by the community and acts as an intermediary between them and the national health system whilst receiving support and resources from the village or community health centre (World Bank, 1994).

Prior to the introduction of prescription charges in the UK, Bangladesh began using an essential drugs list to better target and supplement its limited health resources. The Indian system of panchayat raj seeks to devolve power down from central to local self-government which will take on the responsibility for community focused héalth at a more appropriate level (Collins *et al*, 1999). Cost recovery programmes, most famously UNICEF's 1987 Bamako Initiative, are paying significant local dividends across Africa. The Bamako Initiative promotes community cost sharing mechanisms in support of primary health care and boasts the recovery of between 40-60 per cent of local health centre operating costs. One study reported the recovery of up to 100 per cent of local recurrent primary health care costs (World Bank, 1994: 160).

The Community Participation Factor

It is now commonly accepted amongst international development practitioners and commentators (Chambers, 1983; Mosley, 1987; Oxfam, 1995, World Bank, 1994) that enabling communities in developing countries to participate effectively in the decision-making, design and implementation of health sector initiatives can significantly enhance and sustain those initiatives. A World Bank review of the role of community management committees in local health centres illustrates the benefits. First, they can hold health care providers accountable to users through dialogue and continuous interaction between the two. Secondly, representation on these committees of a broad ethnic and cultural mix reduces community tensions by providing a platform to air problems and seek solutions. Thirdly, participation in such activities creates a sense of ownership and stakeholdership that in turn encourages people to value and protect their community based services. Finally, community management of health facilities helps to build relationships based on trust between providers and users and empathy with local constraints and conditions, such as poverty (World Bank, 1995: 121).

The examples highlighted above serve to illustrate the differences in policy-making processes, the variance in approaches between primary medical care and primary health care and the potential for community participation in health care delivery functions. Of greater importance to this analysis, they also help to define the extent of the ground that now needs to be made up by those involved in the UK HAZ programme at all levels, whether NHS policy-maker, medical professional or V/CHW.

Lesson Drawing Opportunities Beyond the State

Much of the public policy and policy transfer literature focuses on the state, as evidenced by the specific emphasis that researchers place on networks and the contacts within and between epistemic communities (Haas, 1992), policy communities (Rhodes and Marsh, 1992) and policy transfer networks (Evans and Davies, 1999). These are all to a large extent concerned with the analysis of the role of state organizations, a focus that helps to create artificial limits to the scope of policy learning. This chapter has consistently emphasized the need to broaden the search and incorporate a wider range of policy informants.

The policy transfer literature, and by association, much of the analysis that lies behind it, concentrates on the formal entities of policies, policy instruments, administrative arrangements and institutions. The focus is state centred and neglects those opportunities for broadening the field of policy enquiry that could be gained from considering less-formal 'ideas, interests, behaviours, perceptions and cultures which move or change as much as policies' (Freeman and Tester, 1996: 11). Participants in the 1993 international conference on *Health Sector Reform in Developing Countries* reached consensus in calling for 'an international, horizontal and independent consortium to foster exchange, learning, assistance and institutional growth on health sector reform'. The term 'horizontal' implied equality of partnership amongst all members of the consortium, with no prejudice based on country, type of institution or government. The 'independence' of the consortium's agenda, moreover, was to be assured against bias from any particular donor source or philosophy (Berman, 1995). Participants also noted that the majority of developing country health sector analysis comes from donor agencies involved in development projects. This consortium approach reflects the essence of the argument advanced in this chapter, the need to establish a 360-degree approach to policy learning.

Learning from Smaller, 'Hollower' States: Some Practical Lessons

This chapter has highlighted the need for a broader approach to the search for policy ideas. But what practical steps can be taken to establish this approach to policy learning? Collins *et al* (1999) suggest three specific actions that, although they focused primarily towards learning from developing country experience on health sector reforms, are applicable across a range of policy arenas. First, the establishment of a fact finding mission of UK policy-makers to review developing country experience. Secondly, an end to the one-way, North-to-South traffic in visits by external consultants, by inviting a review of UK programmes from policy makers, community and political representatives and opinion leaders. The aim here would be to challenge consensus by gaining novel perspectives. Thirdly, to promote action research on cross-cultural learning through the periodic exchange of personnel within developed and developing country programmes. International experience needs to align with the work of professional bodies such as the Health Education Authority and the Medical Councils to develop new perspectives and suggest changes to direction on a wide range of programme issues. In addition, those information networks and exchange fora already established by the NGOs, think tanks and other international development institutions, should be resourced and expanded, their expertise made readily accessible to more formal state actors engaged in policy transfer.

The UK policy-making environment itself needs to become a far more receptive and open arena for international learning. Before scanning Southern horizons, policy entrepreneurs in search of fresh information could look first to the experiences of other domestic government departments, institutions or non-governmental organizations. The Department for International Development (DFID) is a major bi-lateral donor of funds and expertise to programmes in developing countries around the world. Its social development advisors and technicians work in collaboration with developing country governments, NGOs and communities to build sustainable social service delivery systems. Through this collaboration, they have built up a substantial database of information that provides a reliable resource for policy-makers in other areas to utilize. It is interesting to note, however, that there is no mention of inter-departmental learning between the departments of health and international development in available data on the origins of HAZ policy formulation. The very same developing country experiences, that this chapter proposes that the HAZ programme can learn from, are those that another arm of the same government has fostered and supported for decades.

How can the currently confined political space, in which NHS policy is formulated, be opened up? An obvious move would be to encourage a broader, deeper range of consultation, in search of fresh policy options, between departments, think tanks, institutions, academics, community representatives, health service users and non-governmental organizations. A forum, along the lines of that taking place in Brazil, could be held periodically to review the state of the nation's health, raise issues and discuss options for change. Such a forum could encourage cross-party, inter-departmental focus on key issues and promote the longer-term sustainability of health policies.

According to Rhodes (1997), the UK government is experiencing a 'hollowing-out' of the state, whereby functions that were traditionally carried out and owned by a centralized state machinery are being gradually 'lost' upwards to the EU, downwards to special purpose bodies and outwards to specialist agencies. Since Rhodes expounded his 'hollowing out of the state' theory the British government has clearly encouraged local authorities to collaborate with private and voluntary sector agencies to improve service delivery, as illustrated in the case of HAZs. In this respect, those developing societies that have by necessity learned how to operate smaller, more appropriate state machinery within tighter budgetary parameters, present fertile opportunities for drawing lessons. The higher levels of community participation and the involvement of non-government organizations in social welfare, described in the Tanzania case study, also offer proven examples of increased ownership of social programmes and self-governance from which both the UK government and wider society could learn.

As an 'action-oriented conclusion about a programme…in operation elsewhere' (Rose, 1991) lesson drawing approaches the issue of policy transfer from a highly voluntary and informal basis. This informality, often actively pursued by non-state actors or agents such as NGOs, academics and practitioners in the field, can promote a dynamic inter-change of knowledge that refuses to limit itself to the artificial North-North orbit enjoyed by the economically advanced nations. An 'alternative' approach to transfer is perhaps best illustrated by the activities of international development organizations, such as the International Institute for the Environment and Development (IIED) or the Institute for Development Studies (IDS) in England, or the host of international and national NGOs who research and network constantly on issues of health, education and poverty alleviation.

Lesson drawing suggests that there is valuable policy information to be gained, not only from direct policy transfer itself, but also from negative lessons. What is not transferred becomes as important as what is transferred. It is at this point within any given policy transfer dynamic that lesson drawing, as a theory of policy development, is perhaps at its strongest. Rose (1991: 4-5) asserts that lesson drawing:

> …requires more than singling out examples of present success elsewhere. The need is prospective: understanding what others do there today is meant to improve conditions here in future… prospective evaluation can give forewarning of failure when conditions necessary to make a programme work in country X are not met in country Y.

However, such foresight is only of value if policy-makers are willing to study all aspects of a given programme in one or more countries, regardless of that country's state of social or economic development. Policy researchers now need to use global prospective evaluation to explore the extent that 'foreign' knowledge may prove compatible, or otherwise, with domestic programming. If '…everyone concerned with public policy unconsciously draws lessons across time and space…[it is what] intelligent people do without thinking' (Rose, 1991: 6), then it is certainly feasible that global communication systems could aid prospective evaluation between developed and developing nations. Prospective evaluation can negate the 'fear' for policy-makers of entering uncharted territory in search of policy solutions. But what of the constraints that appear to limit South-North policy learning? Let us consider these in more detail.

Agents and Structures

Stone (1999: 54) asserts that both 'agency and structural factors will condition the degree of transfer and the character of implementation'. The capacity and purpose of each agent of transfer will inevitably dictate which lessons are drawn, how and why they are 'imported' and the degree to which they are imported whole or in part. Whether or not a potentially viable lesson is drawn is also open to the whim of structures pertaining in the 'importing' country, institution or programme. If those in search of policy solutions are experiencing political, institutional, financial or public crisis, such as an election, institutional reform, loss of confidence in the currency or civil disobedience, the opportunity for transfer is delayed or lost.

'Immature' Policy Environments

Just as their economies, polities and social structures may be considered 'under-developed' in comparison with their Northern counterparts, many developing countries of the Southern hemisphere may be considered to possess comparatively immature policy environments. The inference being that policy developed in such an environment is not coherent or 'developed' enough for transfer to a more mature policy location. There is some truth in this argument regarding the process of policy development. The reality is that policy in a developing country may be constructed in a reactive manner, for example, in response to natural or man-made disasters where the terms of a state of emergency may apply. In the most extreme cases the threat or reality of military coup and subsequent accession to power of an un-elected group can frustrate or even reverse the policy development process.

The Limits to Implementing Collaborative and Partnership Strategies

The adoption of new policy ideas, especially those from external sources, often require the adopting government or department to drop its own reluctance to change. The rhetoric, and to some extent, practice of the 'New NHS' hints at large-scale institutional and street-level change, but the removal of entrenched management positions is difficult and the acceptance of collaborative or partnership working is not yet a reality. In her preliminary audit of the state of partnership working within the HAZ programme, Maddock (1999: 5-6) illustrates the problems associated with change management, '[m]ost players insist the institutions are far from changing, that leaders are uncertain [of] their role and change management know-how, and [that] more sophisticated performance management is needed'. Maddock further cites central government rigidity and its constant demand for joined-up action from local groups and authorities as a major barrier; arguing that 'mainstreaming change concerns not just innovators and cultural shifts, it requires the whole machinery of government to change gear.

Collaborative approaches are new to contemporary UK society, which has a weak community-action oriented base when compared with many developing countries. Even the participatory models of assessing community needs prior to action, that are proving so successful in developing country contexts, are meeting obstacles in UK. Here, any appraisal requires a high degree of local assent and control that must be obtained prior to any further consultation or risk alienating or dividing the community. It must also be linked to imminent action and not be viewed as an experimental or abstract exercise (see West, 1999: 90). There are clearly inherent obstacles to entry-point community collaboration within HAZs and other programmes that rely on building partnerships on many levels. However, all are surmountable, given new approaches to organizational development, the inputs from trained facilitators and the lessons available from positive examples such as CBHC in Tanzania.

Political Reluctance

The lesson drawing literature claims to '...draw upon empirical evidence of programmes in effect elsewhere to create a new programme for adoption at home" (Rose, 1991). However, the reality is that *elsewhere* relates solely to the transfer, exchange, emulation and borrowing of ideas and policies between the like-minded, economically advanced and 'developed' nations of the Northern hemisphere. The transfer is neither comprehensive nor inclusive, allowing little scope for genuine global, multi-directional learning. On the contrary, the literature displays either an astonishing unawareness or conscious ignorance of the potentially fruitful lessons to be drawn from the non-G7, 'developing' countries of the Southern hemisphere. Stone (1999) asserts that this state of affairs '...arises for reasons such as habits of mind, the "special [US/UK] relationship", the historical legacy of empire, or the ease of looking towards other English speaking countries'. She also observes that before June 1997, just when 'the Western world' was opening up to draw economic policy lessons from the 'Asian miracle', the financial bubble burst and policy-makers withdrew in a hurry.

There is, however, evidence that this problem has been identified. Stone (1999: 54-57) asserts that the advent of the AIDS crisis '...prompted health experts, NGOs and officials to look to practices elsewhere as guides to action on..."safe sex" advertising'. The 'elsewhere' that the AIDS practitioners looked to was to nations such as Uganda and the Republic of South Africa, that have consistently led the international field in AIDS response and care over the past decade (see Kennis, 1999). In a similar, though darker vein, the questionable selectivity of latter day and perhaps contemporary policy-makers is considered by Proctor (1999) when he acknowledges that epidemiologists in Nazi Germany in the 1930s had made the crucial link between smoking and heart and lung disease:

...abhorrence of Hitler's regime led to lessons learned being suppressed at the end of the war. It took another 30 years for health awareness campaigns to reach that level of sophistication in Europe and the US [even though] at the end of the war, the Allies were quite happy to apply Nazi findings in rocket science and bacteriological warfare (*The Observer*, 9 May 1999).

Complexity and Alignment

Programme design can also constrain lesson drawing. Dolowitz and Marsh assert that '...the more complex a policy or programme is the harder it will be to transfer'. Rose (1993) hypothesizes that transfer is most likely to occur when programmes have single goals; the problem in focus is simple to understand; a direct relationship between problem and solution is determined; side-effects are perceived to be minimal; a programme's performance in a given environment is known about and the outcomes of its transfer are easily predicted.

What these pre-requisites also suggest however, are the potential difficulties that can arise, should one or more of them not be satisfactorily met. Indeed the inference is that lesson drawing is particularly predicated upon all factors aligning perfectly and simply, whereas reality dictates that the non-alignments and complexities present in any policy environment – whether mature or fledgling – would normally conspire to obstruct the transfer process. It is the overcoming of these obstacles that is the fundamental challenge to agents of transfer. The constraints identified within this chapter, however, are all, to varying degrees, surmountable through rational policy analysis.

In Conclusion: Taking a Southern Perspective

This chapter has sought to highlight an important weakness in current policy transfer activity: its inherent bias towards transfer between developed nations. As such the search for ideas fails to take advantage of the wealth of positive lessons from developing country experience. This claim has been supported to some extent by the limits of the scope of enquiry which has been revealed through a critical appraisal of the policy transfer literature, which rarely broadens its focus beyond the habitual comparators of G7 or OECD countries of the Northern hemisphere. In drawing attention to the previously uncharted Southern perspective, the chapter has argued for a greater role for informal, non-state agents to engage more comprehensively in the active transfer of innovative programme ideas and policy options, from a broader range of sources. A further argument urges less emphasis on studying the process of transfer and more on programme content, the identification of programming requirements and the exploitation of potentially valuable policy oriented lessons.

The empirical evidence presented in the case study analysis, together with the discussion of the opportunities for and constraints to lesson drawing from developing country experience, have provided the basis for some important recommendations for further research in this area. The UK Government's HAZ programme places partnership and collaborative approaches at the centre of its policy on primary health care delivery. However, the policy-makers who are pushing this approach, and many of those who are expected to implement the programme, only have limited experience of how such approaches are developed and made to function effectively. At the same time, the opportunities for drawing lessons from within the traditional 'ring' of comparator countries are few. Alternatively, evidence from developing country experience in the Tanzanian CBHC case study, points to a rich seam for the potential transfer of ideas in the direction of the UK HAZ programme.

This chapter does not envisage or promote the wholesale import of policy-making procedures or community-based programmes from developing countries. Clearly, any transfer, emulation or drawing of policy lessons must be evaluated with regard to the cultural, social, economic and resource environments pertaining in each location. To attempt, for example, to transfer the Brazilian approach to democratic health policy making to the UK would no doubt result in early failure; given the lack of autonomy and constitutional power of the regional authorities. It is also hard to conceive the population exerting the necessary political will to generate policy change, as witnessed by recent electoral turn-outs that in some constituencies amounted to less than twenty percent of those eligible to vote. The simplistic, piecemeal copying of 'exotic' policies, without due depth of indigenous policy analysis is politically dangerous.

The chapter recommends to policy-makers the importance of a 360-degree perspective on the search for ideas. For there is no shortage of potentially valuable South-to-North policy oriented learning to research. To the study of community-based health initiatives can be added micro-finance and credit programmes, such as those operated through the Grameen Bank in Bangladesh. This initiative has successfully provided recoverable loans for income-generation schemes and offers a wealth of lesson drawing opportunity for policy-makers in developed countries. Given the growing disparities between wealth and poverty in UK, the introduction of similar small scale credit facilities, through domestic finance programmes for the socially excluded, could prove extremely beneficial. Prospective evaluation of food and clothing co-operatives in India could reveal opportunities for establishing similar community-based initiatives in developed countries. The methodologies adopted by such programmes suggest that they could be readily transferred into inner-city regeneration schemes, currently underway in UK. The WHO's 'Healthy Cities' scheme in Sheffield, for example, has a remit to expand its programme to include such ideas.

The chapter further concludes that the concept of lesson drawing provides the most appropriate analytical instruments for accessing and enabling the successful transfer of relevant 'foreign' programmes into domestic settings. The concept views programmes as the primary setting for gaining new policy knowledge. It is modified here to also acknowledge the role for informal agents and their activities in importing programme knowledge. These non-state actors and their informal methods are perhaps better placed than their official counterparts to promote 'lateral thinking' in relation to policy problems and to generate potential solutions from a broader range of perspectives. Their political non-alignment and altruistic tendencies place them outside the usual political bounds, allowing greater freedom to search for and share 'new' ideas.

In sum, there is little doubt that important options exist for policy-makers beyond the search parameters encapsulating current policy transfer activity. Further research is now required to access programmes in developing countries in order to add their potential to the body of available policy knowledge to ensure that policy-making is a rational activity.

Chapter 11

Policy Transfer Between Developing Countries: The Transfer of the Bolsa-Escola Programme to Ecuador

Xenia Lana and Mark Evans

Introduction

This chapter attempts to bridge a significant gap in the literature on policy transfer – the tendency to ignore the study of the transfer of policies, programmes and ideas outside the North American-European axis. The case study literature is heavily biased towards the study of processes of policy transfer among developed countries, mainly the United Kingdom and the United States. As Stone (1999: 57) puts it: '...To-date, Western scholars have been more concerned to look at policy transfer between OECD countries than say, transfer between Latin American countries'. There is also a lack of case study literature concerning policy transfer in South-American countries. This is rather a curious oversight, for the literature on social policy and on development studies frequently makes reference to cases of developing countries serving as exemplars to other developing countries in fields such as economic liberalization, community participation, health policy and education (Haagh and Helgo, 2002). For example, the National Training Agencies model, developed initially in Brazil under the labels SENAI and SENAC, was transferred to most Latin American countries (see Tokman and O'Donnell, 1998: 98). As Anthony Nedley demonstrated in the previous chapter, developed countries can and should learn lessons from developing nations. In sum, he advocates the possibility of a 'south-to-north' direction of transfers. This chapter builds on this argument but addresses a different gap in the literature – the lack of studies concerning 'south-to-south' transfers. Thus, the main theoretical contribution of this chapter is to study the applicability of the policy transfer approach to the analysis of transfers between developing countries. It argues that policy transfer analysis is applicable to the study of transfers between developing countries and presents a multi-level framework for examining such processes. It further argues that knowledge institutions play an important role in facilitating and implementing 'South-to-South' transfers.

The main empirical contribution of the chapter is the development of an original case study of the voluntary transfer of the *Bolsa-escola* (School Scholarship) programme from Brazil to Ecuador, named the *Beca escolar* programme. Both are developing countries in South America that share a colonial past, have recently democratized their institutions and face similar socio-economic challenges. The transfer of the *Bolsa-escola* programme was mediated by a Brazilian knowledge institution called *Missão Criança* (Child Mission). Hence, this experience of transfer is appropriate both for testing the assumptions underpinning the study and linking theory and empiricism. The case study approach adopted in this chapter largely rests on qualitative documentary analysis. This includes the examination of primary (for example, governmental and non governmental policy documents) and secondary (literature drawn from the study of policy transfer, development studies and Latin American politics) source materials. In addition, a broad range of elite interviews was conducted with key protagonists involved in the process of policy transfer.

The chapter is organized into three substantive sections and a conclusion. Section one develops a multi-level framework that combines Dolowitz and Marsh's (1996, 2000) inclusive policy transfer framework with considerations of the macro and meso-level contexts of policy transfer drawn from the work of Evans and Davies (1999), Evans with McComb (1999) and Ladi (2003). Section two evaluates the agent of transfer, *Missão Criança,* and considers its role in diffusing the *Bolsa-escola* programme among developing nations: particular attention is given here to the role of a Brazilian policy entrepreneur, Cristovam Buarque, in the process of transfer. Section three presents an analysis of the transfer of *Bolsa-escola* from Brazil to Ecuado using a multi-level policy transfer framework. The concluding section identifies a range of lessons that can be drawn from the case study in order to consider the constraints and opportunities for the practice of policy transfer between developing countries.

Understanding Policy Transfer Between Developed Countries: A Multi-level Perspective

The main research question addressed in this chapter is – what are the constraints and opportunities for the study and practice of policy transfer between developing countries? It will be contended that in certain policy areas, developing countries have much to learn from each other's experiences because of the sharing of similar structural conditions (global economic challenges, colonial legacies, failed institutions, declining social-economic contexts, etc.) and similar problems (illiteracy, infant mortality, parallel power, mass poverty, a large informal productive sector, etc.). The nature of this hypothesis suggests the need for a multi-level approach to the research question that takes into account the macro-level variables that impact upon processes of transfer in developing countries; in short, an account that considers the relationship between structure and agency in the process of policy change. Dolowitz and Marsh's framework (1996; 2000), together with a consideration of the macro and meso-level contexts of policy transfer drawn from the work of Evans and Davies (1999), Evans with McComb

(1999) and Ladi (2003) will be used to address this research problem.

The literature is also deficient in terms of case studies in which the role of knowledge institutions as agents of transfer in developing countries is examined. This is a further glaring omission when one considers their increasing influence in international policy-making. Thus, a further focus of this chapter is to investigate the following subsidiary research questions. In the context of an underdeveloped third sector, what role do knowledge institutions play in the process of transfer in developing countries? What gives them a stake in such processes? It is assumed *a priori* that their increased influence is connected to the state of development of the countries in which money for aid pushes policy change.

In 1996, Dolowitz and Marsh developed a seminal literature review of the main approaches to the study of policy transfer focusing mainly on the work of Rose (1991; 1993), Bennett (1991) and Wolman (1992). The review was organized around a series of questions that formed the basis of a framework for empirical research (Dolowitz and Marsh, 2000). What is policy transfer? Who is involved in transfer? Why transfer? What is transferred? From where? What is the degree of transfer? What factors constrain or facilitate policy transfer? And, how is the process of transfer related to policy 'success' or policy 'failure'?

Dolowitz and Marsh's approach was regarded as more comprehensive than previous studies for two main conceptual reasons. First, their definition of transfer is broad enough to encompass both voluntary and coercive processes of transfer within and between nations. Secondly, the concept of policy transfer is used as both a dependent and an independent variable. In other words, they seek to explain what causes and impacts on the process of transfer as well as how a process of policy transfer leads to a particular policy output. As demonstrated by Dolowitz's (1997) analysis of how the British government learned from American employment policy, the framework provides an extremely useful tool for organizing case study research and classifying the process of transfer under study.

The explanatory power of the model, however, is limited, as it does not provide a detailed account of the role of actors in processes of agenda setting and transfer. Nor do they provide an adequate theorization of the relationship between broader structural processes of economic, political and social change and processes of policy transfer. Moreover, they fail to provide a theoretical model from where hypothesis can be developed and tested. Page (2000: 12), for example, concludes that the researcher should not expect from the policy transfer literature '...firm guidance about how to frame the research questions or how to pursue them empirically'. However, the broad issues raised in their literature review have been successfully used in empirical research for organising case study investigations and focusing the attention of the researcher on critical variables (see Common, 2001; Dolowitz *et al.*, ed., 2000; Evans and Davies, 1999).

In order to develop insights into what happens when developing countries learn from each other, a focus on the meso-level or interorganizational level of analysis is required. Additionally, an investigation of the macro level structures is necessary to explain policy change in such environments. As chapters three, four, five, six, and seven in this volume reveal, Evans and Davies (1999) offer a consistent methodological approach for analysing the process of policy transfer and linking these levels of analysis. Hence this chapter expands the scope of Dolowitz and Marsh's (1996, 2000) model of policy transfer analysis to include an examination of macro-level variables. The understanding of policy transfer and change demands an examination of the macro-contextual variables concerning the countries and organizations involved. Such variables are related to both exogenous and endogenous environmental factors (Common, 2001). Partly following Evans and Davies (1999), this study will investigate the structures and processes facilitating and/or constraining the transfer of the *Bolsa-escola* programme from Brazil to Ecuador. *A priori*, the variables to be addressed by this study are the level of development of the countries and the global economic challenges faced by the region; the impact of structural adjustment policies and the role of international organizations in 'pushing' the implementation of safety-net programmes; the role of ideology and the recent re-democratization of the state and civil society that has been responsible for incorporating new demands on to the public policy agenda. These variables will be investigated in more detail in the case study sections that follow.

A further focus of this perspective is to provide the methodological tools for evaluating the role of knowledge institutions in transferring policies, ideas and programmes between developing countries. A useful framework for the study of the role of *Missão Criança* in processes of transfer between developing countries, particularly in the case of Ecuador seems to be the one devised by Ladi (2000). Ladi's framework draws on the work of Stone (1996) and Evans and Davies (1999) and illustrate the potential roles that think tanks can perform in processes of transfer. In this chapter, however, *Missão Criança* will be defined as a knowledge institution rather than a think tank. This is not an arbitrary distinction. Firstly, think tank is a term that means 'different things to different people' (Stone, 1996: 9), but always carries the notion of the type of policy advocacy performed by North American think tanks which is not always applicable to similar institutions in other countries. For example, in Stone's (1996) comparative study of American and British research institutes, it is claimed that '...think tanks are not involved in the details of policy implementation or the formal decision making process'. Such a characterization holds with regard to American independent research institutes, but is rather limiting in the study of the role of similar institutes in developing countries, especially the ones involved in policy transfer.

The second reason for the preference for the term knowledge institution is that it immediately refers to the main resource that gives organizations such as *Missão Criança* a stake in the political game. Knowledge institutions possess knowledge and it is this asset that '...place[s] them at the centre of policy developments requiring expert advice and technical information' (Ladi, 2000: 208).

Given these considerations it is appropriate to modify Ladi's (2000) framework and define knowledge institutions as non-profit making ·organizations, distinct from government and from academic research institutes, which devote their research production and networking capabilities to providing policy advice with the ultimate aim of influencing policy outcomes. Ladi (2000) uses the stages model developed by Evans and Davies (1999), to identify the potential role of think tanks as agents of voluntary policy transfer. The list is not exhaustive, but provides a starting point for the discussion of the case of *Missão Criança* that will take place in the next section. The framework is presented in Table 11.1.

Hence, in order to understand what happens when developing countries voluntarily lesson-draw from each other, a multi-level approach will be employed. The process of policy transfer will be investigated both as a dependent and an independent variable. With regard to the former, this will allow us to investigate how the structural context of a developing country affects its ability to draw lessons from other developing countries. The case study will identify and examine the process of policy transfer from the perspective of its structural context. Moreover, the process of policy transfer will also be treated as an independent variable. The purpose here is to understand what impact the process of policy transfer and the actors involved have on the policy outcome and the policy environment. An overview of this multi-level framework is presented in Table 11.2.

It is necessary here to briefly observe a critical methodological problem embedded in the study of policy transfer. The study of policy transfer demands outstanding access to policy participants. However, access to these elites can be very difficult as policy transfer networks are an ad-hoc phenomenon (Evans and Davies, 1999: 375). Once the transfer is achieved (or even when it fails) the network ceases to exist. As a result, many of the key actors are often no longer a part, or even in contact with the state and non-state organizations. In this case study, many of the policy participants now occupy positions in other institutions. The chapter also employs a single case-study methodology to investigate policy transfer in developing countries. There are obvious limitations in drawing general conclusions from the analysis of one single case study. However, the depth of the study permits insights that indicate avenues for future research on the peculiarities of voluntary or coercive policy transfer in developing countries and on the role of knowledge organizations in such processes.

Studying Agents of Policy Transfer: *Missão Criança* and the *Bolsa-escola* Programme

The main empirical contribution of this chapter lies in the study of the transfer of the *Bolsa-escola* programme from the Federal District in Brazil to the Ecuadorian Central Government under the programme title of *Beca-escolar*. The *Bolsa-escola* programme consists of monthly cash payments to mothers in the poorest and most vulnerable households. The payment is made on the condition that all children of school age regularly attend classes. Due to its significant impact on both school attendance and short-term poverty, *Bolsa-escola* has served as a model for the development of similar projects by governments in Latin America and Africa. The programme has been or is being introduced in Guatemala, El Salvador, Tanzania,

Table 11.1 The potential role of knowledge institutions in the emergence and development of a voluntary process of transfer

1. *Problem Recognition*: recognition by experts of emerging problems, advice about the need for policy change.

2. *Search for solutions*: independent investigation of potential solutions, which can include research into other political systems.

3. *Contact with agents of transfer*: attempts to become involved in the solution to the problem by lobbying, and through expert commentary.

4. *Emergence of an information feeder network*: knowledge institutions act as information clearing houses; their influence rests on their reputation for expert knowledge on the policy issue

5. *Cognition, reception and emergence of a transfer network*: certain knowledge institutions will be recognized as sharing a commitment to a common value system through their incorporation into the policy transfer network.

6. *Elite and cognitive mobilization:* knowledge institutions assist in coalition building and seek funding to generate more information about the policy problem. Knowledge institutions also act as 'gate-keepers' to the policy network.

7. *Interaction with potential donors*: knowledge institutions help to convene and build consensus in the network through knowledge exchange.

8. *Policy evaluation*: knowledge institutions help in the assessment of cross-national evidence. They often advocate certain solutions.

9. *The formal decision stream*: knowledge institutions have a limited role in formal decision-making.

10. *Implementation*: knowledge institutions monitor and evaluate implementation, provide feedback to government, advise on how the policy can be modified to fit local circumstances.

Source: Developed from Evans and Davies, 1999.

São Tomé, Príncipe and Ecuador, amongst others and is also frequently recommended by international organizations, such as the WB, the IDB, UNCTAD, the ILO and UNICEF.

The *Bolsa-escola* programme is designed to simultaneously guarantee universal basic schooling and to ensure a minimum income to highly impoverished families.

Table 11.2 Multi-level policy transfer analysis

1
Global, International and Transnational Structures

Economic, technological, ideological and institutional structures constrain the autonomy of state actors at levels 2 and 3.

2
The State of Development

The state has limited autonomy from structural forces (economic, technological, ideological and institutional) at the level of strategic selectivity due to reliance on international organizations and events in level 1.

3
Meso-Level: the Policy Transfer Network

A network of indigenous and exogenous agents in resource dependent relationships with some level of autonomy from structural forces at the level of options analysis and implementation in processes of policy transfer. Events at level 3 are largely explained by reference to 1 & 2.

Source: developed from Evans and Davies (1999).

According to the scheme implemented in the Federal District in 1995, the payment of a minimum salary (US$76, in 1999) was directly transferred to families below the poverty line of half a minimum wage per person (Araújo and Aguiar, 2002). The allowance was paid monthly to the mother of the household upon meeting the condition that all children of school age were enrolled and regularly attending classes in public schools. The Federal District's experience has informed the establishment of the programme in other contexts. The scheme:

- represented a shift from traditional social assistance policies based on in-kind donations;
- revealed that targeting was necessary to guarantee universal access to public services and to increase the efficiency of public spending on social assistance programming;
- demonstrated that direct cash transfers are more efficient and prevent corruption, because the administration of the resources is given directly to the beneficiaries; and,
- was delivered at such a scale to produce a real impact on alleviating poverty (ILO and UNCTAD, 2001: 3).

It lies outside the scope of this chapter to provide a detailed review of the *Bolsa-escola* programme, as it was implemented in the Federal District, as we are fundamentally interested in investigating the agents that participated in the development and diffusion of the *Bolsa-escola* programme.

The Policy Environment

The conceptual roots of the *Bolsa-escola* programme were developed in Brazil at the beginning of the 1980s. At that time, it was evident that the import substitution industrialization strategies and the focus on economic growth transformed Brazil into a modern industrialized economy. However, widespread rural and growing urban poverty contradicted the rhetoric that economic growth would lead to poverty reduction. Indeed, social indicators demonstrated the fallacy of the argument that the wealth generated by economic growth would spread through all society in a 'trickle-down' pattern (Buarque, 2000). At the beginning of the 1980s, Brazil's acute disparities in the distribution of national incomes and access to basic public services by the poorest were similar to, or worse than, the 1960s (Pereira and Barros, 2000; Clements and Kim, 1988).

The downturn in the world economy at the end of the 1970s helped to demonstrate the inconsistency of a development model that was highly vulnerable to global economic fluctuations. Brazil was highly indebted and had experienced several unsuccessful macro-economic stabilization plans to curb hyperinflation. Such plans impacted most severely on the living conditions of the poorest sections of society. In 1985, with the end of more than 20 years of military rule, the development model adopted in Brazil since the end of the Second World War started to attract profound and widespread criticism. A discussion group comprised of academics, students, trade unionists and activists formed the University of Brasília (UnB) to debate on and formulate policies to confront national problems, especially the lack of universal access to education. In 1987, a policy proposal emerged from this discussion group involving the payment of a monthly stipend to poor families to keep their children at school (Aguiar and Araújo, 2003).

Policy Entrepreneurship: the Development and Diffusion of the Bolsa-escola Programme

The UnB group was coordinated by Cristovam Buarque, the then Rector of the University. Buarque has played a remarkable role in the development and diffusion of the *Bolsa-escola* programme both in Brazil and internationally. In the following passage, the Brazilian journalist Gilberto Dimenstein (cited in Araújo and Aguiar, 2002: 7) summarizes the nature of Buarque's role in policy advocacy:

It was the former Governor of the Federal District Cristovam Buarque who gave visibility to the idea and seduced the country. He made *Bolsa-escola* not only the cause of an administration but also the cause of his life. Because of his respected scholarship, Cristovam Buarque attracted the attention of UNICEF and UNESCO, which, interested in spreading efficient and low-cost solutions, endorsed *Bolsa-escola* and developed it into a global model.

Buarque is an academic and a politician affiliated to the left-oriented Workers' Party (Partido dos Trabalhadores). In 2002, Buarque was appointed Minister of Education under the Presidency of Luis Ignacio Lula da Silva. He has used his access to academic, political, governmental and development circles throughout his career to create a national and international network in support of *Bolsa-escola*. It is noteworthy that Buarque worked as a consultant for the Inter-American Development Bank (IDB) between 1973 and 1979. His activity as a policy actor provides a textbook example of policy entrepreneurship (see Rose, 1993: 56). Between 1987 and 1994, Buarque created public support for the idea of *Bolsa-escola*. In this period, he presented the project and ensured that it was the subject of public debate in several cities around Brazil. The scepticism faced by Buarque, even inside his own party, is well documented in Araújo and Aguiar (2002). In 1989, Buarque contributed to the development of conditional cash transfer programmes, similar to *Bolsa-escola*, in Venezuela and in Mexico. In 1994, drawing on the work produced within the UnB group, Buarque published the book *A revolução nas prioridades* (Revolution through priorities), in which he developed the ideological foundations to a proposal for a new development model in Brazil. The *Bolsa-escola* programme was included among 103 other reforms (see Buarque, 1994).

Buarque was given his first opportunity to implement *Bolsa-escola* in Brazil when he was elected Governor of the Federal District (Brasília) in 1994. The programme was jointly evaluated by UNESCO and UNICEF three years after its implementation. The evaluation used both quantitative and qualitative data to conclude that the programme had enhanced the quality of life and self-esteem of the families in extreme poverty and had improved school attendance and performance. Additionally, the programme helped to create a positive image for schooling and prevented child labour (UNESCO, UNICEF and POLIS, 1998). Because of the positive results and the low operational costs, UNESCO recommended that the WB and the IDB finance similar projects (Araújo and Aguiar, 2002). The Federal District's experience rapidly became an international reference point. Since then, *Bolsa-escola* has become regarded as one of the best initiatives for confronting child labour and social exclusion in developing countries (*Missão Criança*, 2003). Despite the success of the programme, Buarque was not re-elected in 1998. However, the popularity of *Bolsa-escola* ensured its continuity in the Federal District, although the new administration transformed some of the operational details of the programme.

The Diffusion of the Bolsa-escola Programme in Brazil

The version of *Bolsa-escola* implemented in the Federal District served as a model or an inspiration to similar experiences in other municipalities and states in Brazil. However, it is worth noting that many of the municipal and state programmes in Brazil have not experienced the same impressive results of the Federal District (World Bank, 2001). Lavinas (1999) observes that, in some instances, only a small portion of the target population has benefited and the cash transfer is either too low or has been substituted with 'in kind' donations. Frequently, the programme is not linked to other policies, the continuity of the programme is not guaranteed and there are no defined targets. The ultimate goal of many of these programmes has been to occupy the time of idle children rather than to guarantee the completion of basic schooling. In some cities, for example, there is a rotation of beneficiaries every year (Lavinas, 1999). The haste in putting such programmes into operation and/or the lack of budget resources have been responsible for the problems. In sum, the diffusion of *Bolsa-escola* in Brazil is, in many cases, a good example of Ikenberry's (1990) policy 'bandwagoning'.

In 2001, the Brazilian Federal Government also launched a version of the *Bolsa-escola* programme. In this scheme, the Federal Government funds half of the costs of the programme in municipalities with per capita income and tax revenue below their state average. Evaluations of such programme have demonstrated its efficiency in increasing school attendance. However, given the small size of the cash transfer, the impact on poverty and social exclusion reduction has been minimal (Bourguignon *et al.*, 2001).

The Establishment of Missão Criança

At the end of his term of office in December 1998, Mr Buarque founded a non-governmental organization called *Missão Criança* (Child Mission). Its purpose was to create a national support network for the *Bolsa-escola* programme and to advocate its implementation at the national level (Aguiar and Araújo, 2003). The establishment of *Missão Criança* was made possible by the development of programme expertise during Buarque's administration. Indeed, many of the key experts involved in the implementation of the *Bolsa-escola* programme started working for *Missão Criança* and played a key role in the transfer of *Bolsa-escola* to Ecuador.

Missão Criança is a Brazilian non-governmental organization, independent from any particular political party or religion. It seeks to influence the development of education and poverty alleviation policies, in order to eradicate child labour and guarantee actual universal access to schooling. *Missão Criança* also advises local and state governments, as well as NGOs, on how to implement programmes to promote education. It has participated in the transfer of the *Bolsa-escola* programme to developing countries in Latin America and Africa, such as Honduras, El Salvador, Ecuador, Guatemala, São Tomé and Príncipe and Tanzania (*Missão Criança*, 2003). *Missão Criança* also runs a non-governmental version of the *Bolsa-escola* programme and, because it does not receive governmental subsidies, it has to raise its own funds to finance its activities.

To date, *Bolsa-escola* is one of many programmes that *Missão Criança* has developed to make education a central concern of politicians, businessmen and families. It also seeks to involve civil society in voluntary actions to reduce social exclusion, for example, implementing programmes to promote ecological and cultural awareness, to stimulate healthcare, and to reduce IT and adult illiteracy. By promoting the engagement of voluntaries and the private sector, *Missão*

Criança attempts to spread the idea that child labour and the low levels of schooling are problems that require the participation of the whole society.

Missão Criança has actively promoted the *Bolsa-escola* internationally to governments and non-governmental institutions. *Missão Criança* organizes conferences and takes part in international seminars related to education and child labour eradication. Indeed Buarque personally visited 52 countries between 1999 and 2001 to disseminate the idea and the results of *Bolsa-escola* (Araújo and Aguiar, 2002). *Missão Criança* also generates publications on *Bolsa-escola*, 'universalization' of schooling and promotion of social inclusion. Such publications have been produced to target different sectors of civil society, such as business executives, other NGOs, trade union leaders, and politicians. They highlight the role each of these sectors and individuals can play in promoting education. A set of these publications has been sent to development agencies' offices around the world to promote the idea of *Bolsa-escola*. It is worth noting that such publications not only explain the programme but also inform and advocate its ideological foundations.

In 1999, *Missão Criança* established a partnership with UNESCO to transfer the *Bolsa-escola* programme to Ecuador. The success of the experience led UNESCO to cooperate technically and financially with *Missão Criança* in other projects to transfer *Bolsa-escola*. Since then, *Missão Criança* has worked with local, municipal, state and national governments as well as other NGOs and companies interested in implementing or expanding child labour programmes. Such work includes the identification of local problems and needs and the development of a pilot programme informed by such diagnosis. *Missão Criança* is also often involved technically during the implementation phase, transferring expertise on how to register families, distribute benefits, and evaluate programmes. The borrowing organization has autonomy to determine the operational details of the programme being developed, as long as the fundamental principle of *Bolsa-escola* – the promotion of universal basic schooling – is not altered (Cláudia Camargos, Project Coordinator, *Missão Criança,* author interview, 23 June 2003).

An important component of *Missão Criança's* recent work has been the implementation of a non-governmental version of *Bolsa-escola*. The project is called *Bolsa-escola Cidadã* or 'Citizen's Scholarship' and is currently in operation in cities located in a diverse range of regions of Brazil, rural and urban areas alike. The ultimate objective is to attract the attention and the participation of civil society in tackling problems of social exclusion. As this programme works on a small scale in different contexts, it helps *Missão Criança* to experiment and refine the institutional version of *Bolsa-escola*, adapting it and reformulating it in accordance with the characteristics of each environment. *Bolsa-escola Cidadã* runs with the cooperation of local NGOs, responsible for the execution of the programme. In 2001, the programme involved 3,153 children from 1,173 families in 17 Brazilian cities (*Missão Criança*, 2003). The project is funded exclusively by donations from individuals, the private sector and international organizations, such as USAID, EU, UNICEF, and UNESCO.

International Partnerships

The work of *Missão Criança* is funded and endorsed by several national and international organizations. For example, in Brazil, the coordination and the supervision of programmes and projects of technical cooperation non-commercially received from or transferred to the country are the responsibility of an agency of the Ministry of Foreign Relations (*Agência Brasileira de Cooperação* – ABC). ABC does not carry out the programmes itself but contracts a Brazilian non-profit organization to implement them. The support of ABC to such organizations consists, chiefly, of training and the payment of travel expenses to the consultants (Agência Brasileira de Cooperação, 2003). *Missão Criança* has been invited by the ABC to work on the transfer of *Bolsa-escola* to Guatemala, El Salvador and Mozambique. With the support of ABC, *Missão Criança* has also worked on the transference of specific features of the programme, such as the technology delivering the payment of the stipend through magnetic cards, to Mexico and Ecuador. The consultancy provided by *Missão Criança* is also sponsored by the UNDP. The UNDP pays the experts' fees and travel expenses. It also finances the implementation of the resulting programme or makes possible the transference of funds from other sources. According to Cláudia Camargos, the Project Coordinator at *Missão Criança*, technical and financial partnerships also exist with UNESCO, UNICEF, Oxfam, USAID, the WB and the ILO (Ibid).

The Role of Missão Criança in Processes of Policy Transfer

The definition of a knowledge institution proposed at the outset is applicable to *Missão Criança*, because it uses knowledge to influence the development of public policies related to the improvement of access to education in developing countries as a strategy for addressing problems of poverty and social exclusion. Nevertheless, *Missão Criança* has another distinctive characteristic. It goes beyond policy advocacy through its involvement in policy implementation. *Bolsa-escola Cidadã* is simultaneously part of the research agenda of the organization and a strategy that the institution uses to facilitate policy change. This is an implication of the fact that *Missão Criança*'s policy métier is not exclusive to the state. For example, knowledge institutions devoted to privatization or the advocacy of NPM are by definition precluded from implementing the policies they recommend. Moreover, the quality of the institutions advice is partly derived from its experience of implementation issues in the field. Finally, and most importantly, *Missão Criança*'s policy implementation function may also be explained by the state of development of the country in which it operates which is characterized by the inability of government to respond to the basic needs of the citizenry. This also explains the interest of international organizations in *Missão Criança*, because NGOs are often deemed more accountable and effective than governmental organizations in implementing social inclusion schemes in developing countries.

Missão Criança has a very active role at the problem recognition stage of processes of policy transfer. It uses publications, international seminars, bilateral meetings with governmental and international organizations and fact finding missions to raise awareness of all dimensions of the problem of poverty reduction and the strategies that can be used to alleviate suffering. It attempts to persuade governments in developing and developed nations, as well as international aid agencies that investment in children's education is a rational policy choice. It is significant that relevant international political players such as George Soros, Bill Clinton and Kofi Annan have expressed their support in favour of targeted educational programmes and have all cited *Bolsa-escola* as an example of a successful, rational and relatively inexpensive initiative (see Araújo and Aguiar, 2002: 62-66).

Missão Criança has also contributed to the search for innovative ideas by governments and international organizations. For example, it has investigated the applicability and the feasibility of the *Bolsa-escola* model in African states (Buarque, 2002). *Missão Criança* expertise in this field provides it with the resources to gain access to policy transfer networks. Indeed *Missão Criança* works to create policy transfer networks to facilitate or to fund the implementation of schemes similar to *Bolsa-escola*. It is important to note, however, that in the process of transferring the *Bolsa-escola* programme to Ecuador, it was the WB and the IDB, on the advice of UNESCO, who decided to include *Missão Criança* in the transfer network. *Missão Criança* uses its knowledge and elite mobilization skills to form supportive coalitions and to identify funding possibilities. Moreover, experts from *Missão Criança* travel to other countries to help design and implement new programmes. For example, in 2003 Cláudia Camargos travelled to Guatemala to advise on the transfer of the *Bolsa-escola* programme. (Cláudia Camargos, Project Coordinator, *Missão Criança*, author interview, 23 June 2003).

As a knowledge institution, the role of *Missão Criança* in the decision stage is limited to an advisory capacity. For example, in the case of Ecuador, the decision for the adoption of the programme was taken by the President of the country, in response to conditions laid down by the IMF, the WB and the IDB. However, given the level of participation in programme design and implementation, the role of *Missão Criança* in the evaluation of resulting programmes is also highly significant. Missão Criança often plays a key role in the establishment of monitoring systems and follow-up evaluations of pilot programmes in conjunction with indigenous NGOs.

As we shall see in the next section, in Ecuador, the participation of *Bolsa-escola* finished at this stage.

The Transfer of *Bolsa-escola* to Ecuador as *Beca escolar*

This section examines the role of *Missão Criança* in the transfer of the *Bolsa-escola* programme to Ecuador as the *Beca escolar* programme using the multi-level framework derived from Evans and Davies (1999), Dolowitz and Marsh (1996; 2000) and Ladi (2000).

Global, International and Transnational Forces and the State of Development

In 1999 the Ecuadorian government decided to implement a targeted conditional transfer programme based on *Bolsa-escola*. The objective of the programme was to address structural inequalities that had emerged as a consequence of the country's financial and economic crisis. The economic vulnerability of the Ecuadorian population had already reached its nadir due to the impact of structural adjustment plans on the level of social spending. However, the impact of the 1999 crisis was unprecedented and demanded a dramatic response (World Bank, 1999).

The crisis was provoked by a combination of external shocks: the effects of the Asian and the Brazilian financial crises on international emerging markets; the drop in oil prices (Ecuador's most important export commodity); and, the impact of a natural endogenous disaster (*El Niño*) on agricultural production. Ecuadorian GDP plunged by 7.3 per cent, accompanied by an inflation rate in excess of 50 per cent and a devaluation of 65 per cent in the national currency (the *sucre*) (PPS-MBS, 2003; Sedlacek *et al.*, 2000). A banking collapse followed and led the government to default on its external debt. In a period of less than six months, there was a sharp deterioration in the living conditions of Ecuadorian families. The share of the population under the poverty line of $2 a day per person reached 43.8 per cent. Fifteen per cent of Ecuadorians were unemployed and the minimum salary in real value had decreased by 22 per cent (Lavinas, 1999).

Following rising popular dissatisfaction with the stabilization measures, a political crisis ensued. President Jamil Mahuad was ousted in a short-lived coup organized by indigenous political and military leaders and his Vice-President Gustavo Noboa became president in January 2000. Noboa subsequently established a macro-stabilization plan that involved the replacement of the national currency with the American dollar in an agreement with the IMF.

Ecuador's level of development is responsible for the substantial involvement of development agencies in the process of transfer under study. The dependence of Latin American countries on foreign aid gives institutions such as the WB and the IDB a stake in the region's processes of policy making. In the case of *Beca escolar*, Ecuadorian government needed funding for a social protection policy and sought the help of the Banks. In return, they were granted an important role in the development of the programme. The comparable level of development between Brazil and Ecuador also explains why the Brazilian programme was considered as a model to be emulated. Similarly to Brazil, Ecuador had the available infrastructure and substantial budget for education. Nevertheless, social indicators did not reflect such situation. In 1999, the average of schooling years in Brazil was five to six years. The situation was worse in poorest areas such as the Northeast or the countryside (Lavinas, 1999). In Ecuador, the average of schooling for the period 1990-1999 was 6.7 years. In rural areas, the average was only 4 years of education (Lavinas, 1999). In 1999, in the poorest quintile of the population, only 12 per cent of the children finished primary education. Child labour also plagued both countries. In Brazil, child labour is estimated in 20 per cent (7.6 million) of the children from 10 to 17 years of age (data from 1999 in IBGE, 2001). In

Ecuador, 9 per cent of the Ecuadorian children were working and did not attend school in 1999. In the countryside, this number rises to 16.2 per cent of children (Lavinas, 1999).

Hence, the ineffectivess of educational investments in countries such as Ecuador and Brazil has its roots in the traditional lack of policy coordination and in the wrong focus of the investments (Lavinas, 1999; World Bank, 1999; IDB, 2000). The Brazilian experience was seen as a model to face these structural challenges because it addressed basic schooling directly, demonstrated a potential to promote better policy coordination, and had over 90 per cent of its costs reaching the final beneficiaries (Lavinas, 1999).

The State of Development and the Collapse of Political Institutions

Since the end of military rule, the democratic institutions of Ecuador have been constantly shaken by the developments of economic crises, corruption-related scandals and ruinous party politics (La Hora, 2003). As a result, Ecuador has rarely enjoyed administrative continuity. For example, in the period 1992-1999, the country had six presidents. The ousting of Jamil Mahuad in 2000 caused disruption to the process of policy transfer. This was aggravated by the frequent replacement of ministers responsible for the Education and Social Welfare departments. The upshot was a long and clumsy policy transfer process, in which actors and roles varied considerably over time.

The State of Development and the Role of Policy Belief Systems

In Latin America, external funding agencies promote 'second-generation reforms' (health, education, and social protection), with the explicit objective of achieving the Millennium Development Goals (MDG) for the region. Focused social spending and measures to break the intergenerational cycle of poverty are the prevailing ideology underpinning such reforms. *Bolsa-escola* matched the new orientation of the WB and the IDB and addressed directly or indirectly the three first MDGs (to eradicate extreme poverty and hunger; to achieve universal primary education; to promote gender equality and empower women). This ideological identification conditioned the policy options available for the Ecuadorian officials and led to the adoption of a foreign model rather than the expansion of *Bono Solidario*.

Meso-level Analysis: Understanding the Process of Policy Transfer

The need to provide the poorest households with help was reinforced by the WB in its debt negotiations with President Mahuad in 1999 (Lavinas, 1999; World Bank, 1999). Funding was earmarked for a means-tested conditional safety-net programme linked to education programming (World Bank, 1999). Contrary to Mahuad's wishes the existing social programme, *Bono Solidario* (Solidarity Bonus) was not considered for funding because of improper targeting and its failure to meet WB conditions (PPS-MBS, 2003). Through *Bono Solidario,* a small amount of money ($10) was paid to the head of the household, the elderly and to those who could not work due to mental or physical impairment. In October 1999, Buarque, then President of *Missão Criança,* was invited by the WB and the IDB to present the *Bolsa-escola* programme to Ecuadorian officials. A consultancy project was then set up to devise a programme similar to *Bolsa-escola.* The project group involved experts from the WB and the IDB in partnership with the Ministry of Human Development and the Ministry of Education of Ecuador (World Bank, 1999). UNESCO and *Missão Criança* were also asked to establish a technical group to design *Beca-escolar* and its implementation arrangements. The Banks earmarked 90 million dollars to fund *Beca escolar* in the period 2000-2003, and financed some activities during its development phase.

In the two months that followed, a series of feasibility studies were conducted. These included: an assessment of the educational infrastructure of the country and the legislation for basic education; the development of criteria for informing the selection of the poorest and most vulnerable families in Ecuador; the design of appropriate monitoring procedures, payment methods, implementation and human resource strategies; and, the implementation of pilot programmes. However, due to the politically turbulent policy environment the project could not proceed. But in the aftermath of the overthrow of Mahuad, the process of transfer was resumed under Noboa's administration. In 2000, because of budget restrictions, political disagreements between the Ministries involved and inconsistencies in the system devised to identify the beneficiaries, the first version of *Beca escolar* was repeatedly refined. The responsibility for the programme also changed hands several times: from the defunct Ministry of Human Development to the Ministry of Education and Culture to the National Modernization Council, and finally in January 2001, to the Social Protection Programme in the Ministry of Social Welfare (PPS-MBS). At the end of January 2001, a technical delegation of the PPS-MBS had a meeting with WB and IDB experts in Washington, DC, to discuss the development of the project. At the meeting it was agreed that the Ecuadorian government should devise a final version of *Beca escolar.* However, according to Ecuadorian officials, when the final version was completed, the WB and the IDB abandoned the project:

> ... surprisingly and without explanation, the WB decided to withdraw its funding because it identified other investment priorities. The IDB on the other hand kept to the agreement initially but then decided not to continue the funding. So we decided to go on by ourselves not only with the programme design but also with the implementation (Francisco Enríquez, Senior Civil Servant, Government of Ecuador, *author interview*, 17 September 2003).

In April 2001, the pilot programme was initiated with the technical and financial support of UNICEF, and Ecuador finally established the official national version of *Beca escolar* in 2002. Public resources have subsequently been used to finance the programme.

The decision of the Ecuadorian government to transfer the *Bolsa-escola* programme was informed by a combination of voluntary and coercive factors. The interviews conducted for this research indicate that the President of Ecuador at the time of the transfer had a great interest in implementing a project to protect the country's human capital and, simultaneously, to provide a safety net for the population at greater risk (Marcelo Aguiar, Senior Civil Servant, Government of Ecuador, *author interview*, 15 August 2003, and, Francisco Enríquez, Senior Civil Servant, Government of Ecuador, *author interview*, 17 September 2003). There is evidence, however, that the necessary 'push' for *Bolsa-escola* was precipitated by the political and economic situation combined with the conditionality of the WB and the IDB loan. The reports produced by the Social Protection Programme state the necessity of '...compensating those most affected by the structural reforms of the country' (PPS-MBS, 2002: 3). The interest of the WB and the IDB in introducing and funding social assistance measures in the country is also evident (see WB, 1999 and IDB, 2000). The IDB and the WB's project reports also suggest that the Ecuadorian government had little autonomy in choosing where to search for lessons. Thus, it seems correct to classify this transfer as a 'negotiated transfer', since the Banks had to convince the Ecuadorian government of the rationality behind the implementation of *Beca escolar* and an exchange of resources occurred.

During the initial phase of policy development, coordinated by the WB and the IDB, the Ecuadorian president and the Minister of Education were personally involved in the development of *Beca escolar*. In 2001, responsibility for the programme was transferred to the Ministry of Social Welfare. The participation of *Missão Criança* was fundamental during the process of negotiation between the WB, the IDB and the Ecuadorian government in the adoption of *Beca escolar*. As a private consultant involved in the process confirms:

> The WB decided to contact them because inside the Government there were disagreements over the concept and the details of the programme. The Brazilians became salesmen, and explained to the Government the advantages of the programme and the success it had in Brazil (Francisco Ayala, *author interview*, 17 September 2003).

Prior to this point, *Missão Criança* played an important role in disseminating details of the programme among international funding organizations. In the design of *Beca escolar*, however, *Missão Criança*'s participation was limited to technical assistance.

The Brazilian government was not involved at all in the process of policy transfer to Ecuador in the period 1999 to 2002. As Marcelo Aguiar (former Executive Secretary of *Missão Criança, author interview*, 18 August 2003), explains: '...it was in our interest to have the involvement of ABC, because of the support it provides. But at that time, *Missão Criança* still did not have an agreement with ABC'. In 2003, *Missão Criança* was contacted through the ABC to transfer the technology of payment through magnetic cards to Ecuador. According to Mr Francisco Enriquez (*Author interview*, 27 August 2003), the National Coordinator of the Social Protection Programme in 2000-2001, the version of *Beca escolar* devised with the cooperation of *Missão Criança* was never put into operation at the national level, '...the banks supplied funding in the initial phase, that is, in the design of a programme that was not executed, although some of the elements developed therein were considered in the definitive design'.

A comparison between the original programme, the one proposed by the agents of transfer and the one that was actually implemented confirms the limits to the degree of transfer that occurred. Although these aspirations are clearly linked, the most important difference between the Brazilian and the Ecuadorian programmes is the emphasis by the former on improving literacy rates and the latter on reducing poverty through a financial transfer. In the Federal District, *Bolsa-escola* was based in the Department of Education and was run by an interdisciplinary commission formed by the Departments of Education, Social Development and Labour. In Ecuador, the programme was the responsibility of the Ministry of Social Welfare. In Brazil, the Ministry of Education is responsible for providing educational service and controlling school attendance, while in Ecuador, the *Bolsa-escola* programme is run by a small staff of five officers. Hence, key implementation activities are contracted out to NGOs.

Both documentary analysis and interview data clearly demonstrate that certain features of the *Bolsa-escola* programme are missing from the programme implemented in Ecuador. Their overall goals, instruments and implementation strategies, however, remain very similar. *Beca escolar* was the first conditional cash transfer implemented in Ecuador (PPS-MBS, 2002). Available evidence supports the conclusion that the programme is an emulation of the *Bolsa-escola* programme mediated by *Missão Criança*. The concept and the methodology for its implementation were the product of a process of policy transfer, although certain original features have been culturally assimilated to reflect the Ecuadorian context, especially those concerning implementation issues, such as the form of payment and eligibility criteria. Nonetheless, the core of the programme remains the same.

In Conclusion: 'South' to 'South' Policy Transfer

This chapter has made three main contributions to the study of policy transfer. First, it has made a conceptual contribution through the development of a multi-level approach for investigating processes of transfer between developing countries. Secondly, it has applied this framework to a case of policy transfer between two developing countries. By focusing on a case of south-to-south transfer, it has broadened the scope of the field of enquiry of policy transfer analysis beyond developed countries. Thirdly, in an attempt to advance beyond the study of the role of formal actors, this chapter has focused a significant degree of critical attention on the role of knowledge institutions in advocating, disseminating and implementing policy change in developing nations. There follows a review of the chapter's key theoretical and empirical conclusions.

Opportunity Structures for Policy Transfer in Developing Countries

Intuitively, it is possible to identify at least four opportunity structures for the practice of policy transfer between developing countries. These mostly emanate either from the activities of organizations disseminating foreign experiences or from similar structural variables affecting change in developing countries. First, international funding bodies are frequently disseminating what they call 'best practice'. 'Best practice' refers to policies and programmes that were evaluated by external international agencies and considered to be successful in terms of outcomes and costs. The emulation of 'best practice' by other developing countries is encouraged and even financed by international organizations. This opens up channels for lesson drawing and policy transfer between developing countries. Nevertheless, the limitation of such channels is evident, due to the fact that external funding agencies demand that recipients conform to the dominant ideology of policy-making.

Secondly, the existence of indigenous agencies of technical cooperation in developing countries can and effectively do open up more channels for interaction between developing countries. The importance of agencies such as the Brazilian ABC is that they give developing countries a broader choice in terms of where to look for lessons. By using domestic agencies and seeking alternative funding schemes, developing countries can follow their own agendas regardless of what external agencies have determined to be 'best practice'. Other examples of agencies of cooperation between developing countries are the Community of Portuguese Speaking Countries (*Comunidade de Países de Língua Portuguesa*), which disseminates lessons, for example, between Brazil, the Cape Verde Islands, Mozambique, São Tomé and Príncipe; and, the Andean Community (*Comunidad Andina*), which encourages the exchange of knowledge between Ecuador, Bolivia, Colombia, Peru and Venezuela.

Thirdly, it can be inferred from the case study that policy transfer involving NGOs tends to be extremely common in developing countries. This is mainly because NGOs are deemed to be more accountable, skilled and flexible than governments. Consequently, external funding regimes privilege NGOs' programmes over governmental initiatives. This also reflects the view, widely disseminated by international organizations, that governments should play a coordinating rather than an implementation role.

Fourthly, developing countries experience similar social problems, such as increasing urban violence, unemployment, mass poverty and hunger. The case study reveals that Ecuador and Brazil have to face comparable problems of child labour and high school drop-out rates. Because the Brazilian experience was successful in confronting such problems, it was chosen as a model to be emulated, despite significant social, political, and institutional differences between the two countries.

Processes of Negotiated Coercive Policy Transfer

This case study illuminates some of the key features of negotiated processes of policy transfer in developing countries. The Ecuadorian government was not seeking lessons when they voluntarily contacted the external funding bodies. However, its dependency on foreign capital to implement social protection schemes initiated a process of south-to-south transfer and led to the adoption of a policy that was different from the one that the Ecuadorian officials had in mind. In such a process, the role of a knowledge institution from a developing country was fundamental in terms of convincing the Ecuadorian government about the advantages of transfer and of contributing to the adaptation of the foreign programme. Another interesting aspect of this transfer is that after the WB's and the IDB's withdrawal, the Ecuadorian officials voluntarily decided to implement the project despite the absence of foreign aid.

The case study also demonstrates that a process of policy-making that involves the transfer of knowledge from other settings produces different results in the policy environment. This allows for the important conclusion that processes of policy transfer are distinctive from normal processes of policy-making.

A further conclusion drawn from the case study is that the modification of the original programme is a strategy deployed to minimize implementation problems. The implication of this is that the transfer can still be considered successful, even if the evaluation of the degree of transfer demonstrates that only certain features of the original programme were preserved in the new policy. Hence the analysis of policy content must focus on an assessment of the objectives of inner circle actors and their interests.

Constraints on the Role of Policy Transfer as an Instrument of Rational Policy-making in Developing Countries

The case study identified significant economic, structural and social differences between developing countries that can constrain the emergence of policy transfer networks. For example, Ecuador is a centralized state while Brazil is a federal state. In Ecuador, girls tend to drop-out from school earlier than boys in order to carry out domestic chores. In Brazil, the pattern is the reverse. Ecuador is also a relatively less advanced developing country than Brazil. For example, Brazil's educational infrastructure is more developed and accessible than Ecuador's. As a result of these differences, *Beca escolar* was refined to meet particular indigenous problems such as targeting and implementation coordination. The ILO and UNCTAD have both acknowledged the importance of this process of cultural assimilation. While advocating for the introduction of programmes similar to *Bolsa-escola* in African lesser developed countries (LDCs), they recognize that the implementation of such programmes have to be '...carefully adapted to national circumstances and priorities', since African LDCs are far more rural and are facing the effects of AIDS on household and family structures (ILO and UNCTAD Advisory Group, 2001: ix).

In addition, the absence of administrative continuity provides a substantial constraint on effective policy development in developing countries. Administrative discontinuity can lead to the cessation of policy transfer networks or the modification of its purposes. In the case study, the replacement of both the Ecuadorian President and the Minister of Education, for political reasons, disrupted the process of transferring *Bolsa-escola* to Ecuador, extending the longevity of the process of transfer by two years.

In summary, the multi-level framework has proved a useful approach for analysing the main features of the process of transfer. However, the complexity of the process of transfer in terms of the interaction between structural variables and the actors involved in the process of transfer indicates the limits of the literature in explaining transfer between developing countries. Because of the heavily politicized nature of the policy environment, and, the relationship between knowledge and aid, policy transfer in developing countries demands further examination through the production of more case studies that either corroborate or dismiss the conclusions that have been presented here.

Chapter 12

In Conclusion – Policy Transfer in Global Perspective

Mark Evans

Introduction

This book's main concern has been with identifying the domestic and international circumstances likely to bring about policy transfer, the scope and dimensions of policy transfer and which aspects of the policy transfer framework should and should not be pursued in empirical work. It was hoped that this would allow for the development of a better understanding of the phenomenon of policy transfer and its relationship with global and domestic processes of economic, social and political change. It therefore remains to draw some general conclusions on the implications of our case study findings for the broader study of policy transfer. With this aim in mind my concluding remarks will be organized around the following themes: the domain of enquiry, case study comparison and hypotheses and policy transfer analysis in critical perspective. This will provide an overall assessment of the utility and prospects of policy transfer analysis as a heuristic theory of policy development.

The Domain of Enquiry

Policy transfer analysis can only be distinctive from the analysis of normal forms of policy-making if it focuses on the remarkable movement of ideas between systems of governance through policy transfer networks and the intermediation of agents of policy transfer. This should involve the study of different forms of voluntary and coercive completed transfers, failed transfers and 'in process' transfers between developed countries; from developed to developing countries; and, from developing countries to developing and developed countries. Moreover, while policy transfer analysis remains weak as an explanatory theory of policy change if used in isolation from other theories of policy change, this volume demonstrates that transfer analysts are busy developing a common idiom of theoretical and methodological discourse from which lessons can be drawn and hypotheses developed. These will be presented in the following section.

Policy transfer analysis thus presents a valuable field of study for integrating common research concerns of scholars of domestic, comparative and international politics insofar as it provides a lens for observing both the changing nature of the nation state and the role of state actors and institutions in promoting new forms of complex globalization.

Comparative Lessons – Explaining Policy Transfer

As Table 12.1 shows, there is a general consensus amongst the majority of contributors to this volume that multi-level models of policy transfer analysis that encompass:

- global, international and/or transnational explanations of policy change;
- macro-level explanations of policy change;
- mesó-level analysis of the role of policy transfer networks in mediating policy change; and,
- micro-level analysis of the process of policy oriented learning in and between policy transfer networks,

yield the most comprehensive explanations of policy change. Flores-Crespo, for example, demonstrates the importance of developing a multi-level explanation of policy change in the Mexican education sector in Chapter Eight. He argued that the negotiated policy transfer of the UTs may be viewed partly as a response to the imperatives of globalization (WB, 2000), and, partly as a response to poor performance at the micro-level. Ivanova and Evans found that policy transfer is not only a useful but also a necessary approach for understanding a state in transition. This is because it is an empirical regularity in transition societies for exogenous policy inputs to influence endogenous policy development due mainly to the turbulent nature of the policy environment. They argued, however, that transforming policy transfer into a tool applicable to transition societies depends largely on employing a multi-level model of policy analysis that integrates the policy transfer network approach with macro- and micro-level analysis. This provided an explanation of the outcome of the process of transfer by establishing the following relationships between exogenous macro-level factors (economic, political, ideological, technological) and the network; between the network structure and behaviour and the relationship between individual actors in the network (micro-level) and between the network's structure and the policy outcome.

The empirical chapters in this volume also provide compelling evidence to sustain the claim that processes of political globalization appear to have increased the opportunities for policy transfer to take place. In addition to Crespo's conclusions presented above, Lana and Evans observe the importance of political globalization in guiding the democratic transition in the Ukraine. With regard to the case studies of developed countries, Evans and Ladi both emphasize the role of

Table 12.1 Explanations for policy change

Case Study	Critical Variables
Performance measurement and resource allocation programme (UK DSS) to counter social security fraud.	Voluntary transfer in response to micro-level dissatisfaction; key role for Project Leader, a bureaucrat, as the prime agent of transfer; the policy transfer network; multi-level search leads to hybrid policy outcome; historical ties and the sharing of a common language.
New Deal programme for unemployed 18-24-year-olds (UK)	Macro-level commitment to competition state principles; voluntary transfer building on existing transfer of welfare to work programmes; the policy transfer network; multi-level search leads to hybrid policy outcome; and historical ties and the sharing of a common language.
Ecotrans; an environmental employment programme (Germany)	Voluntary transfer in a positive response to the discourses of globalization and Europeanization; key role for *Understandingbus*, a KI, as the prime agent of transfer; the policy transfer network; EU funding regimes; and, institutional similarities and receptiveness.
Local government reform in a period of democratic transition (Ukraine)	'Voluntary but necessary' reform initially in response to conditions of Washington Nexus; key role for AUC (KI) and USAID as the prime agents of transfer; the policy transfer network; and, donor conditionality and the absence of acceptable institutional memory.
The Mexican Technological Universities	Voluntary transfer of rhetoric and programmes to legitimate conclusions already reached; the transformation of the state; international perceptions and donor conditionality; international education policy community; and historical ties.
New public management type reforms in Hong Kong (TMP, PPS, Efficiency Unit, Trading Funds)	Voluntary transfer (emulation) of rhetoric and programmes to legitimate conclusions already reached; political context (China); international perceptions; and the policy transfer network. *
New public management type reforms in Malaysia (MBS, 'Look East', QCCs)	Voluntary transfer (emulation) of rhetoric and programmes in response to micro-level dissatisfaction; international perceptions; and the policy transfer network. *

Table 12.1 Explanations for policy change (continued)

Case Study	Critical Variables
New public management type reforms in Singapore (PS 21, BFR)	Voluntary transfer (emulation) of rhetoric and programmes (adaptation) to legitimate conclusions already reached; international NPM policy community; and the policy transfer network. *
The *Beca escolar* social assistance programme in Ecuador	The state of development; initially a coercive. negotiated transfer in response to conditions of Washington Nexus; a key role for *Missão Criança* and UNESCO as the prime agents of transfer; the policy transfer network; and institutional similarities and receptiveness.

* Common does not refer to this concept directly but he does emphasize the role of agents of transfer in combination with indigenous bureaucrats in an ad hoc decision structure.

political globalization in facilitating policy transfer in Chapters Four and Five respectively. In contrast, Common highlights the decisive role of economic rather than political globalization with regard to his three case study countries, where substantial democratization or cultural homogenization is not likely to occur in the foreseeable future. He notes that economic development has served to enhance the colonial structures of public administration in all three countries and that the drive for economic development has energized the political systems of Malaysia and Singapore.

With regard to the case studies of developed countries, Evans and Ladi both emphasize the role of political globalization in facilitating policy transfer in Chapters Four and Five respectively; in the former as part of a broader competition state strategy and in the latter as part of a process of Europeanization. In contrast, Evans and McComb's chapter presents compelling evidence that in certain instances, the process of policy transfer itself may be treated as an independent variable that explains why this particular raft of policy proposals was adopted.

It is noteworthy that both Common and Ladi's chapters highlight the importance of discourse in shaping policy outcomes. Common demonstrates how new public management was influential as a discourse; Ladi shows how the discourses of globalization and Europeanization impact upon processes of policy transfer. An understanding of the belief systems that agents of transfer hold is clearly crucial in order to evaluate the influence of the discourse within which the policy transfer process takes place. For example, the central agent of transfer in Chapter Five, *Understandingbus*, had a proactive approach towards Europeanization and globalization. At the same time, although the discourses of globalization and Europeanization were influential in both Germany and Greece, the outcome of the policy transfer process varied. It can be concluded that although the ideational sphere is important, it is interwoven with the material sphere and processes of policy transfer can only be successful if the material sphere is also satisfied. The sustainability and vitality of transfer networks rests on the forging of a consensus between policy actors and agents of transfer that a programme has been found that will deal with the problems that they are facing. In order to achieve such a consensus policy-makers must be convinced that the programme is technically feasible and in keeping with the dominant value systems of the domestic policy domain.

The importance of political reasons for policy change is also highlighted in the volume. In Chapter Seven, Street argues that fundholding was considered as a reform option for Kyrgyzstan simply because it was in vogue in the UK; USAID, in particular, was keen on the policy because of its emphasis on consumer choice. However, the extent to which policy-makers in Kyrgyzstan agreed with fundholding as an appropriate policy option can be questioned. In view of their difficult economic situation, the Kyrgyz were reliant on the support of external agencies and would have been under pressure to develop a reform plan that reflected donor perceptions of the situation and their analysis of the way forward. Lacking an established 'epistemic community', the Kyrgyz did not have a knowledge base from which to reject donor suggestions.

In keeping with Barry's (1975: 86) argument that '...fruitful analogy will suggest new lines of enquiry by provoking the speculation that relationships found in the one field may hold, mutatis mutandis, in the other as well', a set of hypotheses can be generated from these case study findings in order to guide the identification of potential independent and dependent variables for future policy transfer research. These include some normative, as well as analytical propositions.

Global, International and Transnational Explanations of Policy Change

Hypothesis 1: *Processes of globalization provide opportunity structures for policy transfer to occur* (see Chapters Three, Five, Six, Seven, Eight, Nine, Ten and Eleven).

Hypothesis 2: *Processes of policy transfer facilitated by processes of globalization can lead to divergent or convergent policy outcomes* (see Chapters Five, Nine and Eleven).

Hypothesis 3: *Processes of Europeanization provide opportunity structures for policy transfer to occur* (see Chapter Five).

Hypothesis 4: *Processes of policy transfer facilitated by processes of Europeanization can lead to divergent or convergent policy outcomes* (see Chapter Five).

Hypothesis 5: *Discourses, such as new public management, globalization or*

Europeanization, provide opportunity structures for policy transfer to occur (see Chapters Five and Nine).

Hypothesis 6: *In most instances, coercive negotiated forms of policy transfer demonstrate the weakness of state actors in decision processes and reflect their broader state of development. Such states are particularly vulnerable to international policy agendas established through the Washington Consensus. This is particularly evident in transition states or states emerging from conflict* (see Chapters Six, Seven, Eight and Eleven).

Hypothesis 7: *The dissemination of 'best practice' by international organizations, KIs and think tanks in the international domain provides opportunity structures for policy transfer to occur* (see Chapters Six, Seven, Nine and Eleven).

Hypothesis 8: *KIs play a key role in facilitating opportunity structures for policy transfer in developing countries* (see Chapter Six), *between developing countries* (see Chapter Eleven) *and in developed countries* (see Chapter Five).

State-centred Explanations of Policy Change

Hypothesis 9: *Changes in government can provide an opportunity structure for policy change to occur* (see Chapters Three, Four, Five, Six, Seven, Nine and Eleven).

Hypothesis 10: *New Governance has facilitated cross-sectoral opportunities for policy transfer. Hence, the private sector is increasingly used as a source of policy learning due to its expertise in particular areas e.g. banks and credit card fraud detection, management, risk assessment or logistics* (see Chapters Three and Nine).

Hypothesis 11: *The existence of indigenous agencies of technical cooperation in developing countries provides opportunity structures for policy transfer between developing countries* (see Chapter Eleven).

Hypothesis 12: *The sharing of similar social problems can provide an opportunity structure for policy transfer to occur* (see Chapters Three, Four, Five, Ten and Eleven).

Hypothesis 13: *Developing countries can engage in policy transfer for tactical reasons to increase their relative autonomy from international forces. This often leads to the transfer of rhetoric rather than substantive policy content* (see Chapters Nine and Eleven).

Hypothesis 14: *Macro-level commitment to competition state principles in developed countries provides opportunity structures for policy transfer to occur* (see Chapters Three and Four).

Hypothesis 15: *General processes of state transformation provide opportunity structures for policy transfer to occur* (see Chapters Three, Four, Six, Seven, Eight, Nine and Eleven).

Hypothesis 16: *The sharing of a common language provides opportunity structures for policy transfer to occur* (see Chapters Three, Four and Eleven).

Hypothesis 17: *The sharing of historical ties provides opportunity structures for policy transfer to occur* (see Chapters Three, Four and Seven).

Hypothesis 18: *State actors in developing countries can increase their autonomy from international forces by ensuring that key development programmes are financed by the state* (see Chapters Six and Eleven).

Hypothesis 19: *In most instances, voluntary forms of policy transfer demonstrate the relative autonomy of state actors in decision processes and reflect the broader state of development* (see Chapters Three and Four).

Organizational-centred Explanations for Policy Change

Hypothesis 20: *Micro-level dissatisfaction provides opportunity structures for policy transfer to occur* (see Chapters Three, Four, Five, Nine and Eleven).

Hypothesis 21: *Policy transfer is introduced to legitimate conclusions already reached* (see Chapters Seven and Nine).

Hypothesis 22: *Changes in organizational leadership can provide an opportunity structure for policy change to occur* (see Chapters Three, Four, Five, nine, and Eleven).

Hypothesis 23: *Public organizations in both developed and developing countries do not always have the expertise to tackle the problems they confront and increasingly look outside the organization for the answers to problems* (see Chapters Three, Four, Five, Six, Seven, Eight, Nine and Eleven).

Hypothesis 24: *The sharing of institutional similarities provides opportunity structures for policy transfer to occur* (see Chapters Three, Four, Five, Eight and Eleven).

Hypothesis 25: *Negotiated forms of policy transfer can precipitate voluntary policy transfer* (see Chapter Eleven).

Hypothesis 26: *Policy transfer networks largely determine the content of policy transfer outcomes* (see Chapters Three, Four, Five, Six, Seven, Nine and Eleven).

This last hypothesis requires further elaboration through the investigation of a set of dependent variables that help policy analysts to unpack the process of policy transfer. The policy transfer network approach involves the application of an 'ideal-type' policy cycle to the analysis of processes of policy transfer. By this we refer to the stages through which a policy can, but does not always, pass. As this emphasis infers, this stagist approach is associated with what has been traditionally termed rational decison-making, which rarely provides an exact account of the real world of policy-making. Nonetheless, the policy transfer network approach has *additionality* as it proves a useful heuristic device for organizing our case study analysis and studying the process of policy transfer. In Mackenzie's terms it provides a 'criteria of relevance'. The majority of authors in this volume adopt this approach for heuristic reasons.

Comparative Lessons – Policy Oriented Learning

The policy transfer network approach helps us to simplify a complex process of policy development in order to comprehend the multiplicity of factors that shape these unusual policy-making processes.

The Scope of Search Activity

Hypothesis 27: *Setting limits on the scope of learning activity may severely prejudice the capacity of a policy transfer network to engineer successful policy change* (see Chapters Seven and Eight).

Hypothesis 28: *The time-scale that is established to search for policy ideas informs the scope of enquiry and almost inevitably draws policy-makers to easily accessible exemplars that share similar ideological commitments and normally a common language* (see Chapters Three and Four).

Hypothesis 29: *Multi-level search activity creates a pathology for hybrid forms of cross-national and cross-sectoral policy transfer and consequently policy and programme copying is very rare* (see Chapters Three and Four).

Agenda-setting

Hypothesis 30: *The nature of the state determines the type of actors involved in the process of policy transfer* (for example, compare Chapters Three and Four with Chapters Six, Seven and Eleven).

Hypothesis 31: *Highly technocratic voluntary policy transfer networks have significant autonomy from counter forces elsewhere in the endogenous bureaucracy. The power of state actors in such networks can often be undermined by their lack of expertise and over reliance on agents of transfer* (see Chapter Three).

Hypothesis 32: *Policy transfer networks are characterized by resource dependency and include state and non-state actors such as international knowledge institutions, corporate bodies and policy entrepreneurs* (see Chapters Three, Four, Five, Six, Seven, Eight, Nine and Eleven).

Hypothesis 33: *The ability of non-state actors to penetrate policy transfer networks and gain a status of acceptance in decision-making processes depends on both their cognitive and elite mobilization skills and their compatibility with the common policy belief system underpinning the network* (see Chapters Three, Four, Five, Six, Seven, Eight, Nine and Eleven).

Hypothesis 34: *The density of the policy transfer network has a significant impact on the outcome of the process of policy transfer. The close-knit structure of the network provides it with significant autonomy that contributes to the successful outcome of the policy transfer* (see Chapters Three, Four, Five, Six, Seven, Eight, Nine and Eleven).

Hypothesis 35: *In order to ensure that transition societies are insulated from inappropriate policy transfer the driving force for the creation of policy transfer networks should be of indigenous origin* (see Chapters Six, Seven, Eight, Nine and Eleven).

Hypothesis 36: *Policy transfer networks involve the development of inner circles of policy-making participants who often promote new forms of complex globalization in the attempt to adapt state action to cope more effectively with what they see as global 'realities'* (see Chapters Three, Four, Eight, Nine and Eleven).

Hypothesis 37: *Policy transfer networks in transition societies should retain as much independence from exogenous actors and their resources as possible* (see Chapters Six, Seven, Eight, Nine and Eleven).

Hypothesis 38: *In transition societies, independent and partnership relations with donor agencies and the right balance between local and foreign actors within the network are central to its ability to engineer policy change* (see Chapters Six, Seven, Eight, Nine and Eleven).

Hypothesis 39: *The receptivity of indigenous institutional structures and processes is a key determinant of policy oriented learning* (see Chapters Three, Five, Six, Seven, Eight, Nine and Eleven).

Hypothesis 40: *Historical legacies are a key determinant of policy oriented learning* (see Chapters Six and Nine).

Hypothesis 41: *The creation of policy transfer networks provides an opportunity structure for the creation of further policy transfer networks* (see Chapters Four, Six, Seven and Eleven).

Agents of Policy Transfer and Policy Learning

Eight main categories of agents of transfer can be identified in the case studies in this volume that play a key role in policy transfer networks: bureaucrats (see Chapters Three, Four, Five, Six, Seven, Eight and Nine); politicians (see Chapter Eleven); policy entrepreneurs (see Chapters Three, Four, Nine and Eleven); global financial institutions and international organizations (see Chapters Six, Seven, Eight, Nine and Eleven); KIs (see Chapters Five, Six and Eleven); and, supra-national organizations (see Chapter Five). But how do they influence the process of policy oriented learning?

Hypothesis 42: *Policy transfer networks can act as agents of globalization* (see Chapters Three, Four and Five) *or counteragents to globalization* (see Chapters Nine and Eleven).

Hypothesis 43: *Agents of policy transfer are often carriers of particular policy belief systems and use their membership of formal and informal international policy networks to disseminate international policy agendas* (see Chapters Three, Four, Five, Six, Seven, Eight and Nine).

Hypothesis 44: *Policy transfer network actors act as gatekeepers to the decision structure and filter out forms of policy-oriented learning that are incompatible with the dominant belief system* (see Chapters Three, Four, Five, Six, Seven, Eight, nine and Eleven).

Hypothesis 45: *Agents of policy transfer, such as KIs, play a key role in facilitating policy-oriented learning through imparting technical advice and providing evidence-based knowledge to advocate certain policy options over others* (see Chapters Five, Six and Eleven).

Hypothesis 46: *Knowledge institutions provide an ongoing opportunity structure for policy transfer* (see Chapters Five, Six and Eleven).

Comparative Lessons – What is Transferred?

The case studies in this volume provide evidence of the transfer of: policy goals (see Chapters Three, Four, Five, Six, Seven, Eight, Nine and Eleven); policy design and content (see Chapters Three, Four, Five, Six, Seven, Eight and Eleven); policy instruments and programmes (see Chapters Three, Four, Five, Six, Seven, Eight and Eleven); institutions (see Chapters Four, Six, Seven, Eight and Eleven); policy style (see Chapters Three, Four, Five, Six, Seven, Eight and Eleven); ideology (see Chapters Three, Four, Five, Six, Seven, Eight and Eleven); negative lessons (see Chapters Three and Nine); rhetoric (see Chapters Five and Nine); and, ideas (see Chapter Nine). These observations stimulate the following hypotheses:

Hypothesis 47: *Soft transfers, ideas, concepts and attitudes, are less remarkable than hard transfers, implemented policies and programmes* (contrast Chapters Five and Nine with Chapters Three, Six and Eleven).

Hypothesis 48: *The content of policy transfers normally reflects areas where indigenous state actors lack expertise. This hypotheses holds in both developed and developing countries* (see Chapters Three, Four, Five, Six, Seven, Eight, Nine and Eleven).

Hypothesis 49: *Agents of policy transfer that can bridge the indigenous knowledge gap can become important players in policy transfer networks* (see Chapters Three, Four, Five, Six, Seven, Eight, Nine and Eleven).

Hypothesis 50: *The content of policy transfers is often informed by notions of 'best practice' disseminated by international organizations, KIs and think tanks in the international domain* (see Chapters Five, Six, Seven, Eight, Nine and Eleven).

Hypothesis 51: *The content of policy transfers in developing countries often takes the form of conditions imposed by the Washington Consensus in return for grants or loans* (see Chapters Six, Seven, Eight, Nine and Eleven).

Hypothesis 52: *Ideological considerations play a key role in informing the content of policy transfers* (see Chapters Three, Four, Five, Six, Seven, Eight, Nine and Eleven).

Comparative Lessons – Degrees of Transfer

There are four main options on how to incorporate lessons into a political system and all four are illustrated in the case study chapters in this volume – copying (see Chapters Six, Seven and Eight), emulation (see Chapters Four, Five, Nine and Eleven), hybridization (see Chapter Three); and, inspiration (see Chapter Nine). These observations stimulate the following hypotheses:

Hypothesis 53: *Copying occurs more often in developing countries than in developed countries due to external interventions in the decision process by international organizations and donors* (see Chapters Six, Seven and Eight).

Hypothesis 54: *Copying is a function of limited search activity* (see Chapters Six, Seven and Eight).

Hypothesis 55: *Hybridization tends to be a function of multi-level search activity* (see Chapter Three).

Hypothesis 56: *Emulation leads to locally sensitive policy transfer* (see Chapters Four, Five, Nine and Eleven),

Hypothesis 57: *Inspiration may be viewed as a policy instrument for absorbing the negative impact of globalization. In policy transfer idiom this means marginal adjustments to the status quo* (see Chapter Nine).

Hypothesis 58: *Inspiration may be viewed as a policy instrument for responding to the discourses of globalization* (see Chapters Five and Nine) *and Europeanization* (see Chapter Five). *In policy transfer idiom this often leads to marginal adjustments to the status quo* (see Chapter Nine).

Comparative Lessons – Obstacles to Transfer

We are interested here both in the capacity of policy transfer networks to forge policy change and the ability of the policy to realize its objectives in meeting particular societal needs. The case study evidence derived from both incomplete cases of policy transfer and problems confronted in completed processes of policy transfer, suggests that the following factors can act as constraints on successful policy transfer: limited search activity (see Chapters Seven and Eight); the receptivity of existing environmental structures and institutional cultures (see Chapters Three, Four, Five, Six, Seven, Eight, Nine and Eleven); lack of political, human, technological and/or economic resources (see Chapters Six, Seven, Eight, Nine and Eleven); complexity (see Chapters Three, Four and Five); lack of regard for indigenous practices and existing policy systems (see Chapters Six, Seven, Eight and Nine). As Figure 2.1 in Chapter Two has already illustrated, these obstacles can be divided into three broad sets of variables: 'cognitive' obstacles in the pre-decision phase, 'environmental' obstacles in the implementation phase and international and public opinion. These variables do not exist in a vacuum; they interact in complex and often unexpected way and inform the process of policy transfer. Hence, they must be clearly understood by practitioners in order to develop the appropriate strategy for engaging in policy transfer. The interaction between these 'cognitive' and 'environmental' obstacles and the forces of international and domestic public opinion (depending on the nature of the state) inform the completion or otherwise of the process of policy transfer. These observations stimulate the following hypotheses:

Hypothesis 59: *Cognitive obstacles in the pre-decision phase of the process of policy transfer can enhance or constrain policy development* (see Chapters Three, Four, Five, Six, Seven, Eight, Nine and Eleven).

Hypothesis 60: *Environmental obstacles during the process of policy transfer can enhance or constrain policy development* (see Chapters Three, Four, Five, Six, Seven, Eight, Nine and Eleven).

Hypothesis 61: *International opinion during the process of policy transfer can enhance or constrain policy development in developing countries* (see Chapters Six, Seven, Eight, Nine and Eleven).

Hypothesis 62: *Domestic opinion during the process of policy transfer can enhance or constrain policy development* (see Chapters Three, Four, Five, Six, Seven, Eight, Nine and Eleven).

Hypothesis 63: *Setting limits on a policy transfer network's scope of learning activity may severely prejudice its capacity to engineer successful policy change* (see Chapters Seven and Eight).

Hypothesis 64: *In transitional societies the effectiveness of policy transfer programmes are largely determined by the degree to which the essential components of a national culture are preserved within the policy transfer design and inappropriate foreign content is filtered out in a process of cultural assimilation* (see Chapters Six, Seven, Eight and Nine).

Hypothesis 65: *Public organizations are unlikely to engage in policy transfer if the policy is too complex and difficult to implement* (see Chapter Three).

Comparative Lessons – Prospective Policy Evaluation

The case study findings have proved particularly useful in helping to identify potential obstacles to policy transfer (see hypotheses 59-65) and in providing insights for practitioners on how to develop the type of learning organization conducive to the facilitation of successful policy transfer (see hypotheses 27-9, 53-8, 32-5, 37 and 39). Moreover, Evans and McComb provide some practical insights into how to design representative policy transfer networks, while Nedley highlights some practical steps that should be adopted in approaching policy learning. Nedley further concludes that the concept of lesson drawing provides the most appropriate analytical instruments for accessing and enabling the successful transfer of relevant 'foreign' programmes into domestic settings.

Policy Transfer Analysis in Critical Perspective

Several research problems were encountered with the policy transfer approach during the process of empirical investigation that require further theoretical consideration and empirical research.

First, as Street correctly observes, it is often difficult to explain why policy transfer takes place. In his case study, there appeared to be prima facie evidence to suggest that the reform programme was undertaken voluntarily in collaboration with external donor agencies, in response to severe economic crisis. But, having invited external assistance, it is less clear whether specific policy proposals were entered into voluntarily. Fundholding may have been voluntarily adopted if it was believed that it would be the best strategy to promote the health of the population or because local bureaucrats and doctors felt it would best advance their own interests. But the policy choice also reflected indirect coercive pressures by USAID pushing an ideological agenda. In practice it is likely that processes of voluntary and indirect coercive transfer merged in this instance. It may well be that this is the norm, particularly when donor agencies are part of the transfer network. After all, policy transfer is more likely to be successful if coercing agents convince members of the policy transfer network that the transfer is in their interests or if the alternatives are perceived to be less palatable. As Lana and Evans revealed, this clearly occurred in the transfer of the *Bolsa-Escola* Programme from Brazil to Ecuador. These two case studies reveal the difficulty of disentangling dependent and independent variables and establishing clear causal pathways in policy transfer analysis.

Secondly, demonstration that policy transfer has taken place demands excellent access to key informants in informal decision-making processes. Such access is not often possible either in developed or developing countries. This is a common problem in the study of public policy-making, which often undermines the practicality of engaging in formal modelling such as public choice theory. In policy transfer analysis an emphasis should be placed on building a preponderance of evidence in support of a particular narrative of policy development; multi-level analysis helps this endeavour. Moreover, this is why it is important for policy transfer analysts to generate more 'in process' case studies and particularly those with implementation perspectives.

Thirdly, while at the meso-level of analysis the policy transfer network approach appears to have a high degree of relevance, several shortcomings can also be identified with the approach. As Chapter Three shows, consultants are generally paid fees, which presents a financial motive for their involvement in a policy transfer network. This is at odds with the expectation that all participants share basic policy values. It is also evident from the case studies that it is crucial to conceptualize policy transfer networks as a potential site for a healthy competition of ideas between different bureaucratic interests. Consequently, the role of the practitioners operating existing policy programmes deserve greater attention.

Most importantly, the policy transfer network model does not provide a general theorization of policy change that accounts for all processes of policy transfer. It can only provide a partial account of policy change emanating from the relationship between the structure of the network and the agents operating within them and the network and the policy outcome. If applied in isolation from macro-analysis, this overlooks the potential for the existence of a causal relationship between the network and the environment in which it operates. Moreover, at the same time, the network is interpreted, reinterpreted and constrained by participating actors. Hence, the complex, interactive relationship between network (structure) and agency needs to be analysed in any study of policy transfer. This volume has demonstrated that this problem can be overcome if a multi-level perspective is adopted that combines macro-, meso- and micro- levels of analysis for examining the impact of relationships between the policy environment and the network and the network and network actors on policy outcomes.

Finally, contrary to initial claims that policy transfer networks are a short-lived ad-hoc phenomenon set up with the specific intention of engineering policy change, Ivanova and Evans and Lana and Evans show that in some instances, they can become more permanent entities. In the Ukraine, the AUC policy transfer network now provides an ongoing opportunity structure for policy transfer. At some time in the future, when the need for policy transfer diminishes, this 'permanent' policy transfer network may well evolve into an epistemic community that resembles those in the West. Nonetheless, the argument remains that once the structure of resource dependencies within a network is broken, the life of a policy transfer network comes to an end. This remains a key distinction between policy transfer networks and other forms of policy network. Moreover, the key element of the case in defence of establishing policy transfer analysis as a distinct mode of enquiry from the study of normal forms of policy-making largely rests on the discovery that policy transfer involves unique forms of network.

There are, however, obvious limitations in inferring general conclusions from nine case studies. More research is required both in terms of developing a greater range of case study investigations of different forms of policy transfer and in identifying the range of constraints that condition the success of policy transfer in different policy environments. Further study of the anthropological aspects of these constraints warrants detailed examination. This study has also paid limited attention to the patterns of policy transfer network formation in transition states. Research should be undertaken to examine the recruitment/exclusion patterns that inform the composition of policy transfer networks as well as internal structural variables such as the competitive struggle between interests, and the balance of strategic resources. This type of analysis can be extended to inform an account of the capacity building, evolution, transformation and ultimately the termination of these networks. Assuming the need to demonstrate the pragmatic value of the study of policy transfer networks in a transitional environment, the effectiveness of particular strategies for building policy networks could be examined further by developing a series of indicators around the themes of resource dependency, participation, transparency, capacity building, sustainability and further policy learning opportunities.

Street also observes that a crucial message emanating from this study is that the interpretation of examples of policy transfer may depend on the perspective adopted by the analyst. The analytical approach one adopts can predetermine the conclusions that are drawn from empirical analysis about the nature of the process and the outcome of policy transfer. This suggests the importance of using rigorous validation criteria such as those presented in Chapter Two and investigating counterfactuals in order to ensure the value of any knowledge claims generated from policy transfer analysis.

The policy transfer approach should be adapted to respond to these theoretical and methodological weaknesses.

Parting Shots

This study has met its three main aims highlighted in the introductory passages to this book. It has demonstrated the value of adopting a multi-level, interdisciplinary framework for analyzing processes of policy transfer, provided the basis for an explanatory model of policy transfer through the identification of a broad range of critical variables for further empirical investigation and helped to bridge an empirical gap in the literature through the presentation of case studies of policy transfer between and from developing countries. The case study evidence presented in this volume has ably supported two central arguments. Policy transfer can be a rational and progressive learning activity but only if the policy that is transferred is compatible with the value system of the recipient organization, culturally assimilated through comprehensive evaluation, and, builds on existing organizational strengths. Moreover, policy transfer analysis can only be distinctive from the analysis of normal forms of policy-making if its focuses on the remarkable movement of ideas between systems of governance through policy transfer networks and the intermediation of agents of policy transfer. Policy transfer analysis is best concerned with the study of discernible and remarkable features of contemporary policy change not otherwise explained. The daily diffusion of knowledge, intentional or otherwise, at the micro level within organizations or between organizations in a system of governance is not remarkable in the context of policy transfer either in terms of process or of fact. These transfers are best the subject of normal policy studies.

Bibliography

Abel-Smith, B. and J. Falkingham (1995), Financing Health Services in Kyrgyzstan: the Extent of Private Payments (London: LSE Departments of Health and Social Policy and Administration).

Adler, E. and P. Haas (1992), 'Conclusion: epistemic communities, word order, and the creation of a reflective research program', International Organisation, 46: 367-90.

Agência Brasileira de Cooperação (2003), Official Website (http://www.abc.mre.gov.br).

Aguiar, M. and C.H. Araújo (2003), Bolsa-escola: educação para enfrentar a pobreza (Brasília: UNESCO).

Almond, G. (ed.), (1990), A Discipline Divided: Schools and Sects in Political Science (London: Sage Publications).

Alpin, C. and S. Walsh (1998), 'Over and Under Education in the UK Graduate Labour Market', Studies in Higher Education 23: 17-34.

American Enterprise Institute (1987), The New Consensus on Family and Welfare (Washington, DC: AEI).

ANUIES [National Association of Universities and Higher Education Institutions] (2000), La Educación Superior En El Siglo XXI Lineas Estratégicas De Desarrollo (México: ANUIES).

Araújo, C.H. and M. Aguiar (2002), A força de uma idéia: a história da Bolsa-escola (Brasília: Missão Criança).

Arias, F. and J. Patlán (1998), 'El Trabajo De Los Estudiantes Y Su Relación Con Algunos Aspectos Demográficos: El Caso De La Facultad De Contaduría Y Administración-Unam', Revista De La Educación Superior, No. 107.

Aristotle (1984), The Athenian Constitution (London: Penguin Books).

AUC Brochure (1998), The Association of Ukrainian Cities (Kiev: Tarhan).

AUC Electronic Magazine (1997-1999), Ukrainian City (Kiev: Tarhan).

AUC Information Bulletin (1998), People and Power, No.1 (Kiev: Tarhan).

AUC Information Bulletin (1998), People and Power, No.2 (Kiev: Tarhan).

AUC Information Bulletin (1998), People and Power, No.3 (Kiev: Tarhan).

Audit Commission (1996), What The Doctor Ordered (London: HMSO).

Avksentyev, O. (1998), 'The Administrative Functions of the State and Local Self-Government', in M. Sazonov (ed.), Political Science (Kharkov: Folio).

Bachtler, J. et al (2001), 'The transfer of EU regional policy to the countries of central and eastern Europe: Can one size fit all?', ESRC Future Governance Programme, http://www.hull.ac.uk/futgov/.

Barnés, F. (1999), 'Universidad Responsable, Sociedad Solidaria', in Proceso Weekly, No. 1163, 14th February.

Bartolucci, J. (1994), Desigualdad Social, Educación Superior Y Sociología En México (México:Cesu-Unam, Porrúa).

Baines, D.L. and D.K. Whynes (1996), 'Selection Bias in GP Fundholding', Health Economics 5: 129-140.

Benefit Fraud Inspectorate (1998a), Securing The System: A Report By the Director General (Harrogate: BFI).

Benefit Fraud Inspectorate (1998b), The Measurement Challenge (Harrogate: BFI).

Benefit Fraud Inspectorate (1998c), Blackpool Borough Council: Report By the Benefit

Fraud Inspectorate (Harrogate: BFI).

Benefit Fraud Inspectorate (1998d), *Strand 3: Measurement Project Initiation* (Harrogate: BFI).

Bennett, C. (1991a), 'Review Article: What is Policy Convergence and What Causes it?' *British Journal of Political Science*, 21: 215-233.

Bennett, C. J. (1991b), 'How States Utilise Foreign Evidence', *Journal of Public Policy*, 11, 1: 31-54.

Bennett, C. (1997), 'Understanding Ripple Effects: the Cross-National Adoption of Policy Instruments for Bureaucratic Accountability', *Governance*, 10: 213-233.

Bennett, C. and M. Howlett (1992), 'The Lessons of Learning: Reconciling Theories of Policy Learning and Policy Change', *Policy Sciences* 25: 275-294.

Berger, S. and R. Dore. (eds.), (1996), *National Diversity and Global Capitalism* (Ithaca and London: Cornell University Press).

Berman, P. (1995), 'Health Sector Reform in Developing Countries: Making Health Development Sustainable', *Health Policy*, 32 (April-June).

Biersteker, T. (1992), 'The "Triumph" of Neoclassical Economics in the Developing World: Policy Convergence and the Bases of Governance in the International Economic Order', in J. Rosenau and E. Otto Czempiel (eds.), *Governance Without Government: Order and Change in World Politics* (Cambridge: Cambridge University Press).

Blair, T. (1996), *New Britain. My Vision of a Young Country* (London: Fourth Estate).

Blaug, M. (1974), *Education and the Employment Problem in Developing Countries* (Lausanne: ILO).

Bloor, K. and A. Maynard (1993), 'Expenditure in the NHS During and After the Thatcher Years' (York: Centre for Health Economics, University of York).

Bloor, K., A. Maynard, and A. Street (2000), 'The Cornerstone of Labour's "New NHS": Reforming Primary Care', in Smith, P.C. (ed.), *Reforming Markets In Health Care: An Economic Perspective* (Buckingham: Open University Press).

Boltvinik, J. (1998a), 'Privatizar La Unam?', *La Jornada*, 20th February.

Boltvinik, J. (1998b), 'Recorte A Universidades Y Bm', *La Jornada*, 4th December.

Boltvinik, J. (2000), 'Evolución Heterogénea De La Pobreza En México 1970-1995', in J.M.Tortosa (ed.), *Pobreza Y Perspectiva De Género* (Spain: Icaria).

Bonefeld, W. and P. Burnham (1998), 'The Politics of Counter Inflationary Credibility in Britain, 1990-94', *Review of Radical Political Economics*, 30: 32-52.

Borowitz, M. and S. O'Dougherty (1997), 'Inverting the Pyramid', *World Health*, 5: 16-17.

Borzel, T. (1999), 'Towards Convergence In Europe? Institutional Adaptation To Europeanization in Germany and Spain', *Journal of Common Market Studies* 37: 573-96.

Boston J., J. Martin, J. Pallot and P. Walsh (eds.), (1996), *Public Management: the New Zealand Model* (Auckland: Oxford University Press).

Boukhalov, O. and S. Ivannikov (1995), 'Ukrainian Local Politics After Independence', American Academy of Political and Social Science, *Annals*, 140: 126-136.

Bourguignon, F. (2002), 'The Growth Elasticity of Poverty Reduction: explaining heterogeneity across countries and time periods', in T. Eicher and S. Turnovski (eds.), *Growth and Inequality* (Cambridge, MA: MIT Press).

Bourguignon, F. *et al.* (2000), *Ex-ante Evaluation of Conditional Cash Transfer Programs: the Case of Bolsa Escola. William Davidson Working Paper*, 516. [http://www.worldbank.org].

Bracho, T. (2000), 'Poverty and Education in Mexico, 1984-1996', in F. Reimers (ed.), *Unequal Schools, Unequal Chances* (Harvard University: DRCLA).

Brewer B. (1998), 'Convergence in Public Sector Management', Asia-Pacific Conference, City University of Hong Kong, 6-7 June.

Brown, P. (2001), 'Skill Formation in the Twenty-First Century', in P. Brown, A. Green and

H. Lauder (eds.) *High Skills. Globalization, Competitiveness and Skill Formation* (Oxford: OUP).

Buarque, C. (1994), *A revolução nas prioridades: da modernização técnica à modernização ética* (São Paulo: Paz e Terra).

Buarque, C. (2000), *Bolsa Escola: a new understanding of the poverty problem and a new tool against poverty through the education of poor children*, presentation for the II General Assembly of the Parliamentary Conference of the Americas, Puerto Rico.

Buarque, C. (2001a), *Bolsa-escola: an education and poverty reduction program. 100 frequently asked questions* (Brasília: Missão Criança).

Buarque, C. (2001b), *What is Bolsa-escola?* (Brasília: Missão Criança).

Buarque, C. (2002), 'Bolsa-escola: a poverty recovery plan for Africa putting children first', VIII Conference of Ministers of Education of African Member States (MINEDAF VIII), Tanzania, 2-6 December 2002 (Brasília: Missão Criança).

Buarque, C. (2003), *O que você pode fazer para ajudar a erradicar o trabalho infantil no Brasil* (Brasília: Missão Criança).

Büchel, F. (2002), 'The Effects of Overeducation on Productivity in Germany – The Firms' Viewpoint', *Economics of Education Review*, 21: 263-275.

Business Times (1994), 'Changing Civil Service To Meet Goals', Business Times (Malaysia), 8 Feb.

Cabinet Office [UK], (1999), *Modernising Government* (London: Stationery Office).

Callinicos, A. (2003), *The Anti-Capitalist Manifesto* (Cambridge: Polity).

Cantwell, J. (1992), 'The Internationalisation of Technological Activity and its Implications for Competitiveness', in O. Granstand, L. Hakanson and S. Sjolander (eds.), *Technology Management And International Business* (Chichester: Wiley).

Carlen, P. (2001), 'Governing the governors: telling tales of managers, mandarins and mavericks', *ESRC Future Governance Programme*, http://www.hull.ac.uk/futgov/.

Carter, N. (1989), 'Performance Indicators: "Backseat Driving" Or "Hands Off" Control? *Policy and Politics*, 17: 131-138.

Cerny, P.G. (1990), *The Changing Architecture of Politics: Structure, Agency, and the Future of the State* (London and Thousand Oaks, Ca: Sage).

Cerny, P.G. (1994), 'The Dynamics of Financial Globalization', *Policy Sciences*, 27: 319-342.

Cerny, P.G. (1996), 'Globalization and Other Stories: the Search for a New Paradigm for International Relations', *International Journa*, 51: 617-37.

Cerny, P.G. (1997), 'Paradoxes of the Competition State: the Dynamics of Political Globalisation', *Government and Opposition*, 32: 251-74.

Cerny, P.G. and M. Evans (2000), 'New Labour, Globalisation and the Competition State', *Harvard Papers* 70, Center for European Studies, Harvard University.

CGUT (2000a), *Universidades Tecnológicas. Mandos Medios Para La Industria* (México: Sep-Ut-Noriega).

CGUT (2000b), *Coordinación General De Universidades Tecnológicas*, http://cgut.sep.gob.mx.

Chambers, R. (1983), *Rural Development: Putting The Last First* (London: Longman).

Chen J. (1997), 'Government Relates to the Public as Individuals', *Straits Times*, 7 December. /658.009s cHE

Chen M. (1995), *Asian Management Systems* (London: ITP).

Chen, R. (1998), *Experiences and Problems in the Current Administrative Reform in China* (Guangdong: Guangdong Higher Education Press).

Cheung A. (1996), 'Efficiency as the Rhetoric: Public-Sector Reform in Hong Kong Explained', *International Review of Administrative Sciences*, 62: 31-47.

Civil Service Bureau, Hong Kong Government (1999), *Civil Service Into The 21st Century –*

Civil Service Reform (Government Printer: Hong Kong).

Clements, B.J. and K.S. Kim (1988), *Foreign trade and income distribution: the case of Brazil, Working Paper* 108, The Helen Kellogg Institute for International Studies.

Coleman, W. (1994), 'Policy Convergence in Banking: A Comparative Study', *Political Studies*, Vol. XL11: 274-92.

Collins, C., A. Green and D. Hunter (1999), *NHS Reforms and Learning From Developing Country Experience* (Nuffield Institute for Health: Leeds).

Collins, C., A. Green and D. Hunter (1999), *NHS Reforms and Learning From Interpretation of Policy Context*, Health Policy 47: 69-83.

Committee of Public Accounts (26 March 1998), *Twenty-Seventh Report: Measures To Combat Housing Benefit Fraud*, Press Notice, HC366 (London: HMSO).

Common R. (1999a), 'Accounting for Administrative Change in Three Asia-Pacific States: the Utility of Policy Transfer Analysis', *Public Management*, 1: 429-438.

Common R (1999b), *Public Management and Policy Transfer in Southeast Asia*, D.Phil. Thesis, Department of Politics, University of York, England.

Common, R. (2001), *Public Management and Policy Transfer in Southeast Asia* (Aldershot: Ashgate).

Common, R. (2004), 'Organisational Learning in a Political Environment: Improving Policy-making in UK Government', *Policy Studies*, 25: 72-97.

Coombs, P. (1985), *The World Crisis in Education: the View from the Eighties* (New York/Oxford: OUP).

Corney, R. (1994), 'Experiences of First Wave General Practice Fundholders in Southeast Thames Regional Health Authority', *British Journal of General Practice* 44: 34-37.

Cortés, F., D. Hernández, E. Hernández-Laos, M. Székely and H.Vera, H. (2002), *Evolución Y Características De La Pobreza En México En La Última Década Del Siglo XX,* Serie: Documentos De Investigación (México: Sedesol).

Coulter, A. and J. Bradlow (1993), 'Effect of the NHS Reforms on General Practitioners' Referral Patterns', *British Medical Journal,* 306: 433-437.

Daugbjerg, C. and D. Marsh (1998), 'Explaining Policy Outcomes: Integrating the Policy Network Approach with Macro-Level and Micro-Level Analysis', in D. Marsh (ed.), *Comparing Policy Networks* (Buckingham/Philadelphia: Open University Press).

Davies, J. (1996), 'Urban Regime Theory in Critical Perspective: A Case Study of Regeneration Policy in the London Borough Of Merton', *York Papers in Policy and Politics*, No.3 (York: University of York).

Davies, J. and M. Evans (1998), 'Unpacking Policy Transfer Analysis: the Case of Local Agenda 21', University of York, Department of Politics Working Paper, No. 14 (York: University of York).

Davies, H., S. Nutley and P. Smith (eds.), (2000), *What Works? Evidence-based Policy and Practice in Public Service Policy* (Bristol: Policy Press).

Deacon, A. (2000) 'Learning From the US? The Influence of American Ideas Upon "New Labour" Thinking on Welfare Reform', *Policy and Politics*, 28: 5-18.

Dearlove, J. (2000), 'Globalization and the Study of British Politics', *Politics*, 20: 111-118.

Denes, C. A. (2003), 'Bolsa escola: redefining poverty and development in Brazil', *International Education Journal*, 4: 137-47.

Department of Health [UK] (1989a), *Practice Budgets for General Medical Practitioners* (London: HMSO).

Department of Health [UK] (1989b), *Terms of Service for Doctors in General Practice* (London: HMSO).

Department of Health [UK] Connold, A. and J. Rowley (1999), 'Our Healthier Nation', Government White Paper (London: Department of Health).

Department of Social Security [UK] (1996), *Social Security Departmental Report 1996/97*

To 1998/99 (London: HMSO).

Department of Social Security [UK] (1998), *Facts And Figures*, www.dss.gov.uk.

Department of Social Security [UK] (1996), *Social Security Departmental Report 1996/97 To 1998/99* (London: HMSO).

Department of Social Security [UK] (1998), *Facts And Figures*, www.dss.gov.uk.

Doh J.C. (1994), 'Budgetary Reforms: Lessons From Malaysia And Singapore', in I. Scott and I. Thynne (eds.), *Public Sector Reform: Critical Issues and Perspectives* (Hong Kong: AJPA).

Dolowitz, D. (1997a), 'British employment policy in the 1980s: learning from the American experience', *Governance* 10: 23-42.Dolowitz, D. (2000), 'Introduction', *Governance* 13: 1-4.

Dolowitz, D. (1997b), 'Where's the State? The Political Process of Globalisation', in C. Hay and D. Marsh (eds.), *Demystifying Globalization,* (London: Macmillan).

Dolowitz, D., R. Hulme, N. Ellis and F. O'Neal (2000), *Policy Transfer and British Social Policy* (Buckingham: Open University Press).

Dolowitz, D. and D. Marsh (1996), 'Who Learns What From Whom: A Review of the Policy Transfer Literature', *Political Studies*, 44: 343-57.

Dolowitz, D. and Marsh D. (1998), 'Policy Transfer: A Framework for Comparative Analysis', in M. Minogue, C. Polidano and D. Hulme (eds.), *Beyond the New Public Management: Changing Ideas and Practices in Governance* (Cheltenham: Edward Elgar).

Dolowitz, D. and D. Marsh (2000), 'Learning from abroad: the role of policy transfer in contemporary policy-making', *Governance* 13: 5-24.

Dolton, P. and A.Vignoles (1998), 'Overeducation. Problem Or Not?' in M. Henkel and B. Little (eds.), *Changing Relationships Between Higher Education and the State* (London: Jessica Kingsley).

Dowding, K. (1995), 'Model or Metaphor? A Critical Review of the Policy Network Approach', *Political Studies*, 43: 136-158.

Dowding, K. (2001), 'There Must Be End to Confusion: Policy Networks, Intellectual Fatigue, and the Need for Political Science Methods Courses in British Universities', *Political Studies*, 49: 89-105.

Dunleavy, P. (1994), 'The Globalization of Public Services Production: Can Government be 'Best' in World?', *Public Policy and Administration*, 9: 36-64.

Durand, V. and M. Smith (1997), 'La Educación Y La Cultura Política En México: Una Relación Agotada', *Revista Mexicana De Sociología*, 59: 41-74.

Easton, D. (1965), *A Framework For Political Analysis* (N.J.: Prentice Hall).

Ekins, P. (1986), 'Learning from the South', in *The Living Economy: A New Economics in the Making* (London: Routledge and Kegan Paul).

Efficiency Unit [Hong Kong] (1995), *Serving the Community* (Hong Kong: Government Printer).

ERSC Future Governance Program (2000) *Introduction to the Future Governance Research Programme*, http://www.futuregovernance.ac.uk/.

European Commission (2000), *Leonardo Da Vinci: Das Gemeischaftliche Aktionsprogramm In Der Berufsbildung* (Brussels: European Commission).

Evans, M. (2000), 'The New Constitutionalism and the Impact of Spill-Over', *Public Policy and Administration*, Vol. 15: 5-24.

Evans, M. (2003), *Constitution-making and the Labour Party* (London: Palgrave).

Evans, M. (2004), 'Post-war Reconstruction and Public Administration', in S. Barakat (ed.), *Reconstruction after war: Peace, humanitarianism and development* (London: IB Tauris, forthcoming).

Evans, M. and P.G. Cerny (2003), 'Globalisation and Social Policy', in N. Ellison and C.

Pierson (eds.), *Developments in Social Policy 2* (London: Palgrave), pp. 19-40.

Evans, M. and P.G. Cerny (2004), 'Globalisation and Public Policy Under New Labour', *Policy Studies*, Vol. 25, 1: 84-107.

Evans, M. and J. Davies (1999), 'Understanding Policy Transfer: A Multi-Level, Multi-Disciplinary Perspective', *Public Administration*, 77: 361-386.

Evans, M. with P. McComb (1999), 'Policy Transfer Networks and Collaborative Government: the Case of Social Security Fraud', *Public Policy And Administration*, 14: 30-48.

Eyestone, R. (1977), 'Confusion, Diffusion and Innovation', *American Political Science Review*, 71: 441-453.

Faux, J. and L. Mishel (2001), 'Inequality and the Global Economy', in W. Hutton and A. Giddens (eds.), *On The Edge. Living With Global Capitalism* (London: Vintage).

Ferreira, F. and P. Leite (2003), 'Policy Options for Meeting the Millennium Development Goals in Brazil: Can micro-simulations help?' *World Bank Policy Research Working Paper*, No. 2975, February 2003, www.worldbank.org.

Finance Branch [Hong Kong Government] (1989), *Public Sector Reform* (Hong Kong: Hong Kong Government Printer).

Finance Branch [Hong Kong Government] (1995), *Management of Public Finances* (Hong Kong: Hong Kong Government Printer).

Flores-Crespo, P. (2002a), *An Analysis of the Relationship Between Higher Education and Development By Applying Sen's Human Capabilities Approach. The Case of Three Technological Universities in Mexico*, Ph.D Thesis, Department of Politics, University of York, England.

Flores-Crespo, P. (2002b), 'En Busca De Nuevas Explicaciones Sobre La Relación Entre Educación Y Desigualdad. El Caso De La Universidad Tecnológica De Nezahualcóyolt', *Revista Mexicana De Investigación Educativa*, 7: 537-576.

Flores-Crespo, P. (2000), 'Un Acercamiento Al Criterio De Equidad. Breve Discusión Con Referencia Al Conflicto De La Unam', *Debates Magazine*, Universidad De Antioquia, Colombia, 28: 16-19.

Flores-Crespo, P. and S. Ruiz De Chávez (2002), 'Globalización, Gobierno Y Transferencia De Políticas Públicas. El Caso De La Educación Superior En México', *Education Policy Analysis Archives*, 10, 41, www.epaa.asu.edu/epaa/v10n41.html.

Freire, P. (1993) [1970], *Pedagogy of the Oppressed* (London: Penguin Books).

Freire, P. (1996), *Política Y Educación* (Mexico: Siglo XXI).

Fukuyama, F. (1992), *The End of History and the Last Man* (New York: Free Press).

Furlong, P. (2001), 'Constitutional Change as policy transfer; policy transfer as constitutional change', *ESRC Future Governance Programme*, http://www.hull.ac.uk/futgov/Papers/APSAFurlongPau.pdf.

Garrett, G. (1998), *Partisan Politics in the Global Economy* (Cambridge: Cambridge University Press).

Giddens, A. (1998), *The Third Way: The Renewal of Social Democracy* (Oxford: Oxford Polity Press).

Giddens, A. (2002), *Runaway World. How Globalization is Shaping Our Lives* (London: Profile).

Gilbert, A. (2001), 'Power, ideology and the Washington consensus: the development and spread of Chilean Housing policy', *ESRC Future Governance Programme*, http://www.hull.ac.uk/futgov/.

Gleason, W. (1998), 'A History Ukraine Can Use', *Kyiv Post*, Issue 031.

González-Casanova, P. (2001), *La Universidad Necesaria En El Siglo XXI* (México: Era).

Governo do Distrito Federal (1995), Decreto n. 16.270 de 11 de Janeiro de 1995.

Governo do Distrito Federal (1995), Portaria n. 16 de 9 de Fevereiro de 1995.

Governo do Distrito Federal (1998), Decreto n. 19.391 de 3 de Julho de 1998.

Gray, A. (1998), 'New Labour-New Labour Discipline', *Capital and Class*, 65: 1-8.

Gray, V. (1973), 'Innovation in the States: a diffusion study', *American Political Science Review*, 67: 1174-85.

Greener, I. (2001), 'Social Learning and Macroeconomic Policy in Britain', *Journal of Public Policy*, 21: 1-22.

Grossmann, A. (2000), *Transfer Project Ecotrans: Final Report* (Berlin: Understandingbus).

Grossmann, A., P. Umbsen, and R. Furth (1998), *Headways Opening Employment Opportunities For Unemployed People In The Environmental Sector* (Berlin: Understandingbus).

Haagh, L. and C. Helgo (eds.), (2002), *Social Policy Reform and Market Governance in Latin America* (London: Palgrave).

Haas, E. (1980), 'Why Collaborate? Issue-Linkage And International Regimes', *World Politics*, 32: 357-405.

Haas, P.M. (1989), 'Do Regimes Matter? Epistemic Communities and Evolving Policies to Control Mediterranean Pollution', *International Organisation*, 43: 377-403.

Haas, P.M. (ed.), (1992), *Knowledge, Power, and International Policy Coordination*, Special Issue of *International Organization*, Vol. 46, No. 1, Winter.

Haas, P.M. (1992), 'Introduction: Epistemic Communities and International Policy Coordination', *International Organization* 46: 1-36.

Hall, P. (1993), 'Policy paradigms, social learning and the state: the case of economic policy-making in Britain,' *Comparative Politics*, 25: 275-96.

Hall, S. (1985), 'Authoritarian Populism: A Reply', *New Left Review*, 151: 115-24.

Hambleton, R. and M. Taylor (eds.), (1993), *People in Cities: A Transatlantic Policy Exchange* (UK: SAUS).

Hay, C. (1996), *Re-Starting Social and Political Change* (Buckingham: Open University Press).

Hay, C. and D. Marsh (eds.), (1997), *Demystifying Globalization,* (London: Macmillan).

Heclo, H. (1974), *Modern Social Politics in Britain and Sweden* (New Haven: Yale University Press).

Hinchliffe, K. (1987), 'Forecasting Manpower Requirements', in G. Psacharopoulos (ed.), *Economics of Education: Research and Studies* (London: Pergamon).

Hirst, P. and G. Thompson (1996 and 2000), *Globalisation In Question* (Cambridge: Polity Press/Blackwell).

HKDF Policy Committee [Hong Kong] (1998), 'Reform Of Government – Towards An Agenda', *Hong Kong Democratic Foundation Newsletter*, 9: 5-7.

Hoberg, G. (1991), 'Sleeping With An Elephant: the American Influence on Canadian Environmental Regulation', *Journal of Public Policy*, II: 107-132.

Hofstede, G. (1980), *Culture's Consequences* (Beverly Hills, Ca.: Sage).

Hogwood, B. and B.G. Peters (1983), *Policy Dynamics* (Brighton: Wheatsheaf).

Holden, C. (1999), 'Globalisation, Social Exclusion and Labour's New Work Ethic', *Critical Social Policy*, 19: 529-538.

Hollis, G. and K. Plokker (1998), *Waking Sleeping Beauty: Towards a Sustainable Provision of Social Services in Transitional Countries* (Brussels: Tacis Services DG IA, European Commission).

Hon. M. and No K-Y. (1999), 'Civil Service Revamp Not Against Basic Law', *South China Morning Post*, 10 March.

Hood C. (1991), 'A Public Management For All Seasons?' *Public Administration*, 69: 3-19.

Hood C. (1995), 'Contemporary Public Management: A New Global Paradigm', *Public Policy and Administration*, 10: 104-117.

House of Commons [UK], Social Security Committee (1998), *Social Security Reforms:*

Lessons from the United States of America (HC 82, London: HMSO).

Howie, J., D. Heaney, and M. Maxwell (1995), *General Practice Fundholding: Shadow Project – An Evaluation*, (Edinburgh: University of Edinburgh).

Huque A., S. Lee and A. Cheung (1998), *The Civil Service in Hong Kong: Continuity and Change* (Hong Kong: Hong Kong University Press).

Hutton, W. (1995), *The State We're In* (London: Cape).

Hyndman, N.S. and R. Anderson (1998), 'Performance Information, Accountability and Executive Agencies', *Public Money and Management*, April-June.

IBGE (2001), *Pesquisa Nacional por Amostra de Domicilios. Trabalho Infantil.* [www.ibge.gov.br]

IDB (2001), *The Social Program* Progresa *Breaks Extreme Poverty Cycle in Mexico*, www.iadb.org/exr/PRENSA/2001/cp9101e.htm.

IDB (2000), *Perfil II – Ecuador – Programa de Proteccion Social*. Proyecto EC-0190, www.iadb.org/exr/doc98/pro/uec0190.pdf.

Ikenberry, J.G. (1990), 'The International Spread of Privatisation Policies: Inducements, Learning and Policy Bandwaggoning', in E. Suleiman and J. Waterbury (eds.), *The Political Economy of Public Sector Reform* (Boulder: Westview Press).

ILO and UNCTAD Advisory Group (2001), *The Minimum Income for School Attendance (MISA) Initiative: Achieving International Development Goals in Africa Least Developed Countries* (Geneva: ILO).

Inkeles, A. (1981), 'Convergence and divergence in industrial societies', in M. Attir, B. Holzner and Z. Suda (eds.), *Directions of change* (Boulder: Westview Press), pp. 3-38.

Ishaq, M. (1999), 'Foreign Direct Investment in Ukraine Since Transition', *Communist and Post-Communist Studies*, 32: 91-109.

James, O. (2001), 'Business Models and the Transfer of Business-like Central Government Agencies', *Governance*, 14, 2.

James, O. and M. Lodge (2003), 'The Limitations of "Policy Transfer" and "Lesson Drawing" for Public Policy research', *Political Studies Review*, 2003: 179–193.

James, S. (1996), 'Obstacles to Policy Transfer', 'Policy Transfer: the Global Spread of Ideas, Policies and Institutions', ESRC Research Seminar, 26-27 October 1996.

Jessop, B. (1990), *State Theory, Putting Capitalist States in Their Place* (Cambride: Polity Press).

Johnstone, P. and I. McConnan (1995), 'Primary Health Care Led NHS: Learning from Developing Countries', *British Medical Journal*, 311: 891-892.

Jones, C. (1996), *Using Participatory Appraisal in the UK Health Sector: Assessing Palliative Care Services*, Consultants Report on Bradford and Keighley Districts, 101323.3337@compuserve.com.

Jones D. (1999), 'Public Administration in Singapore: Continuity and Reform', in H. Wong and H. Chan (eds.), *Handbook of Comparative Public Administration in the Asia-Pacific Basin* (New York: Marcel Dekker).

Jones, T. and T. Newburn (2001), 'Learning from Uncle Sam? Exploring US Influences on British crime control policy', *ESRC Future Governance Programme*, http://www.hull.ac.uk/futgov/.

Jordan, A., and J. Greenaway (1998), 'Shifting Agendas, Changing Regulatory Structures and the 'New' Politics of Environmental Pollution: British Coastal Water Policy, 1955-1995', *Public Administration*, 76: 669-694.

Joseph, K. (1972), 'The Cycle Of Deprivation', Speech to Conference of Pre-School Playgroups Association, 29 June.

Joseph, K. (1974), 'Britain: A Decadent New Utopia', Speech, Birmingham 19 October, Reprinted in the *Guardian*, 21 October.

Judge, K. (1999), *Tackling Social Exclusion: Is There A Third Way?* Inaugural Lecture At

UKC, May, 1999.

Judge, K. (1999), *Health Action Zones: Learning To Make A Difference. Findings From a Preliminary Review of Health Action Zones and Proposals For a National Evaluation* (London: Department of Health).

Kent, R. (1999), 'Reform in Mexican Higher Education: An Overview of the 1990s', *International Higher Education*, spring, http://www.bc.edu/bc_org/avp/soe/cihe/direct1/news15/text7.html.

Kerr, C., J. Dunlop, F. Harbison, and C. Myers (1973), *Industrialism and Industrial Man* (London: Penguin Books).

King, D. and M. Wickham-Jones (1999), 'From Clinton to Blair – the Democratic Party Origins of Welfare to Work', *Political Quarterly*, 70: 62-74.

Kingdon, J. (1996), *Agendas, Alternatives And Public Policies* (New York: Harper Collins).

Kleinman, M. (1998), 'Social Exclusion: New Deal, Old Barriers', *The Guardian*, 30 August 1998.

Know How Fund Team (1996), 'Rationalisation of Hospital Services in the Geographical Area of Bishkek' (London: London Health Economics Consortium).

Kushanryev, Y. (1995), 'Self-Government Again', *Holos Ukrainy*, No.150.

Kuzio, T. (ed.), (1998), *Dynamics of Post-Soviet Transformation: Contemporary Ukraine* (New York: M.E. Sharpe).

Lächler, U. (1998), *Education and Earnings Inequality in Mexico*, http://www.worldbank.org.

Ladi, S. (1998), Policy Transfer, Globalisation and Think Tanks: the International Dialogues Foundation and Youth Employment, Dissertation for MA in Public Administration and Public Policy, Department of Politics, University of York, England.

Ladi, S. (2000), 'Globalization, Think-Tanks and Policy Transfer', in D. Stone (ed.), (2000), *Banking on Knowledge: The Genesis of the GDN* (London: Routledge).

Ladi, S. (2002), *Globalization, Europeanization and policy transfer: a comparative study of knowledge institutions*, PhD Thesis, Department of Politics, University of York, England.

La Hora (2003) *Ecuador – Historia Contemporanea*, www.dlh.lahora.com.ec.

Lasswell, H. (1970), 'The Emerging Conception of the Policy Sciences', *Policy Sciences*, 1: 3-14.

Latapí, P. (1996), *Tiempo Educativo Mexicano I* (México: UAA-UNAM).

Latapí, P. (1997), *Tiempo Educativo Mexicano IV* (México: UAA-UNAM).

Latapí, P. (1998), *Tiempo Educativo Mexicano V* (México: UAA-UNAM).

Latapí, P. (2000), *Tiempo Educativo Mexicano VI* (México: UAA-UNAM).

Lavinas, L. *et al.* (2001) *Assessing local minimum income programmes in Brazil* (Geneva: ILO-WB).

Lavinas, L. (1999) *The appeal of minimum income programmes in Latin America* (Geneva: ILO).

Layard, R. (1997), *What Labour Can Do* (London: Warner).

Leftwich, A. (2001), *States of Development* (Cambridge: Polity Press).

Leibfried, S. (2000), 'National Welfare States, European Integration and Globalization: A Perspective for the Next Century', *Social Policy and Administration*, 34: 44-63.

Leon, D., L. Chenet *et al.* (1997), 'Huge Variation in Russian Mortality Rates, 1984-94: Artefact, Alcohol, Or What?' *Lancet*, 350: 383-388.

Lesage, M. (1993), 'The Crisis of Public Administration in Russia', *Public Administration*, 71: 121-133.

Levi, M. (2001), 'Money-laundering and its regulation', *ESRC Future Governance Programme*, http://www.hull.ac.uk/futgov/.

Levy, D.C. (1986), *Higher Education and the State in Latin America: Private Challenges to*

Public Dominance (Chicago: the University of Chicago Press).

Levy, D.C. (1994), 'Mexico: Towards State Supervision? Changing Patterns of Governance in Mexican Higher Education', in G. Neave and F. Van Vught (eds.), *Government and Higher Education Relationships Across Three Continents. The Wind of Change* (London: IAU-Pergamon).

Levy, D.C. (2000), 'Framing the Problem: How a Changing Latin American Higher Education Opens the Door for Community Colleges', paper presented at the Seminar on *New Options For Higher Education in Latin America: Lessons from the Community Colleges Experience*, Inter-American Development Bank and the Harvard Graduate School of Education, 4-8 September.

Levy, J. (1994), 'Learning And Foreign Policy: Sweeping A Conceptual Minefield', *International Organisation*, 48: 279-312.

Lightfoot, E. (1999), 'Connecting Policy Transfer with Ideology: A Study of Great Britain's Failed Emulation of the Americans with Disabilities Act', *American Political Science Association Annual Conference*.

Lindblom, C.E. (1977), *Politics and Markets: The World's Political-Economic Systems* (New York: Basic Books).

Livingstone, D.W. (1999), 'Lifelong Learning and Underemployment in the Knowledge Society: A North American Perspective', *Comparative Education*, 35: 163-186.

Lorey, D.E. (1993), *The University System and Economic Development in Mexico Since 1929* (Stanford: Stanford University Press).

Lukes, S. (1974), *Power: A Radical View* (London: Macmillan).

Lund, B. (1999), 'Ask Not What Your Community Can Do For You: Obligations, New Labour and Welfare Reform', *Critical Social Policy*, 19: 447-462.

Lynn L. (1998), 'The New Public Management: How to Transform a Theme into a Legacy', *Public Administration Review*, 58: 231- 237.

Macintosh, M. (1997), 'Managing Public Sector Reform: the Case of Health Care', *Working Paper*, No. 37, Development Policy and Practice Research Group (Milton Keynes: Open University Press).

Maddock, S. (1999), *Managing The Development of Partnerships and Modernisation* (North West Change Centre), http://www.york.ac.uk/depts/poli/pac/paper/maddock.htm.

Mahathir M. (1983), 'New Government Policies', in K. Jomo (ed.), *The Sun Also Sets: Lessons in 'Looking East'*, (Petaling Jaya: Insan).

Majone, G. (1991), 'Cross-National Sources of Regulatory Policy Making in Europe and the United States', *Journal of Public Policy*, 11: 79-106.

Malcolm, L. (1993), 'General Practitioner Fundholding: Experimental Sideshow Or Main Event of the NHS Reforms?', *New Zealand Medical Journal* 106: 183-186.

Manas Programme Unit (1995), *Manas National Programme on Health Care Reform (1996-2006)* (Bishkek: Ministry of Health).

Marín, A. (1998), 'La Globalización Y Su Impacto En La Reforma Universitaria Mexicana', *La Universidad Mexicana En El Umbral Del Siglo Xxi, Visiones Y Proyecciones* (México: ANUIES).

Marinker, M. (1984), 'Developments in Primary Health Care, in G. Teeling Smith (ed.), *A New NHS Act For 1986?* (London: Office of Health Economics).

Marmor T. (1997), 'Global Health Policy Reform: Misleading Mythology or Learning Opportunity?' in C. Altenstetter and J. Bjorkman (eds.), *Health Policy Reform, National Variations and Globalization* (Basingstoke: Macmillan).

Márquez, A. (1999), *El Costo Familiar Y/O Individual De La Educación Superior* (México: ANUIES).

Marsh, D. (ed.), (1998), *Comparing Policy Networks* (Buckingham/Philadelphia: Open University Press).

Marsh, D. and R.A.W. Rhodes (eds.), (1992a), *Policy Networks in British Government* (Oxford: Clarendon Press).

Marsh, D. and R.A.W. Rhodes (1992b), 'New Directions in the Study of Policy Networks', *European Journal of Political Research*, 21: 181-205.

Maruyama, M. (ed.), (1993), *Management Reform in Eastern and Central Europe: Use of Pre-Communist Cultures* (Aldershot: Dartmouth).

Massey, A. (1997), 'In Search of the State: Markets, Myths and Paradigms', in A. Massey (ed.), *Globalization and Marketization of Government Services* (Basingstoke: Macmillan).

May, P. (1992), 'Policy Learning and Failure', *Journal of Public Policy*, 12: 331-354.

Maynard, A. (1986), 'Performance Incentives in General Practice', in G. Teeling Smith (ed.), *Health Education and General Practice* (London: Office of Health Economics).

McAdam, D. and D. Rucht (1993), 'The Cross-National Diffusion of Movement Ideas", *Annals AAPS*, 528: 56-74.

McGrew, A. and G. Lewis (1992), *Global Politics* (Cambridge: Blackwell).

McKee, M., J. Figueras, and L. Chenet (1998), 'Health Sector Reform in the Former Soviet Republics of Central Asia', *International Journal of Health Planning and Management* 13: 131-147.

McKenzie, R. and D. Lee (1991), *Quicksilver Capital: How the Rapid Movement of Wealth Has Changed the World* (New York: Free Press).

Missão Criança (2000), *Beca-escolar: um proyecto para America Latina y el Caribe.* (Brasília: Missão Criança).

Missão Criança (2003), *Official Website*, http://www.missaocrianca.org.br.

Mokhtar, K. (2001), *Policy Transfer in Critical Perspective: the Case of the Privatisation of Malaysian Airlines*, PhD Thesis, Department of Politics, University of York, England.

Mosley, P. (1987), *Overseas Aid: Its Defence And Reform* (Sussex: John Spiers).

Mossberger, K. and H. Wolman (2001), 'Policy transfer as a form of prospective policy evaluation', *ESRC Future Governance Programme*, http://www.hull.ac.uk/futgov/.

Muñoz-Izquierdo, C. (1994), *La Contribución De La Educación Al Cambio Social* (México:Gernika).

Myers, C.N (1965), *Education and National Development in Mexico* (Princeton: Princeton University Press).

Nagel J. (1997), 'Radically Reinventing Government: Editor's Introduction', *Journal of Policy Analysis and Management*, 16: 349-356.

National Audit Office (1997), *Measures To Combat Housing Benefit Fraud* (London: the Stationery Office).

Newhouse, J.P. (1982), 'Is Competition the Answer?' *Journal of Health Economics,* 1: 109-116.

NHS Executive (1997), 'The New NHS: Modern, Dependable' (Leeds: NHS Executive).

Nordberg, M. (1998), 'State and Institution Building in Ukraine', in T. Kuzio (ed.), *Dynamics of Post-Soviet Transformation: Contemporary Ukraine* (New York: M.E. Sharpe).

Oakeshott, M. (1976), 'On Misunderstanding Human Conduct: A Reply to my Critics', *Political Theory*, 4: 353-367.

Osborne, D. and T. Gaebler (1992), *Reinventing Government: How the Entrepreneurial Spirit is Transforming the Public Sector, From Schoolhouse to Statehouse, City Hall to the Pentagon*, (Reading, MA: Addison-Wesley).

Osborne D. and Plastrik, P. (1997), *Banishing Bureaucracy* (Reading, Ma: Addison-Wesley).

OECD (1997), *Reviews of National Policies for Education. Mexico; Higher Education* (Paris: OECD).

OECD (2000), *Education at a Glance. OECD Indicators* (Paris: OECD).

OCE (2000a), Comunicado 22: 'La Educación Superior Ante Un Nuevo Siglo', *Comunicados* I: 1-30 (México: OCE).

OCE (2000b), Comunicado 13: 'El Gasto De Las Familias En Educación', *Comunicados* I: 1-30 (México: OCE).

OCE (2000c), Comunicado 2: 'Aumentan Los Recursos Para La Educación', *Comunicados* I: 1-30 (México: OCE).

OCE (2000d), Comunicado 34: 'El Gasto En Educación Superior Y El Conflicto De La Unam', www.observatorio.org.

OCE (2000e), Comunicado 4: 'Los Dilemas De Las Universidades Tecnológicas', *Comunicados* 1: 1-30. (México: OCE).

Oliynyk, V. (1999a), 'Time to Live According to the Laws of One's Own Land', *Holos Ukrainy*, No. 151.

Oliynyk, V. (1999b), 'There is no alternative to Self-Government', *Region*, 12.

Olsen, J. and B.G. Peters (1996), 'Learning From Experience?', in J. Olsen and B.G. Peters (eds.), *Lessons From Experience: Experiential Learning In Administrative Reforms In Eight Democracies* (Oslo: Scandinavian University Press).

Ordorika, I. (1996), 'Mexican Higher Education in Transition: From Politically to Financially Driven Public Policies', *International Higher Education*, August.

Ornelas, C. and D. Post (1992), 'Recent University Reform in Mexico', *Comparative Education Review* 36: 278-297.

Oxfam (UK and Ireland), (1995), *The Oxfam Handbook of Development And Relief*: Volume 2. (Oxford: OxfamU.K.).

Page, E.C. (2000), '*Future governance and the literature on policy transfer and lesson drawing,'* paper prepared for the ESRC Future Governance Programme Workshop on Policy Transfer, 28 January.

Paz, O. [1970], (1990), *The Other México* (London: Penguin).

Pallán, C., R. López, *et al.* (1995), *La Educación Superior En México*, Colección: Temas De Hoy En La Educación Superior, No. 1 (México: ANUIES).

Panitch, L. and C. Leys (1997), *The End of Parliamentary Socialism. From New Left to New Labour* (London: Verso).

Parsons, W. (1996), *Public Policy: an introduction to the theory and practice of policy analysis* (London: Edward Elgar).

Pawson, R. (2002), 'Evidence and Policy and Naming and Shaming', *Policy Studies*, 23: 211-230.

Pedler, M., J. Burgoyne and T. Boydell (1991), *The Learning Company* (Maidenhead: McGraw-Hill).

Pereira, F. and R. de Barros (2000), 'Education and income distribution in urban Brazil, 1976-1996,' *Cepal Review*, 71.

Peters B.G. (1996), 'Theory And Methodology', in H. Bekke, J. Perry and T. Toonen (eds.), *Civil Service Systems in Comparative Perspective* (Bloomington, Ind.: Indiana University Press).

Peters, B.G. (1997), 'Policy transfers between governments: the case of administrative reforms', *West European Politics*, 20: 71-88.

Peters, B.G. (1998), 'Policy Networks: Myth, Metaphor and Reality', in D. Marsh (ed.), *Comparing Policy Networks* (Buckingham/Philadelphia, Open University Press).

Piraeus Chamber of Small and Medium Sized Enterprises (2000), *Information Leaflet* (Athens: Piraeus).

PND (1989), *Plan Nacional De Desarrollo 1989-1994* (México: Poder Ejecutivo Federal).

PNE (2001), *Plan Nacional De Educación, 2001-2006* (México: Sep).

POLIS and UNICEF (1998), *As famílias beneficiárias do Programa Bolsa-escola do*

Distrito Federal: uma abordagem qualitativa.

Polokhalo, V. (ed.), (1997), *The Political Analysis of Post-Communism: Understanding Post-Communist Ukraine* (Texas: A&M University Press).

PPS-MBS (2002), Programa de Protección Social. Ministério de Bienestar Social. (2002) *Beca Escolar: los primeros dos años,* www.pps.gov.ec.

PPS-MBS (2003), *Programa de Protección Social,* Ministério de Bienestar Social, www.pps.gov.ec.

Price, D., A. Pollock and J. Shaoul (1999), 'How the World Trade Organisation is Shaping Domestic Policies in Health Care', *Lancet* 354: 1889-1892.

Proctor, R. (1999) 'Hitler Health Policy Led Way' The Observer Newspaper: P.16, 9.5.99.

PS21 Office [Singapore] (1995), *The Case for PS21* (Singapore: Singapore Government).

Puryear, J. (1995), 'International Education Statistics and Research: Status and Problems', *International Journal Of Educational Development,* 15: 79-91.

Rech, D. and M. Abramovay (2002), *Relatório de Avaliação/Missão Criança* (Convênio NOVIB/União Européia).

Reich, R. (1991), *The Work Of Nations: Preparing Ourselves for 21ˢᵗ Century Capitalism* (New York: Knopf).

Reséndiz, D. (1998), 'La Vinculación De Universidades Y Empresas: Un Asunto De Interés Público Y Privado', *Revista De La Educación Superior,* Vol 102, No. 106: 55-64.

Reschenthaler, G. and F. Thompson (2001), 'Public Administration in a Period Of Change: Moving To A Learning Organization Perspective', *International Public Management Network Journal,* 1, 1: 1-59.

Rhodes, R.A.W. (1994), 'The Hollowing-Out of the State: the Changing Nature of the Public Service in Britain', *Political Quarterly,* 65: 138-151.

Rhodes, R.A.W. (1996), 'The New Governance: Governing Without Government', *Political Studies,* XLIV: 652-667.

Rhodes, R.A.W. (1997), *Understanding Governance. Policy Networks, Governance, Reflexivity and Accountability* (Milton Keynes: Open University Press).

Ridley F. (1996), 'The New Public Management In Europe: Comparative Perspectives', *Public Policy and Administration,* 11: 16-29.

Risse-Kappen, T. (ed.), (1995), *Bringing Transnationals Back In: Non State Actors, Domestic Structures and International Institutions* (Cambridge: Cambridge University Press).

Robertson, D. (1991), 'Political Conflict and Lesson Drawing', *Journal of Public Policy,* 11: 55-78.

Robinson, D. (1998), 'Rethinking the Public Sector: NGOs, Public Action Networks and the Promotion of Community-Based Health Care in Tanzania', *Working Paper,* No 38, Development Policy and Practice Research Group (Milton Keynes: the Open University Press).

Rocha, S. (2001), *Applying minimum income programmes in Brazil: two case studies* (Geneva: ILO).

Rodgers, P. *et al.* (1995), *Social Exclusion: rhetoric, reality, response.* (Geneva: ILO).

Rodríguez, R. (2002), 'Continuación Y Cambio De Las Políticas De Educación Superior', *Revista Mexicana De Investigación Educativa,* 7: 133-154.

Root H. (1996), *Small Countries, Big Lessons: Governance and the Rise of East Asia* (Hong Kong: Oxford University Press).

Rosamond, B. (1999), 'Discourses of Globalization and the Social Construction of European Identities', *Journal of European Public Policy,* 6: 652-668.

Rose, R. (1991), 'What is Lesson Drawing?', *Journal of Public Policy,* 11: 3-30.

Rose, R. (1993), *Lesson Drawing in Public Policy: A Guide to Learning Across Time and Space* (Chatham House: New Jersey).

Rose, R. (2001), 'Ten steps in learning lessons from abroad', *ESRC Future Governance Programme*, http://www.hull.ac.uk/futgov/.

Rose, R., W. Mishler and C. Haerpfer (1998), *Democracy and Its Alternatives. Understanding Post-Communist Societies* (London: John Hopkins University Press).

Roselle, L. (1990), 'Model Fitting in Communist Studies', in G. Almond (ed.), *A Discipline Divided: Schools and Sects in Political Science* (London: Sage).

Rounds, T. (1997), 'Decentralization and Privatisation: Education Policy in Chile', *Journal of Public Policy*, 17: 107-133.

Ruiz, C. (1997), *El Reto De La Educación Superior En La Sociedad Del Conocimiento* (México: ANUIES).

Rutherford, A. and M. Telford (2001), 'Dealing with people with severe personality disorders', *ESRC Future Governance Programme*, , http://www.hull.ac.uk/futgov/.

Sabatier, P. (1986), 'Top Down and Bottom Up Approaches to Implementation Research', *Journal of Public Policy*, 6: 21-48.

Sabatier, P. and H. Jenkins-Smith (1999), 'The Advocacy Coalition Framework: An Assessment' in P. Sabatier (ed.), *Theories of the Policy Process* (Boulder: Westview Press).

Sabatier, A. and H. Jenkins-Smith (1997), 'The Advocacy Coalition Framework: An Assessment', a paper presented at the Department of Political Science, University of Amsterdam.

Saboia, J. and S. Rocha (2002), *An evaluation methodology for minimum income programmes in Brazil* (Geneva: ILO).

Samoff, J. (ed.), (1994), *Coping With Crisis. Austerity, Adjustment and Human Resources* (London: Cassell-UNESCO).

Sarji A. (1996), *The Chief Secretary to the Government, Malaysia* (Subang Jaya: Pelanduk).

Sakwa, R. (ed.), (1999), *The Experience of Democratization in Eastern Europe* (London: Macmillan).

Salazar, R. (2000), 'Por qué interesa reducir la pobreza?' *Gestión Economia y Sociedad*, 74, www.gestion.dinediciones.com/74/2info.htm.

Sands, T. (1999), *Health Action Zones*, National Health Service Executive: Ministerial Briefing Notes (NHS: Leeds).

Sankey C. (1998), 'The Hong Kong Experience', Emerging Market Economy Workshop on Public Management in Support of Economic and Social Objectives, 10-11 December (OECD: Paris).

Sazonov, M. (ed.), (1998), *Political Science* (Kharkiv: Folio).

Secretary of State for Health [UK], (1989), *Working for Patients*, Cmnd 555 (London: HMSO).

Secretary of State for Social Security [UK], (1998) *Beating Fraud Is Everyone's Business*, Cmnd 4010 (London: HMSO).

Secretary of State for Social Security [UK], (1999), *A New Contract For Welfare: Safeguarding Social Security*, Cmnd 4276 (London: HMSO).

Secretary of State and Minister for Social Security [UK], (1998), *New Ambitions For Our Country*, Cmnd 3805 (London: HMSO).

Seeliger R. (1996), 'Conceptualizing and Researching Policy Convergence', *Policy Studies*, 24: 287-306.

Sen, A. (1999), *Development as Freedom* (Oxford: OUP).

SEP (1991), *Universidad Tecnológica. Una Nueva Opción Educativa Para La Formación Profesional A Nivel Superior* (México: SEP).

SEP (1999), *Informes De Labores 1998-1999* (Mexico: SEP).

SEP (2000), *Profile of Education in Mexico* (Mexico: SEP).

Skilling, G. and F. Griffiths (eds.), (1971), *Interest Groups in Soviet Politics* (Princeton:

Princeton University Press).

Smithies, J. (1992), *Healthgain '92: Information Sheet, Standing Conference*, Belfast (Belfast: Healthgain '92).

Social Security Benefits Agency [UK], (1996), *Benefits Agency Annual Report And Accounts* (London: HMSO).

Stallings, B. (1992), 'International influence on economic policy: debt, stabilization, and structural reform', in S. Haggard and R. Kaufman (eds.), *The politics of economic adjustment: international constraints, distributive conflicts, and the state* (Princeton: Princeton University Press).

Stevens, H. (1995), 'Converging Administrative Systems: Recruitment and Training in the United Kingdom', Working Paper, *The European Institute*, LSE (London: LSE).

Stone. D. (1996a), 'Non-Governmental Policy Transfer: The Strategies of Independent Policy Institutes', paper presented to ESRC Research Seminar, Department of Politics and International Studies, University of Birmingham.

Stone, D. (1996b), *Capturing the Political Imagination: Think Tanks and the Policy Process* (London: Frank Cass).

Stone, D. (1999), 'Learning Lessons and Transferring Policy Across Time, Space and Disciplines', *Politics*, 19: 51-59.

Stone, D. (ed.), (2000a), *Banking on knowledge: the genesis of the Global Development Network* (London: Routledge).

Stone, D. (2000b), 'Non-Governmental Policy Transfer: the Strategies of Independent Policy Institutes', *Governance*, 13: 45-62.

Strange, S. (1986), *Casino Capitalism* (Oxford: Blackwell).

Street, A. and J. Haycock (1999), 'The Economic Consequences of Reorganizing Hospital Services in Bishkek, Kyrgyzstan', *Health Economics* 8: 53-64.

Suplicy, E. (2002), *Renda de cidadania: a saída é pela porta* (São Paulo: Perseu Abrano).

Surender, R., J. Bradlow, *et al.* (1995), 'Prospective Study of Trends in Referral Patterns in Fundholding and Non-Fundholding Practices in the Oxford Region, 1990-4', *British Medical Journal,* 311: 1205-8.

Tedstrom, J. (1998), 'Ukraine's Economy: Strategic Issues For Successful Recovery', in T. Kuzio (ed.), *Dynamics of Post-Soviet Transformation: Contemporary Ukraine* (New York: M.E.Sharpe).

Theodore, N. and J. Peck (1999), 'Welfare-To-Work: National Problems, Local Solutions?', *Critical Social Policy*, 19: 485-510.

Thunhurst, C. and N. Ruck (1991), 'A Lesson in Southern Comfort', *Health Service Journal*, 10 January, pp. 24-25.

Tickell, A. and G. Clark (2001), 'New architectures or liberal logics? Interpreting global financial reform', *ESRC Future Governance Programme*, http://www.hull.ac.uk/futgov/.

Tilak, J.B.G. (1997), 'Lessons From Cost Recovery in Education', in C. Colclough (ed.), *Marketizing Education and Health In Developing Countries* (Oxford: Clarendon Press).

Tinbergen, J. (1959), *The Theory of the Optimum Regime* (Amsterdam: North Holland).

Tokman, V. E. and G. O'Donnell (1998), *Poverty and inequality in Latin America: issues and challenges* (Notre Dame, University of Notre Dame Press).

Torres, C. A. (1991), 'El Corporativismo Estatal, Las Políticas Educativas Y Los Movimientos Estudiantiles Y Magisteriales En México', *Revista Mexicana De Sociologi,*53: 159-183.

Torres, C.A. and A. Puiggrós (1997), (eds.), *Latin American Education: Comparative Perspectives* (Westview Press).

Transition Newsletter (2001), 'Investment With a High Return: Supporting Economics Education and Research in Transition Countries. Minutes of a High-Powered Meeting at the World Bank', Vol. 12, 2, Development Research Group (World Bank/William

Davidson Institute).

Tsang D. (1997), 'Hong Kong Government – Hong Kong Means Business', *M2 Presswire*, 17 Jan.

Tünnermmann, C. (1996), *Situación Y Perspectivas De La Educación Superior En América Latina*, Colección: Temas De Hoy En La Educación Superior, No. 13. (México: ANUIES).

Turner, M. and D. Hulme (1997), *Governance, Administration and Development: Making The State Work* (Basingstoke: Palgrave).

Tushman, M. and D. Nadler (1996), 'Organizing for Innovation', in K. Starkey (ed.), *How organizations learn* (London: International Thomson Business Press).

UNDP (2001), *Human Development Report, 2001* (New York: OUP).

UNESCO (1997), *International Standard Classification of Education*, www.unescos.org/education/i...tion/nfsunesco/doc/isced_1997.htm.

UNESCO, UNICEF and POLIS (1998) *O programa bolsa-escola do Distrito Federal.* (Brasília).

Unger, B. and F. Van Waarden (1995), 'Introduction: An Interdisciplinary Approach to Convergence', in B. Unger and F. Van Waarden (eds.), *Convergence or Diversity?* (Aldershot: Avebury), pp. 1-35.

Understandingbus, (5/11/98), *Subsidy Application To The EU-Commission GD 5* (Berlin: Understandingbus).

University of Piraeus (May 1999), *Minutes of the Meeting for the Ecotrans Project* (Piraeus: University of Piraeus).

University of Pireaus (June 2000), *Ecotrans: Final Report* (Piraeus: University of Piraeus).

Vaughan, M.K. (1975), 'Education and Class in the Mexican Revolution', *Latin American Perspectives*, 2: 17-33.

Veltmeyer, H. *et al.* (1997) *Neoliberalism and class conflict in Latin America: a comparative perspective on the political economy of structural adjustment* (Basingstoke, Macmillan Press), pp. 9-63.

Villa, L. and P. Flores-Crespo (2002), 'Las Universidades Tecnológicas Mexicanas En El Espejo De Los Institutos Universitarios De Tecnología Franceses', *Revista Mexicana De Investigación Educativa*, January-April, 7,14: 17-49.

Vogel, S. (1996), *Freer Markets, More Rules: Regulatory Reform In Advanced Industrial Countries* (Ithaca, NY: Cornell University Press).

Walker, J. L. (1969), 'The diffusion of innovations among American states', *American Political Science Review*, 63, 880-99.

Walker, R. (1998), 'The Americanisation of British Welfare: A Case Study of Policy Transfer', *Focus*, 19: 32-40.

Walt, G. and L. Gilson (1994), 'Reforming the Health Sector in Developing Countries: the Central Role of Policy Analysis', *Health Policy and Planning*, 9: 353-370.

Weiss, Z. (2000), *Bolsa-escola cidadã* (Brasília: Missão Criança).

West, A. (1999), *Participatory Learning And Action*. Volume 35, June 1999.

Weyland, K. (1998), 'Swallowing the bitter pill', *Comparative Political Studies*, 31: 540-568.

Wilkinson, D. and E. Appleby (1998), *Implementing Holistic Government: Joined-Up Action on the Ground* (Bristol: Policy Press).

Wilson, D. (1998), *Exploring The Limits of Public Participation* (Rotherham: DETR Publications).

Wilson, J. (1996), 'Citizen Major? The Rationale and Impact of the Citizen's Charter', *Public Policy And Administration* Vol. 11, No.1 Spring.

Wincott, D. (1999), 'Globalization and European Integration', in C. Hay and D. Marsh (eds.), *Demystifying Globalization,* (London: Macmillan), pp. 168-190.

Winiecki, J. (1997), 'The Transformation to the Market: At High Cost, Often With Long Lags, And Not Without Question Marks', *Journal of Public Policy*, 17: 251-267.

Wolman, H. (1992), 'Understanding Cross National Policy Transfers: the Case of Britain and the US', *Governance*, 5: 27-45.

World Bank (1993), 'Investing In Health', *World Development Report* (Oxford: Oxford University Press).

World Bank (1994), *Higher Education. The Lesson of Experience* (Washington DC: World Bank).

World Bank (1994), *Better Health in Africa: Experience and Lessons Learned* (Washington DC: World Bank).

World Bank (1995), *Staff Appraisal Report: Health Project in Kyrgystan* (Washington DC: World Bank).

World Bank (1995), *World Development Report: Workers in an Integrating World* (New York: Oxford University Press).

World Bank (1996), *Poverty Lines: Investing in Education* (Washington DC: World Bank). World Bank (1999), *Ecuador - Human Capital Protection* (Washington DC: World Bank).

World Bank (2001), *World Development Report 2001* (Washington DC: World Bank).

World Bank (2001), *Brazil: An Assessment of the Bolsa Escola Programs* (Washington DC: World Bank).

World Health Organisation (1978), *Declaration of Alma-Ata*, International Conference on Primary Health Care (WHO).

Wyatt, A. and S. Grimmeisen (2002), 'Background to the Development of the Toolkit', in CMPS, Cabinet Office, *International Comparisons in Policy-making Toolkit* (Ascot: CMPS).

Xia, S.Z. (1998), *Administration* (Zhongshan: Zhongshan University Press).

Yin, R. (1994), *Case study research: design and methods* (London: Sage).

Index